"Sometimes one simple question can unlock unlimited possibilities. And sometimes one simple book can open doors that we never even knew existed. *What's Here Now?* is both that question and that book. I am so excited for Jeanne and for this book, and I can only imagine all the ways that it will help people find God and themselves in the most obvious and unexpected places!"

Bob Goff, author of the *New York Times* bestsellers
Love Does, *Everybody Always*, and *Dream Big*

"Jeanne Stevens has been a trusted friend for many years. She lives and leads from her soul and has the kind of wise and authentic voice we all need in our lives. I'm grateful for how she has been a voice in my life."

Annie F. Downs, *New York Times* bestselling author of
That Sounds Fun, sought-after speaker, and podcaster

"I've sat under many preachers but under only a few pastors. Jeanne's ability to see into a soul is unmatched. Her pastor's heart and prophet's discernment have set her apart from a crowded culture of wordsmiths and with a small number of soulsmiths. I trust Jeanne with everything, and I'm proud to be able to tell the world that their world is about to become much richer with her words in *What's Here Now?*"

Carlos Whittaker, author and host of the *Human Hope* podcast

"Jeanne is a trustworthy guide, a person who has pursued depth and groundedness in a world that values fast and flashy. Her wisdom is a gift, and her authenticity is an invitation."

Shauna Niequist, *New York Times* bestselling author of
Present Over Perfect, from the foreword

"Raise your hand if you ever donate too much of today to thoughts about yesterday. Raise your hand if you ever spend too much of today focused on what might happen tomorrow, next week, or next year. Why is it so hard to live in the only moment we really have access to—today? Jeanne Stevens knows and is here with a personal invitation to return to the present. If you're ready to live in the now instead of the later or someday, read this book!"

Jon Acuff, *New York Times* bestselling author of *Soundtracks*

"Jeanne has always been thoughtful and brilliant. She's someone I've been inspired by through her truthful storytelling and her wise and honest advice. I've known Jeanne for many transitions in her personal life. This is the book we all need now. I trust her and her words. Most importantly, I trust Jeanne's actions. The words written in this book are a gift for now and for generations to come because they are truly God-inspired."

Latasha Morrison, author of *Be the Bridge*, speaker, reconciler, and bridge builder

"Jeanne Stevens is the voice we so desperately need at this moment. With earned authority and authentic vulnerability, she calls people to the place where Jesus wants to transform their souls. I have seen the fruit of her ministry firsthand at Soul City Church, and I'm so excited for her to share with the world what this church has been receiving all these years."

Nona Jones, author of *Success from the Inside Out*, speaker, and leader

"Jeanne has given us a delightful invitation into presence. Something we all could use more of and something this book helps make more accessible and desirable. Her insight, honesty, and humor are refreshing and help make this book not only easy to read but easy to practice."

Daniel G. Amen, MD, author of *You, Happier* and *Change Your Brain, Change Your Life*

"Jeanne Stevens is a leader worth following and a voice worth listening to. She is someone who is grounded in a deep faith, honesty, vulnerability, and humility. She has over twenty-five years of serving in the trenches of everyday leadership. Jeanne offers a wise and prophetic perspective for the challenges and the opportunities we all face. She can be trusted because she practices the principles she preaches!"

Jo Saxton, author, speaker, podcast host, and leadership coach

"Jeanne is a wise and winsome guide to finding our deepest longings satisfied not in the story just out of reach but in the story right in front of us. *What's Here Now* is a timely and timeless resource on this personal but universal journey toward hope."

Katherine Wolf, author of *Suffer Strong* and *Hope Heals*

"Jeanne is a proven leader and has become a trusted voice for those exploring or returning to faith. Her new book, *What's Here Now?*, draws from her personal story and ministry experience. Enjoy!"

Andy Stanley, author, communicator, and founder of North Point Ministries

"Jeanne is a soul-full woman. She is committed to practicing presence in her everyday life and committed to sharing that practice with others. In our overly distracted world, *What's Here Now?* is like a lighthouse, calling us back to what matters most: presence. I am so grateful for this book and so excited for others to read it—and more importantly, practice it."

Rebekah Lyons, cofounder of Q Ideas and bestselling author of *Rhythms of Renewal*

"Jeanne Stevens is a rare gift to my life, the church, and the world. For over twenty-five years she has lived what she teaches and has built something beautiful at Soul City Church. I am so excited for her to share her deep wisdom and transformational teaching with the world through her new book, *What's Here Now?* I believe God wants to use this book—and this woman—to change your life."

Bianca Juarez Olthoff, author of *How to Have Your Life Not Suck*, speaker, and copastor of The Father's House

"*What's Here Now?* is a masterclass in learning to hold space for you. Jeanne Stevens writes in such an honest and human way that guides you to live freely to this present moment. She teaches you to honor what's really stirring within and all the ways the past and future are relentlessly trying to hold you back. A must-read!"

Steve Carter, pastor and author of *The Thing Beneath the Thing*

"Jeanne Stevens is first and foremost my friend. For some fifteen years now I've had the privilege of sitting in the front row and cheering on her life, family, church, and leadership. She is a gifted voice with a way of speaking right to what matters most. And she does it all with a real sense of humility, vulnerability, and generosity. I can't wait for you to read her new book, *What's Here Now!*"

Jeff Henderson, author of *Know What You're FOR*, leader, and pastor

"*What's Here Now?* is a must-read! Jeanne Stevens is someone I know who not only writes beautifully on the spiritual practice of presence but lives it out."

Jamie Kern Lima, *New York Times* bestselling author of *Believe IT* and founder of IT Cosmetics

"*What's Here Now* is a beautiful reminder that there couldn't be a better moment to embrace your very own life than *now*! Jeanne has always been a fresh voice for me, as she is a trailblazer in soulful living. As I turned the pages, it was as though I was joining her again on that precious path, this time awakening to the power of presence and practical ways on *how* to live that out. Her vulnerability is breathtaking, as it is an invitation to be kind to your truest self as you embark on your own journey with God."

Lauren Tomlin

"I have been a fan of Jeanne Stevens for many years. The life she has lived and the church she and Jarrett have built are something beautiful—and so is this book! With all that we have going on in the world and in our lives, it's easy to lose ourselves. This book helps us find ourselves. To get back to what matters most: presence. I believe this book will be one you will not only love but will come back to again and again."

Eugene Cho, author of *Thou Shalt Not Be a Jerk* and *Overrated*

WHAT'S HERE NOW?

WHAT'S HERE NOW?

HOW TO STOP REHASHING **THE PAST** AND REHEARSING **THE FUTURE**— AND START RECEIVING **THE PRESENT**

Jeanne Stevens

Revell

a division of Baker Publishing Group
Grand Rapids, Michigan

Published by Revell
a division of Baker Publishing Group
PO Box 6287, Grand Rapids, MI 49516-6287
www.revellbooks.com

Printed in the United States of America

Library of Congress Cataloging-in-Publication Data
Names: Stevens, Jeanne, author.
Title: What's here now? : how to stop rehashing the past and rehearsing the
    future—and start receiving the present / Jeanne Stevens.
Description: Grand Rapids, MI : Revell, a division of Baker Publishing Group,
    [2022] | Includes bibliographical references.
Identifiers: LCCN 2021046722 | ISBN 9780800740856 (cloth) | ISBN 9781493436408
    (ebook)
Subjects: LCSH: Contentment—Religious aspects—Christianity. | Regret—Religious
    aspects—Christianity. | Anxiety—Religious aspects—Christianity. | Stress
    management—Religious aspects—Christianity.
Classification: LCC BV4647.C7 S74 2022 | DDC 241/.4—dc23/eng/20211005
LC record available at https://lccn.loc.gov/2021046722

Author is represented by The Christopher Ferebee Agency, www.christopherferebee.com

Baker Publishing Group publications use paper produced from sustainable forestry practices and post-consumer waste whenever possible.

22   23   24   25   26   27   28   7   6   5   4   3   2   1

To Jarrett, Elijah, and Gigi
a.k.a. Team Stevens
You are my favorite people to be with.
I love our Here and Now.

This book is written for every person seeking to live life in the here and now. Your willingness to be here, be you, and fully belong in the present moment is the greatest gift you can give yourself. My prayer is that these words allow you to feel held and simultaneously set free.

Contents

Contents

Part 3 Receiving the Present

Foreword

The question *What's here now?* is about embracing reality, about living honestly right here and right now. A wise friend of mine says that true spiritual maturity is nothing more and nothing less than consenting to reality, and I love that. I love it, and to be honest, for most of my life I've been terrible at it.

An object lesson: recently I hurt my leg. I wish I could tell you that I hurt it training for a marathon or practicing aerial yoga or something, but the truth is I'm now at an age when one sustains injuries just by walking or bending down. That's what happened: I bent down and felt a sharp pain in my calf muscle. Braided in with the physical pain were frustration and shame: How old *am* I? How out of shape *am* I?

My first impulse was to ignore it, walk it out, keep going—business as usual. I mentioned it to my husband, Aaron, and he teased me lovingly, joking about my tendency to push through and end up prolonging the pain I was trying so hard to ignore.

"Crazy idea," he said. "What if this time you did something wild, like stay off of it? Hear me out: What if you rested and let yourself heal, and also didn't beat yourself up and make yourself feel bad for being hurt?"

"Nope," I said. "I think I'm going to stay with my normal two-pronged plan of shaming myself and pretending nothing's wrong." I smiled. This is a conversation we've been having for twenty years—it's hard for me to admit pain, fragility, or weakness of either the physical or spiritual variety. So I ignore reality and usually end up making things worse.

In a surprising turn of events, though, that day I followed Aaron's advice. Instead of walking to the grocery store with a friend, I asked her if we could meet for coffee. I changed dinner plans so I'd only have to walk a few blocks instead of a few miles.

When I woke up the next morning, I felt notably, considerably better. This was a whole new world to me: honoring my body, feeling my feelings, consenting to reality. It's a silly example, of course, but I've spent most of my life pushing through pain, both physical and otherwise, and choosing to honor my body and my feelings is still something like a new trick—I'm always a little shocked when it works.

That's the central wisdom of this book: for all of us who've been taught to push through, pretend, and perform, *What's here now?* has the potential to be a life-changing question. If you've been rewarded, like many of us have, for denying your feelings and pushing down pain, this book is a revelation, an invitation to an entirely new way of living.

I've known Jeanne for more than twenty years. When we met, it was easy to see that she was a strong person, a strong leader. Over the years, I've watched her become not only strong but truly wise. I've watched her become a trustworthy leader, a person who has submitted herself to the arduous process of true transformation.

From time to time, when Jeanne and I have the chance to spend a few hours together or catch up on the phone, I'm reminded of who we both were all those years ago when we first met—ambitious and energetic, intense and bold. And I'm grateful for God's grace in both our lives, that while that energy and intensity still remain in our spirits, these days they're accompanied by tenderness, empathy, curiosity—things you only learn the hard way. Things you only learn by asking over and over *What's here now?* and grappling deeply with the answers, even—especially—the answers that are hard to hear.

Jeanne is a trustworthy guide, a person who has pursued depth and groundedness in a world that values fast and flashy. Her wisdom is a gift, and her authenticity is an invitation.

I'm so excited about the journey you're about to begin, and I can't wait to see what comes to life in you as you start asking that powerful question, *What's here now?*

Shauna Niequist

Introduction

Earth's crammed with heaven, and every common bush afire with
God, but only he who sees takes off his shoes; the rest sit round
and pluck blackberries.

Elizabeth Barrett Browning, *Aurora Leigh*

L ocation, location, location. That's it. That's the secret. If you
can figure out your location, you will find what every person
has always been seeking: peace." My friend said *location* over and
over again, causing me to wonder if he had some kind of secret
real estate side hustle or maybe, like me, had watched one too
many hours of HGTV. (But let's be honest, is there ever too much
Chip and Jo Jo?) While I am no real estate wizard, I have bought
and sold enough homes and even done my fair share of renovation projects. So, I get it: the single greatest determining factor in
the price of a house is its location. But the location he described
didn't seem like any place I'd ever been. It almost felt like he was
reading an enticing advertisement that was too good to be true.

- It's a place free from tension.
- Absolutely no worry or anxiety are present.

17

- The lonely are liberated.
- The fearful find faith.
- The foundation is firm, and it's established in love.

It sounded like some kind of dreamy Narnia 2.0, and for just a moment I thought he was about to say there was even a river flowing with milk and honey.

His description intrigued me, so I leaned in, wanting to know more, and when he said, "That location is here," I was beyond baffled. *How? Where?* I thought we were just sitting in his living room. And while his home was beautifully decorated and felt welcoming and warm, it did not feel like a place that matched the brochure he was selling. With total delight, he announced, "We are in it, in this now moment. You can come as you are. No passport. No ticket. It's free of charge and available to all." The more he characterized the location, the more I sensed that the place he was describing was not a place I had been and certainly did not think I was currently in. I was sitting in his living room, part of a circle of lovely people. We were listening to one another's stories, and it was a wonderful experience, but my reality was not what he had just detailed.

Something felt off inside of me. I was here, in the now, but somehow I didn't feel present. As my soul's deepest longing and my real life cascaded together, I realized he was talking about a spiritual location . . . and every fiber of my being was begging to get to the place he described, but I felt lost and without a map and with no idea how to get there. Tears welled up in my eyes. I desperately wanted to be in that location.

I found myself in that living room on a crisp fall morning because I was hoping for a breakthrough, as I desperately wanted to avoid a full-blown breakdown. I had spent the past few years in an all-out holy hustle, and my human doing was running out. The irony within the business I had started was that I was working for God. You would think this has a whole lot of benefits, and it does.

The only problem was the more work I did for God, the more the work of God was slowly deteriorating inside of me. I believed in what we were building. I was all in. I was seeing lives transformed. But I knew the way I was living had an expiration date on it. All my "efforting" had just about dried up any effort left in me. The present moment seemed confusing and complex, like someone had turned a blender on inside me and all my emotions were mixed up—fear, sadness, isolation, exhaustion, loneliness.

My life felt like the opposite of the fantasyland my friend described. I felt drained and dull and unsure if the life I'd created was the life I wanted to keep living. On the outside, everything looked fine, but on the inside, I desperately wanted to know, *How do I live IN the presence of God?* Richard Rohr says, "We cannot attain the presence of God because we're already in the presence of God. What's absent is awareness."[1]

I had sung songs and prayed prayers asking for God to reveal his presence, and what I came to understand was that his presence was already here. What was missing—and perhaps more importantly *who* was missing—was me. I began to get curious. If I was missing . . . then where was I? Over the coming years, that moment in that living room led to countless opportunities to follow the breadcrumbs to where my soul had learned to hide. There were some well-worn paths, and I realized along the way that there were many others hiking the same trails.

One of the greatest gifts that has served as my compass and guide was a question to help me navigate to the place I longed to be:

What's here now?

It's a simple question, and simple was what I was craving. My insides felt twisted and chaotic. My soul felt like the junk drawer in my kitchen that I regularly try to ignore. I needed simple. Four steps were four too many. Ten directives were too directive.

Something to memorize felt like too much work, and I've never been good with memorization. *What's here now?* That I could remember. It was a way for me to breathe. Pause. Look around and look within to locate myself and pay attention to what was really going on. Like those maps in the mall with the big red dot—YOU ARE HERE. The question helped me pay attention to the parts of me I had ignored for far too long.

* * *

When I first started practicing the question, I felt strange and clumsy, like a kid trying to ride a bike for the first time. I knew I would eventually get it, but I kept turning the wrong way. Forgetting to pedal at the right times and often falling off and needing to begin again. My friend Jim, the present location expert from the living room, told me about a simple app called Mind Jogger, in which I could type in anything I wanted and tell it to send me as many random alerts on my phone throughout the day as I chose. I quickly downloaded it and typed in WHAT'S HERE NOW? I made a promise to myself and God that anytime—and I mean anytime—it popped up, I would take a deep breath, pause, and answer the question.

In the beginning I was surprised how often, when the question popped up, I would be hanging out in the past. I was not physically there, of course, but I was living there in every other way. Mulling over what happened in the previous meeting. Replaying what I said to my kids in a moment of frustration earlier that day. Wishing someone had spoken up earlier about the problem I was now solving. I had already lived it, but I was trying to relive it—as if that would change what had occurred. I was in the physical here and now, but my feelings and thoughts were rehashing my past, and I came to realize it was showing up in my body, which was regularly tense. Trying to relive the past was like digging through my own personal scrapyard looking for clues as to why I was experiencing the thoughts and feelings that were surging through my being.

We can gain much by uncovering the patterns and themes of our stories, and I am certainly an advocate for doing so and have gleaned much learning and healing by sitting on a counselor's couch or in a circle of group therapy and digging in the dirt of my past. But the chapters we wrote in the past are not the stories we are living today. Most of us don't realize the suffering we shovel back into our lives when we replay the past. The past is a great place to learn from, but it's a terrible place to live.

We are not who we once were, and our experiences do not need to be our existence today. Keeping one foot in the past keeps us from receiving the gift of the present. When we go back into our closets of shame, lowlands of loss, and gullies of guilt, we rip ourselves out of the present moment and miss out on how God is moving in the now.

It wasn't just the past I had earned frequent flyer miles visiting. I was also a platinum member with my own VIP lounge when it came to touring through my future. I'm a natural visionary and entrepreneur brimming with a new idea every five minutes, so leaving the present to vacation in the future was my preferred place to be. I came out of the womb as a starry-eyed dreamer. I have stacks on stacks of journals filled with ideas. There is nothing wrong with beholding a beautiful future filled with possibility and hope. God invites us to dream and envision—but not as a means of avoiding the present.

> **The past is a great place to learn from, but it's a terrible place to live.**

The idealist gets to be everything they have ever wanted to be in the future. They get to imagine and envision better days. They get to see themselves at the perfect weight, living in the dream house with the dream person and creating the dream family, all while doing the dream job. The optimist loves the future because they get to escape and avoid whatever current dissatisfaction they are experiencing. They get to play on an idealized playground where all their troubles are reduced and their hopes are finally fulfilled. The pessimist also finds the future as a port in their present storm. The pessimist, who prefers the title "realist," is lured into the future down the well-worn path of worry, anxiety, and fear. In the future the realist can think through all the worst-case scenarios, strategize all the ways life could throw them a curveball, and prepare themselves to avoid whatever unfavorable situation they experienced in the past. They get to borrow future possibilities and make them present realities.

Thinking about both the past and the future are ways we contemplate life—but the problem with only thinking about life is that it's an ineffective way to transform it. In the wise words of Father Rohr, "We do not think ourselves into new ways of living, we live ourselves into new ways of thinking."[2] The only place where we actually live is in the present moment.

I was a novice at best at *being* in the present moment with myself and God . . . let alone inviting others into that moment. In the beginning when *What's here now?* would pop up on my phone, I would sometimes just look at it and say, "I don't know. I am here. In my office. Sitting at my desk staring at the blinking cursor on the screen. . . . But I'm not sure if I'm really here." Yet that was enough to start with. I was bringing awareness to the reality that I was not present, and often I would then take a deep breath and whisper a prayer: "God, help me be here. With you, in this now moment."

The more I practiced paying attention to the question, the more I could see and experience God's love holding me with every inhale and exhale. When our lungs expand and contract, God is affirming there is nothing to prove and no other place to be than right here, with him. To practice his name. *Emmanuel*—God with us.

As I learned to rest in the present, I began to sense the nudge to unlearn some other things that were no longer of service to me. To live aware of God's presence means recognizing we have spent a large portion of our lives blind to it. I love how Jesus says in Luke 11:34, "When your eyes are healthy, your whole body also is full of light." When we open our eyes to the present moment, we wake up. We come out of the trance of stumbling and fumbling through this life and wake up to beauty, wonder, and miracles. We start seeing that there is an effortless way of living in flow with God. We get to experience what living in a prayerful presence is: far beyond bowing our heads, folding our hands, and closing our eyes. Rather it is lifting our heads, opening our hands, and looking at life with eyes wide open to the present movement of God.

Once I got comfortable with welcoming the question into my life, I began to do three things; I would try to simply notice what was happening in my body, my heart, and my mind.

- What am I sensing in my body?
- What am I feeling in my heart?
- What am I thinking in my mind?

Sensing, feeling, and thinking. We are all capable of doing these before we ever speak a word or take a step. Babies and kids are naturals at living in the present moment and often are some of the best professors on how to live there. When a baby is hungry, they sense it in their body, they think it in their mind, and they feel it in their emotions. The combination of those three things causes a reaction—the baby cries. When a child is feeling bored with their current activity on the playground and wants to feel the excitement of trying something new, and they see someone else over on the swings smiling, the child runs from the slide to the swings.

● ● ●

Our bodies, hearts, and minds are constantly communicating, but many of us have put a lock around them, and over time we somehow misplaced the key. This book is that key. You are not meant to rehash the past or rehearse your future. You are made for the present. The greatest gift you can give yourself is a willingness to be in the now.

As I learned how to find my own location in the present, I finally understood that now is always where God is. The present is God's zip code. "If I go up to the heavens, you are there; if I make my bed in the depths, you are there" (Ps. 139:8). We can never not be in the presence of God, but we often forget to get present to God's presence.

Living outside of the present is like choosing to eat vanilla ice cream for the rest of your life. There is nothing wrong with vanilla. It is the most common flavor. But when you realize there are flavors like brambleberry crisp, brown butter almond brittle, and, even better, salted peanut butter with chocolate flecks, you start to see that life in the present is a gorgeous multifaceted mystery engaging every one of your senses. It is the most sacred and holy invitation each of us gets: to participate as the here and now unfolds.

You are made for the present.

As we do so, we come to see that we can't really experience anything if we're not present to it. When we experience the sacred unfolding of life, we are transformed along the way. In the present we see that every common bush is ablaze with God's glory and love, and as we take off our shoes on the holy ground of our lives, we see we were never meant to sit around plucking blackberries for all our days.

Somehow in the pausing and being we discover who we are. We recognize that all those years we spent trying to control life or worry about life kept us from being participants in life. We move from being human doings to actual human beings.

What's here now? is perhaps the simplest question ever asked and yet the hardest one to answer. All the world is clawing at us to stay busy, keep hustling, return to the well-worn grooves that have gotten us this far, and ignore the question. But if you are willing, *What's here now?* has the potential to transform your life. It has the power to help you be here, be you, and belong.

PART 1

Rehashing the Past

1

······································

Blame

I Take Thee to Be My Life Coach

The past is a foreign country; they do things differently there.

L. P. Hartley, *The Go-Between*

Bless me, Father, for I have sinned. This is my very first confession." These were the words I was coached to say when
I walked into the dark, intimidating mahogany box to offer my
inaugural confession. I was seven years old, and while I was far
from angelic, my list of sins was undoubtedly not going to sound
any alarms. I was raised Catholic because my parents were raised
Catholic and my grandparents were raised Catholic. If I ever get
around to doing my Ancestry.com personal history lesson, I'm
sure I'll find a spun-out line of Catholics in my story.

While my seven-year-old self was far too naïve to give a theo-
logical lecture on the practice of confession, I knew why I was
committed to going through with the act. Going to confession
was the gateway to communion, and I was tired of sitting through

27

Sunday mass week after week watching my parents get the complimentary bread and juice while I stayed in my seat. I was savvy enough to know that a little hit of carbs and sugar could quickly turn a boring situation around.

My seven-year-old fellow sinners and I sat in the dimly lit church as the thick aroma of incense infused the air, each of us anxiously waiting for our name to be called. I silently rehearsed my list of sins. First, it would be hard not to put the many different disputes between me and my brothers on the list. Second, I'd have to include that time I lied to my mom about how far I went on my bike ride down the prairie path with my neighborhood friends.

I had these two offenses on my trespasses list, even though I was still unsure what a spiritual trespass was. And then I heard them call, "Jeanne Pieczynski." That's my maiden name. I spent twenty-three years praying to marry a Jones or Smith. When I met my husband, Jarrett, and found out his last name was Stevens, I knew the relationship could advance to the next phase; the fact that I was falling madly in love also helped.

"Jeanne Pieczynski." They called my name a second time. I nervously tucked my light brown hair behind my ears and clutched my children's Bible like a comforting security blanket. Standing up, I flattened out my skirt and straightened my posture as I walked to the back of the church. My palms were sweaty as I recited my opening line under my breath.

I opened the creaky door, looked inside, and saw a kneeler and a chair. I quickly chose the kneeler, and as I situated myself, the thick, forest green, velvet curtain on the other side of the box opened up. Before I could get my opening line out, the priest said, "Hi, Jeanne. Welcome to your first confession; there is nothing to be nervous about." I nodded, still very nervous.

"Dear Father, I have sinned; bless me, this is my first confession," I said. The words fell out in the wrong order, but before I could repair my fumble, the priest said, "What would you like to talk about, Jeanne?" I weighed my options. I knew what I *didn't* want to talk about. I was a pretty decent conversationalist, so I knew I could either dance around a few different topics while avoiding the inevitable or just go right to the deep end. I decided to launch straight in, no small talk. No setup. Just one long, run-on sentence.

"I lied to my mom last week about how far I rode my bike on the prairie path my mom said I could only go to the end of the path and not cross the street but there were no cars and we were fine and I had been down that way so many times before and I really wish she would just let me start crossing the path because I am seven now oh and I also fight with my brothers sometimes most of the time they start the fights because I am just trying to play piano in the dining room and they come in and interrupt with their nerf basketball games so really the only reason I am sometimes unkind is that they are always bugging me."

I verbally vomited my two sins without pausing to breathe, and I was resolved *not* to take responsibility for either of them. Blame was my getaway car to avoid any penance for my sins. Blame felt better than remorse, and if the priest believed my excuses, I would waltz out of that dark little box with a free pass and counterfeit forgiveness.

While I didn't really have a conscious knowledge at the time of what I was doing, I paid in full for what blame has been selling from the beginning of time: giving away responsibility for my actions to someone or something else. Isn't that the way it is with blame? It allows us to put the fault elsewhere by transferring responsibility. At first glance, this sounds like a brilliant equation to absolve us of any wrongs, yet the tension lies in the way we get through blame's narrow passageway. It's usually by accusation, punishment, humiliation, or criticism, and the last time I checked, 0.0 percent of people make progress and take relational steps forward using such destructive and emotionally damaging behaviors.

Like a convincing con artist lurking in the shadows of our past, blame's ambition is to become a necessary function in our lives as we subtly learn to rely on its dependable behavior that rescues us from taking healthy responsibility and living with honest accountability. We blame:

- When life deals us a card we wouldn't have chosen.
- When a relationship moves in a direction we would not have steered toward.
- When someone tries to back us into a corner, and we feel pressure to carry more weight than we're willing to bear.

The mind is quick to point a finger elsewhere, desperate to push away the responsibility we are unwilling to hold. Most of the time this tendency is buried beneath years of built-up blaming behavior, and we don't even realize how much we rely on old, dependable blame. Blame becomes an unconscious way we maneuver through the world—like an optical viewfinder of how to look at our lives rather than take responsibility for them.

Primary Patterns

Blame is a topic as wide as the ocean, but I want to focus our conversation on how blame impacts our ability to be in the present moment with God, ourselves, and others. I want to help us better understand how blame diligently works to keep us locked in the past and outside of how God is at work in our present lives. So much of my understanding about blame comes from research I've done periodically, but there has been no better research than my own life, as I can attest to being a card-carrying blame addict since I entered that confessional at age seven.

When we are unwilling to be accountable for our actions, blame is always there to direct, defend, and even deceive us out of taking responsibility for ourselves. The trickery of blame is that it never begins with blatant or blaring announcements. Blame rarely comes into the room making bold declarations that it's about to bulldoze anyone and everything in its path. It just starts dozing, and all those near its route usually end up feeling the bulldozer's presence. The fascinating thing about blame is that it almost always gets stronger and more defined the more it's used. Each time we return to it, it's like the brain knew to leave behind breadcrumbs of remembrance pointing us back to the last time blame allowed us to escape the pressure we assumed responsibility would put on us.

In my experience, blame has three primary patterns when it shows up in our lives: directing, defending, and deceiving. These are blame's most reliable blocks to keep us disconnected from God, ourselves, and one another.

I know we are still getting to know one another, and this is only chapter 1, but you need to know something about me right at the top: I absolutely love alliteration. It helps me remember things that are important while bringing out the preacher in me who has spent twenty-five years crafting memorable phrases and sticky statements in sermons that get my friends Zoie and Tamara always shouting back with an "Amen." Consider yourself warned.

Now, back to the three Ds.

Directing

Blame's first move usually begins with directing attention, responsibility, and accountability away from itself. Blame will always search out ways to try to change another person's behavior by controlling, coaching, or accusing in order to shift responsibility elsewhere. If blame can turn up the lights on something or someone else's actions, it can forgo any responsibility it is unwilling to absorb. Like a movie director yelling "Action!", directing blame starts to call, create, and control the narrative so the responsibility never points to the actual person needing to absorb it.

I love my kids, Elijah and Gigi. They are incredible. They are fun, thoughtful, and creative. They are wildly unique and truly two of my favorite people to spend time with. They still go to one another's rooms each night before they head to bed to say I love you. It makes my heart warm and gooey every time I hear them in the upstairs hallway. I could literally write chapters upon chapters about how I feel about them. They own my heart in ways I never thought possible. But somewhere along the way they both became expert blamers. Both could easily win Academy Awards when it comes to directing blame onto someone else.

"Did you feed the dogs?" I ask. "No, it's not my turn."

"Did you set the table?" I ask. "I did it last night. Why don't you ask her about the last time she set the table?"

"Did you fold the laundry that I washed and dried for you?" I ask. "Do you know how much homework I have? I don't have time to fold my laundry."

It's like they somehow signed up for a secret online class I never knew about, which taught them martial arts maneuvers on how to direct away responsibility. But this wild skill of pushing the attention onto someone or something else is not just something kids are good at doing. Anyone who has deflected responsibility knows what it feels like. We convince ourselves that owning up would be too hard, so we direct attention elsewhere.

You're late for a meeting. "Wow, traffic was such a beast this morning."

You forgot to respond to an email you said you would respond to. "Do you have any idea how much is on my plate?"

You said something you wish you hadn't. "Well, it is mostly true, and I needed to get it off my chest."

Directing responsibility elsewhere is a skill most of us acquired somewhere along the way, and we've kept it in our relational back pocket to pull out whenever taking responsibility for something feels a little too raw or vulnerable. And directing is not the only party trick blame likes to use.

Defending

Anyone skilled in the ability to blame has probably been their own defense lawyer. Like a litigator who knows their way around the judge, jury, and courtroom, they are adept at citing all the important facts to shift the blame. Pushing the attention of the problem onto someone else. Lawyering up in their tone, bravado, and nonverbal communication. Seeking to shut down and completely turn around an argument. The defender is skilled in the ways of getting out of responsibility.

Jarrett and I may have missed our calling in life because both of us have mastered this skill. No wonder our kids are already expert blamers. Early in our marriage our fights were somehow won or lost based on who was better at their defense. Whoever showed up ready to play and to take the other down was the one who remained standing in victory—until we realized that winning a fight on defense, whether the facts were true or not, never satisfied. We were fighting about content that was ultimately meaningless and not fighting for the greater context of having a thriving marriage.

As if directing and defending weren't enough, the skilled blamer usually has one last trick if all else fails, and sadly it's the skill of deceit.

Deceiving

I remember when I first heard Jeremiah 17:9, "The heart is deceitful above all things and beyond cure. Who can understand it?" I even remember wanting to deceive myself into not believing that passage was true. How could the heart be deceitful? Then I started doing some good and hard soul work on my own heart and realized that my heart wants what my heart wants. And usually when the heart wants something, it will go to great lengths to have it.

When we don't want to feel the weight of responsibility, the heart will do whatever it can to move away from any possible pain it might experience, and deceit is one of the heart's most reliable moves. Spinning tales. Making up half-truths. Not owning up to something. These are usually the early seedlings associated with deceit. When these work in our favor, it's just one more affirmation for blame that it has accomplished what it set out to do.

• • •

Sadly, every time blame shows up in our lives, and we follow its seductive song, we cut ourselves off from living in the present moment and therefore cut ourselves off from intimacy and connection with God. Whether we direct, defend, or deceive, it's impossible to do those things while rooting ourselves in the present moment, because every one of those behaviors wraps the crook of its theater cane around our neck and pulls us back to the past. To the behavior, moment, or activity we are directing, defending, or deceiving our way around.

Henri Nouwen says, "To live in the present, we must deeply believe that what is most important is in the here and now."[1] When we let blame run the show in our lives, we're locking ourselves in some moment in the past that has a hold over mind, heart, body, and soul. We have somehow convinced ourselves that taking responsibility will do us in. That it will radically reorient the present from how we want to live it.

This is not true.

The truth is reframing blame can pull us back to the center. Pull us into the now, into the presence of God, in a way that is rooted in grace, mercy, and out-of-this-world love.

But we have to be willing to answer the question, *What's here now?* To lovingly allow the real answer to come to the surface. To avoid pushing it down or letting blame take the lead again. To let the real fear surface. To acknowledge that blame is in the driver's seat and begin to offer ourselves a new way.

Wife or Life Coach? ·

Jarrett and I were probably six or seven years into our marriage when we had one of those conversations that would alter the role blame played in our relationship. I don't think I knew just how defining a conversation it would be when I was wading through the middle of it. Honestly, I just wanted to get out of it. But the gifts I received in that conversation were necessary truths I needed to hear to take some big steps in reclaiming the power blame had taken in my life.

I don't even remember what the incident was that had us putting on our boxing gloves, ready to pull out all our well-developed blame behavior, but we were in the midst of throwing around some upper-cuts, side jabs, and Billy Blanks–style kicks when Jarrett launched into a so-liloquy. (Sidenote, we are both skilled with words and speak for a living, so when one of us goes into speech mode, we usually know a good windup is coming.)

> **Reframing blame can pull us back to the center.**

He said, "You know, I have been thinking about our wedding day a lot lately. I've been reflecting on our friends and family who were there. Remembering our photographer who walked around with an open flask all day, the music, the beautiful gardens at Cantigny, and how we stayed till the very last song dancing the night away. It was such an amazing day."

I agreed, reluctant to say anything else because I was unsure where he was headed.

He continued, "You looked so beautiful—radiant and bright. I couldn't believe at that moment that we were sharing lifelong vows. But as I think back to that moment, I am having a hard time remembering when I said in my vows, 'and I take you, Jeanne, to be my life coach.' I remember saying a whole lot of other things, but for the life of me, I just can't remember that promise. And yet, that's what I feel like I've gotten. I feel like around every corner is a conversation that usually is about why something is my fault, and then you coach me on how to fix it. I don't feel like I have an advocate or ally. I feel like I have an accuser at best, and I don't even think that's the kind of coaching I would want from a life coach. I wanted a wife when I made those promises to you in front of that church with our family and friends gathered around. I wanted a partner. Sure, someone I knew I would fight with at times, but someone who was more concerned in fighting for me and for us."

Tears puddled in my eyes. A lump in my throat bobbed up and down. Jarrett's humor mixed with his potent honesty brought me straight into the power of the present moment. He was lovingly (albeit painfully) inviting me to see that blame was winning in our relationship.

That conversation was a turning point for me. I didn't fight it. I didn't direct it. I didn't lawyer up and try to defend why I had to be his life coach. I didn't look for ways to deceive my way out of it. I allowed the present moment to be what it was. I had hurt the love of my life. I'd put blame into the soil of our relationship, and the fruit coming up was far from fresh and reliable. Blame certainly was not good soil to grow a healthy marriage in.

The gift Jarrett offered me that day was not all that different from the opportunity I could have taken in that dark black box decades earlier, the gift of confession. I was still that seven-year-old who went looking for someone to blame; I'd just found a new way to do it. I blamed through "coaching," a more socially acceptable way of directing, defending, and deceiving.

As painful as that conversation was, I look back on that moment with gratitude and delight. I am beyond thankful for Jarrett's courageous willingness to playfully call out a behavior that had settled into my life and was wreaking havoc in my relationship with him, myself, others, and God.

As I got myself into counseling and found an actual life coach, I began to realize that blaming was the behavior I'd picked up to skip out of personal responsibility. The funny thing: I am a wildly responsible person. Blame only showed up when I didn't want to be responsible for a behavior that felt too scary or vulnerable. One of the biggest issues with blame is that it keeps us from solving our problems because of its uncanny ability to redirect our focus to the *perceived* problem instead of the *real* problem.

Some of the work I began to do then is work I continue to do now. It requires patience and openness to genuinely ask myself the sacred question that this book is all about: *What's here now?* When we let that question rumble around, even for just a moment, when we allow ourselves to settle into the present and begin to discern the emotional energy of blame lurking somewhere in the vicinity, we give ourselves an opportunity to come into presence with God. And more good news? For every movement toward blame, there is another movement away from it.

Get Clear

When directing blame shows up, it is often trying to divert attention from the content at hand. But instead of directing, a great way to come back into the present moment with God is to seek clear content.

To get clear with yourself.

What's really going on in this situation?

Why do I want to ignore any responsibility?

Why am I so ramped up and committed to being right about this situation?

Is there another way to look at the content of what is happening here?

So much of this step is about trying to remain unattached from needing to prove we're right. To let the content offer just the facts versus the stories associated with the facts.

Blaming so often comes when the mind makes up stories about what the facts mean. For example, one day I asked Jarrett to pick something up for me at Target. (This happens on the regular because I love Target, and if I ever go missing, just look for me there.) When he came home, I greeted him, noticed there was no Target bag in his hand, and asked, "Hey, did you go to Target for me?" He instantly said, "Oh, I'm so sorry. I totally forgot."

I could feel blame nipping at the heels of my mind. *Of course he forgot. It wasn't a priority to him. He always forgets things.* It's wild how quickly blame wants to sabotage. It was there in a matter of seconds.

It's important to get clear on the content, because the content doesn't have feelings or motives. The content is that I asked Jarrett to go to Target. He did not go. He said he forgot. It was my mind pulling up past stories and directing a steaming pile of blame onto the situation that kept me from being in the present moment with Jarrett.

I could have asked him more about the content he offered me, "I forgot," but instead I picked up blame's breadcrumbs and followed them down a trail of disconnection.

Getting clear on what is going on is an opportunity to step out of blame that pulls us into the past and come into the present moment as we choose to let the content just be clear content. It's an opportunity to pay attention to the now moment instead of a past story.

Get Curious

Another way to escape the trap of blame is to get curious. Blame always has a closed and convinced kind of posture, with arms crossed and heart locked. But you can choose a different posture. Asking *What's here now?* brings you into the present moment with all you are holding and grappling with. Instead of being closed, invite openness and curiosity. Instead of needing to be right, get curious about seeing the situation, story, or experience through different eyes. Curiosity is such a powerful tool for practicing presence. It is rooted in hope with branches that always bear fruit.

Get Conscious

When we blame, we give away our power and get ourselves stuck in an unconscious loop. While it's a natural human tendency to blame, every time we do it, we pull ourselves away from the present moment. It's almost like we turn off the lights and sleepwalk instead of seeing how God is moving in the here and now. We lock ourselves up in a past story, perhaps one of trauma or pain, believing that moment defines all our reality.

> When we blame, we give away our power and get ourselves stuck in an unconscious loop.

Laying down deception and choosing to get conscious is a gift that allows us to come into the daylight hours. To drink in the moment for what it really is, not what we want it to be. There may still be frustration and anger and disappointment. But at least we can name them and accept ourselves for being right where we are in the present moment.

When I think back to that seven-year-old me who was ripe with fear and desperate to avoid condemnation, I have so much compassion and love for her. She just wanted to get it right. To be right. It was and is a beautiful desire.

What that little girl needed to hear so many years ago are the same words anyone struggling with blame still needs to hear: "May almighty God have mercy on you, and having forgiven your sins, lead you to eternal life. May the almighty and merciful Lord grant you indulgence, absolution, and remission of your sins. Amen."

2

Shame

Who Told You?

Shame derives its power from being unspeakable.
Brené Brown, *Daring Greatly*

Living in a big city means we know there is always something going on. Our neighborhood has had a massive growth spurt in the last few years, and many trendy restaurants have moved in. So, one of our favorite things to do on date night is to check out the cool, new, and up-and-coming spots. Recently some friends told us about a great new place that had just opened. They said, "It's young and hip and vibey," then followed their description with this disclaimer: "We're not sure if it's your scene, but you might like it if you go early enough." *Early enough? What do they think I am, minutes away from a retirement home?* I was determined to prove I was young, hip, and vibey, so we got a reservation and went to check it out one night.

Even though I could tell their recommendation had a baked-in undertone that we might be aging out of the cool category. Even though I'm a middle-aged woman with two teenagers. Even though I have to visit my magician hairstylist, Kristine, every ten or twelve weeks to cover up the gray hair popping through. Even though I would prefer to be in bed by nine o'clock every night. Regardless, in my mind I am still hardly a day over twenty-nine.

But when we entered the restaurant, reality was hard to ignore. I think my gray roots revolted and poked out the second we walked through the door. We were clearly the oldest people there. The vibe, the lighting, the music, and the people radically communicated we were not the target demographic, though we had a great meal and loved the ambiance and energy. We did ask multiple times if there was a quieter spot to sit—and, yes, by nine o'clock I was already craving my pjs and a warm bed.

While Jarrett paid the bill, I went to the restroom. I did not expect the women's room to be as much of a scene as the rest of the restaurant. Girls were taking pics, posing in front of the mirrors with their phones, and laughing as they tried out different filters, and while I was washing my hands, I overheard a conversation that piqued my interest.

One girl said to her friend, with lots of concern in her voice, "Are you OK?" The other girl said, "Yeah, why?" She said, "I was starting to worry about you because you haven't posted a selfie in like two days, and I wondered what was wrong."

Two emotions instantly surged through me: part of me had to keep myself from giggling, and the other part had to hold myself back from crying. I realized somewhere along the way in a selfie-obsessed world, people were losing their true selves at a rapid speed. And behind every photo posted were forty-three that didn't make the cut. The girl's genuine concern for her friend was not connected to something she'd shared in a personal and vulnerable conversation but due to watching her selfie game on her Instagram feed.

After I walked out of the bathroom and returned to my un-vibey life, I couldn't get the conversation I overheard out of my mind. The pressure and burden we put on ourselves and one another to be OK, or to find a filter to make it all look OK, is not OK. Somewhere along the way the seductive and shameful lullaby that the curated life is better than the credible life has left us sleepwalking through our present lives.

I imagine you've had moments of pretending to be someone you're not. Pretending to feel something you didn't really feel. Pretending to know something you didn't totally know. I bet you've put a filter on your photo or maybe even taken a picture, looked at it, and then asked someone to take a better one because it didn't capture the perfect reality you wanted to portray. Spending a disproportionate amount of energy on a self you think you are supposed to be, you end up forgetting the true self God created you to be. The temptation to impersonate and to filter your actual life is so appealing because shame knows how to subtly corrupt and corrode your thoughts into believing that camouflage and cover-ups are the only way to make it through this life.

> The pressure and burden we put on ourselves and one another to be OK, or to find a filter to make it all look OK, is not OK.

You can almost always count on a curated life to leave you feeling overwhelmed but somehow underwhelmed at the same time. Simultaneously you feel like you are too much but not enough. The curated life whispers against your internal urge to tell the truth about who you are and instead tells you to keep it covered up and hidden. That voice from your past that is trying to live in your present is the voice of *shame*.

While we live in a linked-up world and have the power to experience more connectivity than ever, so many of us miss out on the blessing of belonging. The lives we share are, in many ways, not our real lives. We have become personal advertisers with a devoted marketing plan that hides anything and everything we are ashamed of.

Recognizing Shame

When your insides don't match your outsides, and when there are so many categories flying through your mind of what you should be that keep you from who God created you to be, you can be certain that an invisible shackle of shame has wrapped itself around your ankles. It is dragging you out of the present to try to fight your past with the very thing that will never be able to defeat it: more shame.

Shame is an invisible villain. You can't see it, but you feel it every time it invades the present moment. Many times the words *shame* and *guilt* are used synonymously. But they are different.

Guilt says I *made* a mistake.
Shame says I *am* a mistake.

Guilt and shame are certainly not the most popular of feelings. They have never been crowned king or queen of the emotional homecoming court. But they each have a different effect on our lives. Healthy guilt from mistakes we've made can lead us to conviction and change. But shame feels like a storm cloud that rolls into our lives and permeates every part of our being, causing us to believe that we are a mistake.

Shame can come from

- things you've done or things done to you
- things you've said or things that have been said to you
- something that occurred last week or something that occurred decades ago
- unemployment or unprocessed grief

- divorce or depression
- addiction or uncontrollable anger

Shame is something we all experience at some level, from slight embarrassment to deep regret and humiliation. Shame lurks in the dark and has the power to destroy the human mind, heart, and soul because it alters our neuropsychological state every time we experience it.[1]

The impact of shame eclipses any simple definitions we try to give it.

- I could say that shame lives in phrases like, "I'm not smart enough," or "I will never measure up." And that would be true.
- I could say that shame lives in feelings or sensations that arise when a painful memory flashes through your consciousness. And that would be true.
- I could say that shame shows up in bedrooms and closets and bathrooms every time you catch yourself in the mirror and begin to think self-condemning thoughts. And that would be true.

All those experiences and so many more lead to shame's powerful presence in our thoughts. Shame can embed itself into the essence of our human experience, and when given permission it will always leave us isolated, condemned, and believing we are unworthy of love.

A while back I was speaking at a conference and ran into someone I hadn't seen in many years. I had been her son's youth pastor, and Jarrett officiated her son's wedding. I was thrilled to see her, and asked, "How is your son?" The first thing she said was, "Well, he married the wrong person. He's walked away from God, and his life is a total disaster."

Before I could respond, her condemnation continued. "I mean, he's happy, but I don't even know who he is, and I'm pretty sure he's ruined his life." I could feel the judgment and shame in her voice, and while listening to her I felt my anger rising. It took every molecule of self-control in my body not to speak up, and I thought, *God, there are a lot of things I want to say, and I'm pretty sure they are not the same things you want me to say.*

So I kept my thoughts to myself, and I kindly tried every social cue I knew to exit the conversation. I physically backed myself away from her as I said, "Well, I am so glad we ran into one another." But she leaned in and continued talking, shoveling more and more shame onto her son until I just couldn't listen anymore. I respectfully interrupted her and said, "I wonder if you would be open to some of my thoughts."

Oh no, what had I done? I was trying to get out, but before I realized it, I'd stepped in deeper.

She said, "Oh, yes, Jeanne. I've always appreciated your wisdom." I thought, *I don't think you are going to think I'm very wise ever again*, but I said, "I'm glad I ran into you, and I am not sure this is what you want to hear, but your son needs your love, not your judgment. Shaming him is going to cause him to run from you, but loving him just might be the thing that opens his heart up to you. I wonder what it would look like if you found joy in being your son's mom instead of his judge."

These were not the words she expected. I could tell she was looking for me to jump on her bandwagon of condemnation, and when I didn't take the bait her eyes widened in surprise. I assured her of my love for her and her son, and I wished her well before lovingly leaving the conversation.

Shame has a simple goal: to get you to believe you are unworthy of love. Shame will use any available tool to demolish the hope that transformation is possible. I love the way Brené Brown describes the impact of shame on the human soul. She says, "Shame corrodes the very part of us that believes we are capable of change."[2]

Shame says this is as good as it gets. You are going to live this way for the rest of your life, and your past will always define your present. Shame is devoted to making sure that when you ask *What's here now?* you never get to the answer. Shame wants to take you back and lock you up in your previous experiences so you can't even feel what is happening in the now.

Shame is not a new problem, but at one point it was an unknown experience for humans. All the way back in the garden of Eden, the Bible tells us, "Adam and his wife were both naked, and they felt no shame" (Gen. 2:25).

> **Shame has a simple goal: to get you to believe you are unworthy of love.**

It's pretty easy to pay attention to the physical state of Adam and Eve: they were naked. Hello, whoever said the Bible was boring? Good for them. But it's not just their physical state that gets a mention. The emotional state of Adam and Eve is even more important and is clear: they felt no *shame*. Any number of emotional descriptors could have been used at this moment.

- They felt no fear.
- They felt no anxiety.
- They felt no worry.

God could have used any number of adjectives, but he wanted it made clear they had no shame. They didn't even know the feeling. They had never even entertained the thought or the lie that shame most wants us to believe: *there must be something wrong with me.* God knows the impact shame can have on our lives; I think that's why he never intended for you and me to experience it.

If you know the story, you know that Adam and Eve, who felt no shame, decided to do the one thing God asked them to *not* do. They took the fruit from the tree in the center of the garden, and in an instant shame entered their world—and our world. The Bible says "Then the eyes of both of them were opened, and they realized they were naked; so they sewed fig leaves together and made coverings for themselves" (3:7). Soon after, Adam blamed Eve for making him eat the fruit, which is the first recorded moment of a man blaming a woman for all his problems, and for the first time they hid from God. Blame, shame, and hiding, never part of their lives before, instantly took over.

They hid because of their shame, but God went looking for them.

> But the LORD God called to the man, "Where are you?"
>
> He answered, "I heard you in the garden, and I was afraid because I was naked; so I hid."
>
> And he said, "Who told you that you were naked? Have you eaten from the tree that I commanded you not to eat from?" (vv. 9–11)

What a profound and beautiful question God asks: *Where are you, and who told you these lies that you now believe about yourself?* I love God's playfulness at this moment. Let's be honest; it isn't as if God can't see them and doesn't know where they are. God always wins at hide and seek. But I am so moved by his goodness. The heart of God wants to know, *At what point did you believe the lie that this is who you are?* God ever so gently tries to draw Adam and Eve into the present by lovingly whispering, *What's here now?* He sees that what just happened in their immediate past is keeping them from being in the present. The peace of God is always in the present, so if we aren't in the present, we will not experience God's peace or his presence.

What happened in the garden that day began a pattern of elevating the voices, stories, and experiences in our lives above what God says about us. God knows that when shame is present, we run from his presence. Shame is not what God designed. But shame is what so many of us have learned to put on in our lives. Every time we do, we leave the power of the present moment and lock ourselves up in the past. We condemn ourselves and our present lives and any future hope of who we might become.

● ● ●

I didn't really notice when shame first showed up in my life. It wasn't as obvious as it was in Eden. It entered beyond the mechanics of speech and left a feeling exclusively tied to one word in my life: *enough*. Well, to be more accurate: *not enough*. When I first started asking myself *What's here now?* I realized my mental location was almost always hanging out in the past, recalling memories of not feeling like I was enough and then looking for credible facts to back it up.

This is not the exclusive memory contributing to one of my more noticeable shame triggers, but I have a memory of a middle school math teacher, Mr. Tews. (Yes, his name was totally ironic.) He was a sweet man and well-meaning, but I remember asking questions one day, struggling to understand some complex math, and he said, "Jeanne, I have explained this to you before. I don't understand why you aren't getting it." His statement was true. He had explained the concept to me before. I had even gone in after school to try to get it, but it just was not connecting. And when he said that out loud, shame floated into my being and cemented a belief I carried for years: *I will never be smart enough.*

I felt embarrassed and stupid, and that started a pattern of pretending I understood things even when I didn't, because I didn't want to feel that way again. I even started nodding my head when people were talking as a way to look like I knew what was being said, even if I didn't. I told myself to not ask for help, and that certainly did not help—because the more I stayed inside my head and hid my need, the more I struggled. This led to all kinds of shame and to lies I started to believe about myself, which somehow kept me locked up in a middle school classroom in my past, believing it was better to play small, hide, and pretend.

This deafening lie of not believing I was smart enough kept company with others I'd welcomed into my private shame tribe. I distinctly remember another moment in middle school when a boy I really liked found out through a friend that I liked him. (Sidenote: the fact that any of us survive being preteens is a sheer miracle that deserves so much more praise!) The adrenaline of all the feels was exciting and terrifying at the same time. And even though it was decades ago, I can return to that moment in my mind in an instant. I was smack-dab in the center of everything that makes middle school clumsy and challenging. It was the '80s, and I was endearing but lovingly awkward, if I do say so myself. I was in a developing body I didn't know how to live in. I had braces and glasses. My hair had always had a slight curl in it, but puberty turned my locks into a Bob Ross hair double.

With my secret out in the open, I decided to find this boy after school. I stood just past the buses where he walked every day to get home. I saw him coming and mustered up all my courage. He walked right up to me, and before I could say a word, he declared with a surprising amount of confidence, "Hey, Jeanne, I want you to know you're cool, but you're the girl the guys want as a friend, not as a girlfriend." And he then went on to tell me about one of my friends whom he liked, and he wondered if I could check into if she might be interested in him.

The message was clearly delivered, and a new shame wormed its way into my mind that afternoon. *You are never going to be the most attractive and you will never be pretty enough, so your role is play to the middle and stay average.*

I am not smart enough and *I am not pretty enough* were not my only "enough" lies, but they were some of the noisier ones. At times they directed me to hide and play small. Other times they directed me to take on more, trying to prove them wrong by being overly competent and reliable. I got good at hiding under my pile of beliefs, and every time I did, I left the present and tied myself up in a straitjacket of shame.

* * *

Shame is no respecter of persons. It is not partial to a certain gender, ethnicity, age, or socioeconomic category. Shame goes after any and all humans. After spending decades holding sacred space for people as they share their stories, I have been able to detect a common theme when shame starts to decay the life force of a person: the corrosion always begins in the mind.

I remember a guy saying to me, "I guess it's easier to not let anyone know what's really going on in my mind. I am a successful financial analyst. I have a beautiful wife and three great kids. We live in an upscale suburb. My kids go to a private school. I am well respected, and I grew up with every possible privilege available to me. And yet I feel lost and unclear on who I am, what difference I make on the planet, if my work matters, or if my voice is necessary. I can't get my boss to value me, and I am starting to wonder if it's because I don't know if *I* know how to value me."

Another woman, in tears, said, "I don't know how to enjoy sex. I love my husband and I know he loves me. But every time we start to connect intimately, I can't stop thinking about my own body and what it once was and what it will never be."

There are endless stories, life situations, and opportunities for shame to find its way into your present, but the preferred passageway for shame to enter your life is always through the mind. When you travel to the thoughts of your past that are still hanging around in your present, shame looks for any open door to sabotage and bring condemnation.

You Are Not Your Shame

Like an annoying and invisible sliver, shame agitates your mind just enough to keep you from being able to be present. Most people, after a few unsuccessful attempts to get rid of a sliver, start to self-protect and learn to live with the irritation instead of seeking help to remove the problem. Shame can work the same way. It is good at self-protection and making excuses. Shame knows that if you begin to remove the sliver, it will be in the place where it never wants you to go—in the now.

The present is like kryptonite to your shame, because when you begin to ask *What's here now?* you get to see that in this now moment you are *not* your shame, and your shame is not you. The past is good at seducing you into thinking that living with your shame slivers is better than finding freedom from them. Shame always tries to fool you into thinking that if you find success or power, you will no longer feel unworthy or small. But listening to shame's lies will always push the sliver in deeper and shackle you to self-rejection, believing the only credible way out is through a filtered and curated life.

Shame likes to suggest all kinds of excuses for leaving the present moment to rehash the past, but when you welcome the question, *What's here now?*, you begin to cross the border into the only place where shame can be removed from your life: the present. Even if there is a current circumstance wrapping itself tightly around your life and throwing shaming shade, you have the power within you to say, "Shame, you are not welcome here." This takes time and practice. There is no silver bullet or a snap of the fingers to make shame disappear, but the longer you do the work and invite the question, the more shame loses its power in your life and eventually begins to fade away. Shame wants you to believe that the past is the only place to stay and that you can never get out of it. But hope is always boldly singing from the present that it's never too late to do something different.

I had to learn how to pause, take a deep breath, and lovingly tell myself, *Jeanne, you are not in that math class anymore, and you are no longer standing on that sidewalk waiting for a boy to tell you that you are just the girl all the boys want as a friend.*

You are here. In this now moment. I remind myself those were moments that happened, but they're no longer happening. They played a part in my story but are not the central narrative of my story. I get to decide how big or small of a sliver they are in my life.

You have the same power. How you think impacts how you live. There will always be someone who doesn't see your worth. One of the quickest ways to remove shame from your life and live in the present is to never let that person be *you.*

I didn't realize how much my own shame triggers and thoughts kept me locked up and cut off from parts of myself. I also didn't realize how many lingering shameful thoughts from the past were hijacking me and keeping me from living in any present freedom. I wasn't taking my thoughts captive; my thoughts were holding me captive. I'd allowed my own self-limiting beliefs to lock me up. But as I started to turn the lights on in the dark cell of my thoughts, the fog started to clear and I began to see how my past insecurities were driving my current performance and pretending tendencies. I also began to see that the keys to freedom had been in my own hands all along, but shame kept trying to keep them hidden from me.

> There will always be someone who doesn't see your worth. One of the quickest ways to remove shame from your life and live in the present is to never let that person be *you.*

Trade Condemnation for Conviction

It's the stories of shame from the past that we keep alive that take us out of practicing the present moment. Asking *What's here now?* gives us permission to direct light onto our shame. Instead of saying, "I'm not enough," we get to lovingly see that we are human—and so nothing human can be foreign to us. We get to practice self-compassion and empathy. We get to re-belong to ourselves and one another instead of hiding in the dark. We get to boldly declare we are more than enough and experience freedom from self-condemnation.

But so many of us have become skillful at shaming ourselves, forgetting that God says, "Therefore, there is now *no condemnation* for those who are in Christ Jesus" (Rom. 8:1, emphasis added).

Often, the greatest enemy keeping you locked in condemnation is your own mind. Being knotted up in the past keeps you believing it would be too much work to detangle all the shame stories. But letting the past have control of the present never invites freedom; it only invites harm. There is not a single perfect person on the planet. We've all done something we couldn't fix. We've all said something and wished we had a life-size eraser to wipe out our regrettable words. We all have someone who could tell a tale or two about us.

Condemnation invites you to return to shame. To return to your mistakes and stay guilty. To do the same thing Adam and Eve did: run and hide from God, believing you are the sum of your shame. Conviction is something different. Healthy conviction is a gift from the Holy Spirit to help us transform. To come out from the dark and to let ourselves be seen in the present.

Condemnation invites harm.

Conviction invites hope.

What's here now? invites you to bring healthy courage and conviction to your shame. Healthy conviction always welcomes the following steps.

1. Examine your shame stories.

Shame can often be uncomfortable, and the mind has developed lots of ways to avoid the discomfort and pretend it's not there. Shame's goal is to devour the soul. But when we get curious about our shame, we prevent it from eating any more of our souls. As you get curious about the shame in your life, allow yourself to explore it with compassion and love.

2. **Practice healthy noticing.**

Allow yourself to step back from the power shame has over you and try to investigate your life from a different perspective. Instead of looking from the inside out, look from the outside in. Be a gentle and kind observer of your own life. How has shame impacted you? What story has it been telling you? What does your shame feel like? How are you holding it in your body? How do you talk to yourself about yourself?

3. **Pay attention to where you hide.**

Living with shame is isolating and lonely. Shame wants you to believe no one would ever understand your situation or want to get close to your real life. Shame tells you to push others away and stay alone. Noticing the urge to detach and disconnect is essential to moving through shame; it is a marker that your shame identity has taken over. When you find yourself feeling isolated, judgmental, and separated, this is a perfect moment to start asking, *What's here now?* and to really be honest as you answer the question.

4. **Share your story.**

Vulnerability is not optional. You are human, so you are vulnerable. The option is in the degree to which you allow other humans to experience your vulnerability. When we share our shame stories with healthy and loving people, shame loses its stronghold in our lives. Brené Brown says, "If we can share our story with someone who responds with empathy and understanding, shame can't survive."[3]

I think the same questions God whispered in the garden of Eden are still being whispered today: *Where are you? Who told you?*

Remember, there is no condemnation for those who are in Christ Jesus (Rom. 8:1). If we are to live in freedom, we must be willing to vulnerably say, "Shame has no power in my life anymore" and to rewrite our story out in the open. What shame hates more than anything is when we reach out and tell our story. Shame wants to keep us at a distance from God and at a distance from others. But do you remember what God did in the garden? He went and looked for Adam and Eve.

God wanted intimacy. Intimacy requires proximity. We have to come out and be seen. The danger of isolation is greater than the risk of intimacy. Secrecy and silence grow shame. Empathy and compassion kill shame. It's safer to come out and be seen as you really are than it is to hide behind something you want people to think you are.

You may have gotten really good at hiding. You may have found filters to cover up all the things you don't want anyone to know. But shame and hiding are twin siblings that whisper lies, telling you that secrecy and silence are the only ways to survive. When you come out from behind the shrubs and allow yourself to experience empathy and compassion, shame's power begins to melt away. You may be fluent at self-condemnation, but when you start to speak to your shame and remind it that it does not get the final word in your story, you start to live in the light. You cling to the truth that if God is in you, shame can't be on you.

> The danger of isolation is greater than the risk of intimacy.

The more you practice living in the present, the more you will move from reacting to past shame to responding with the steadfast appreciation of seeing your shame clearly. You begin to see that past shame is a mere reminder that you have lived—and you are still living. You have overcome some unthinkable difficulties, and you are still standing and breathing and moving through this life.

• • •

I didn't realize shame was blocking me from my own heart. It was holding me back from taking the very important step of leaving my thoughts and living into a wide-open heart. I never expected my shame could become a fuel that propelled me into a deeper experience of belonging. But I began to see that God had not brought me so far to only leave me where I was. I could, in fact, let go of the filters and pretending. I didn't have to hide anymore, and my past stories of destruction could become a present declaration that I was a human being and I belonged to a human experience.

We never have to betray our present because of past pain, and we can boldly declare, "That was then; this is now. I am committed to living in the *now*."

3

. . . .

Grief

Chutes and Ladders

The quickest way for anyone to reach the sun and the light of day
is not to run west, chasing after the setting sun, but to head east,
plunging into the darkness until one comes to the sunrise.

Jerry L. Sittser, *A Grace Disguised*

For multiple years my mom held the title of "room mom chair" at our school and spearheaded all the classroom parties and field trips for the year. She orchestrated everything from pinning beards on Santa and tails on the Easter Bunny to every possible form of guessing the number of candy canes and jelly beans. I come from a woman who gave it her all to add creativity and fun to our classroom celebrations, and I am so grateful for the countless memories I have of my mom hosting the classroom parties for my brothers and me in our elementary years. She worked part-time and used so much of her remaining time and energy to craft lasting moments I still cherish from that season.

While there are many things I thankfully inherited from my mom, sadly, this craftiness for parties and field trips was not one of them. I work full-time, and on a scale of one to ten, my energy level hovers at a minus ten at the thought of creating parties and moments for my kids and their classmates. Don't get me wrong; I love my kids and other people's kids, which is precisely why *not* planning the parties and field trips is an act of love to them and myself.

So, when my kids were young and the first waves of parent emails started coming into my inbox, I made a deal with my kids. I would give it my all each year for their personal birthday parties, but classroom parties were far from my specialty and a hard no for me. I assured them there was some other parent who had a professional Pinterest page ready to go. My compromise was that I would joyfully do one field trip a year with each of them.

Accordingly, when my daughter's sixth-grade day trip to the state capital came up, I was the first mom to sign up as chaperone. I took the day off, and we got all kinds of fun snacks to share on the two-hour bus ride downstate and set our alarms for the early call time of 5:00 a.m. at the school. When the day came it was pouring rain, and the bus was a little late as we all hovered under the school building's overhang. Cheers erupted when the bus finally pulled up, and we began to load up for our trip down to Springfield.

As we got ourselves situated, counting all the kids, making sure that everyone had a buddy, my cell phone rang. It was still really early, and I noticed it was my sister-in-law Anto (short for Antoinette). The noise of the bus was overpowering, and I knew there was no way I would be able to hear her, so I quickly hit decline and texted her.

> Hey, I'm on a bus with Gigi headed to Springfield. Is everything OK?

> Call me Right Away.

My first thought was, *Maybe she needs help with my nephew, Ewan. Maybe their childcare fell through for the day.* And then my next thought caused my heart to sink deep into my chest. *Maybe something is wrong.* I pulled Gigi close and whispered into her ear, "I need to call Auntie Anto really quick." I hunkered down into my seat and dialed her number.

When she picked up the phone, I knew instantly something was wrong. There is nothing anyone can do to prepare themselves for the words they receive in those first moments of shock. Between the tears and screams on the other end of the phone, I heard my sister-in-law say words that still flood my eyes with tears even as I type them.

"Your brother is not breathing. Get off that bus now. I need you."

My memories from the moments following that phone call are scattered. But I can divide my life into two periods: before the call and after the call. That's what loss does. It signals there was a *before* and an *after.* And no one ever signs up for the after. Everything in me wanted to hold out hope that something could be done—maybe paramedics could revive my forty-four-year-old younger brother back to life, maybe my sister-in-law and nephew would not have to bear the title of a widow and fatherless orphan. Yet a deeper knowing I did not want to accept began to invade my heart. The fog of grief was rolling in, and all I wanted to do was pray it away, but grief's fog moves fast and usually arrives with little to no warning. With tears streaming down my face, I launched into a series of decisions over the coming hours and days with what I can now only describe as a holy grace that disguised itself in the form of clarity and wisdom, and it was not of this world's strength.

> That's what loss does. It signals there was a *before* and an *after.* And no one ever signs up for the after.

I was Anto's first call, which also meant I was the first to arrive at their home. What my heart had most feared became a reality. Andy was gone, and as Anto wept, I held her in one arm and baby Ewan in the other. How were we here? How was this possible? How could this have happened? How was I going to lead us through this moment and all the moments still to come? So much of that day and the days to come are filled with blunt and blurry memories. I remember some of the most random moments, like the Uber driver who took me from my daughter's school to my brother and sister-in-law's home. The moment they took Andy's body out of their home. Calling my mom and brother Eddie—the worst phone calls I have ever had to make. All those moments are seared into my mind, but for the life of me I have no idea how I got anywhere during those days. I don't remember driving my car or eating any meals. God gave me the strength to be present when I needed to be, and honestly, everything else faded away. I was somehow in the here and the now—present, but totally in shock. This was not my first dance with grief. Fourteen years earlier, we'd lost my dad in a similar way. In some ways, this current grief felt worse, like a deeper penetration reopening the earlier wound and returning me to the past.

In the coming days, I gripped what needed to be held together—until I no longer could. The night after my brother's funeral, I started spiraling down a fast and furious chute into the unpredictable waves of grief. A tumultuous ocean I had been in far too many times before was back. I was left trying to stay afloat when everything in me just wanted to succumb to a dark and isolating depression.

I remember playing the game Chutes and Ladders as a child. At first, the chutes looked more fun than the ladders, until I realized they would keep me from winning the game. Yet if there is anything dependable about this life, it is that none of us makes it to the end without traveling down some chutes. They come when we experience moments of change, when the unexpected happens: the betrayal, the shattered dream, the disappointment, the diagnosis, the breakup or the divorce, the letting go of someone you love, the loss of a loved one—every one of those chutes is a loss of what was. However, the further I have traveled the terrain of this life, the more I have come to realize that these chutes of life are also the places God does his deepest transformation in our lives, if we are open—but I don't know if anything is more painful to be present to. I don't know a single person who wants to ask, *What's here now?* when they find themselves in an unexpected chute of grief.

It's in the soil of loss and grief where God does deep and transforming work, but no one ever invites this work. We don't lay out welcome mats to loss. We don't sing songs or throw parties for it because loss feels more like a thief. It takes what once was, and we are never the same. Grief leaves us feeling like we are walking through life in a minor key.

All change is a loss. All loss changes us.

Giving In or Going Into

There are seemingly smaller losses in life, and then there are the ones that take our breath away. There is nothing like loss to cause us to cry out, "God, where are you?" When grief enters our lives, we always have a choice: to *give in* to the grief or *go into* the grief.

Giving in to grief leaves us powerless to every painful wave of loss that laps on the shores of our souls. But going into grief, while we still may feel powerless, allows us to eventually emerge with remedies that bring healing to our own souls and the souls of others.

> It's in the soil of loss and grief where God does deep and transforming work, but no one ever invites this work.

The practice of being present with our grief requires so much energy, especially when it feels like a weighted anchor pulling us to the bottom of the ocean. It's no wonder we feel exhausted from treading in the waters of loss. It feels almost impossible to *not* give in to the aches and pains of grief, because whatever or whomever we were forced to bury is not the only one or thing entombed. Entering the dark tomb of grief often leaves us wondering if we are sentenced to keep living while feeling dead to the rest of life. It almost feels impossible to be in the present moment because the loss in our past plays over and over in our minds.

* * *

One of the narratives that has given me the greatest comfort and direction in the different seasons of grief I have walked through is the biblical story of Job. Job, described as the wealthiest person in the East, was a man of importance and influence. His land and livestock were endless. (Picture someone like Jeff Bezos and his endless Amazon boxes.) Then all the powers of heaven and hell come against Job, and he loses everything. His wealth. His land. His livestock. All ten of his children. He is then struck with an intense sickness and disease that will eventually make him an outcast. This man of honor is now humbled and broken down, and Job comes to the end of himself. The chute of loss leaves him with nothing. In the moment when it is all gone, we get to see Job's reaction. Job 1:20 says, "At this, Job got up and tore his robe and shaved his head."

Why did Job tear his robe and shave his head? This was part of the Jewish practice of mourning, the start of shiva, a week of intense lament, mourning, and grief. But Job is also in shock. Everything has been stripped from him. Everything he held dear is gone. Not just his resources but all his children are gone. Can you imagine that degree of loss? Over the years I have walked with different friends through the loss of a child, and I don't know if there is anything that leaves the heart rawer and more exposed. *All* Job's children are dead.

The Scripture continues, "Then he fell to the ground in worship and said: 'Naked I came from my mother's womb, and naked I will depart'" (vv. 20–21).

Job literally falls. The crushing pressure of his loss is immense, yet when he falls to the ground, he worships. He laments, like what we find in many of the psalms. From the depths of his being, he cries out, "I have nothing. I came into this world naked and now I have been stripped of everything I hold dear, and I might as well die!" This is anguish and despair. Honest, vulnerable, authentic grief. Look at what Job says as he worships:

> "The Lord gave and the Lord has taken away;
>   may the name of the Lord be praised."

In all this, Job did not sin by charging God with wrongdoing. (vv. 21–22)

Job acknowledges the mystery of God. That God gives, and while he does not cause the loss, God allows things and people to be taken away. And somehow, even as Job runs through all the stages of grief in a matter of seconds, he finds himself saying, "May the name of the Lord be praised." Even though he doesn't understand, somehow in his despair he deepens his dependence on God.

Most of the book of Job is a picture of how he sinks deeper and deeper into the soil of grief. While Job tries to hold on for dear life to the last dangling thread of hope he has in God, his wife does the opposite. Job allows himself to go into grief, but his wife gives in to grief. At one point she says, "You need to just curse God and die." It's too much. The loss. The ache. The misery. The questions.

And Job responds to his wife, "You are talking like a foolish woman. Shall we accept good from God, and not trouble?" (2:10). While this may not be the most empathetic response between a husband and wife, it is raw and real.

Somehow, even in the midst of the darkest night of his soul, Job's life is a picture to all of us that when we surrender ourselves to God, we surrender to a life that will have both gifts and grief. We will have moments of delight and moments of deep discouragement. Our hearts will expand with pure bliss, and they will also be cracked open and broken in such a way that we wonder if we'll ever be able to carry on.

What we see in Job's life is a deep respect for the loss in his life. He doesn't deny or dismiss it. He respects that it is real and honors that grief has a role to play in his life.

We need to respect the losses in our lives so we can grieve them. We do so by first acknowledging the loss. So many of us give in to grief by throwing an "F" word all over our loss. We say we are *fine* when we are anything but fine. When we suffer the loss of a loved one. A friendship. A job. Even a season of life.

One of the greatest ways to go into grief is by simply naming your loss as a loss. I remember leaving the season of having little ones. My kids didn't need me in the same way they once did. They were more independent and self-sufficient. I didn't need to cut their food for them, and they were ordering their own food at restaurants. I remember the day I went to give Elijah a kiss at drop-off and he gave me a fist bump instead. I held it together in the moment but cried right as I got out of the school. I felt crushed. I had to respect that this season was over so I could be available to the new season I had entered as a mom.

The worst grief and suffering in life are those we reject. When we acknowledge that something or someone has been lost, then we can begin to walk through the stages of grief, over and over and over, until we find acceptance.

* * *

Grief is never the same for anyone, and no one travels the stages of grief the same way—because no loss is the same. But all of us at some point, and sometimes at many points, will need to travel through these stages. They are not linear, and they don't necessarily build upon each other. Often you will cycle through the stages hundreds if not thousands of times as you process through grief.

As a quick refresher, these are the classic stages of grief, first identified and studied by Dr. Elisabeth Kubler Ross.[1]

Denial. Denial is the first stage, and it helps us endure the loss. In this stage, the world becomes meaningless and overwhelming. Life makes no sense. We are in a state of shock. Denial helps us to cope and makes survival possible.

Anger. Anger is a necessary stage of the healing process. We have to be willing to feel our anger, even though it may seem endless. The more you truly feel it, the more it will begin to dissipate and the more you will heal.

Bargaining. Before a loss, it seems like you will do anything to prevent it. "Please God," you bargain. After a loss, bargaining may take the form of a temporary truce. "What if I devote the rest of my life to helping others? Then can I wake up and realize this has all been a bad dream?" We become lost in a maze of "If only . . ." or "What if . . ." statements. We want life returned to what it was.

Depression. This is when we find ourselves in the depths of what our *now* means. Empty feelings arise, and grief enters our lives on a deeper level, deeper than we ever imagined. This stage feels as though it will last forever. It is the appropriate response to a great loss. We withdraw from life and are left in a fog of intense sadness, wondering, perhaps, if there is any point in going on alone.

Acceptance. Acceptance is often confused with the notion of being "all right" or "OK" with what has happened. This is not the case. Most people don't ever feel OK or all right about the loss of a loved one. This stage is about accepting the reality that our loved one is physically gone and recognizing that this new reality is the permanent reality.

All these stages occur as our present loss plucks us out of our past, leaving us knowing that life will never be as it once was. One of the hardest parts of grief is realizing that you cannot grieve what you cannot leave. So much of the pain of grieving is knowing that we are leaving a season, a place, a person—and oftentimes it's not something we would have chosen.

I remember grieving my dad was so hard because I was afraid that if I let myself leave that season, if I let go, I would have to accept the truth that I would not be with my dad again on this side of heaven. It cracked my heart open. I didn't want it to be true, and a part of me didn't want to face the answer to *What's here now?* I wanted to return to the past in the hopes that it would somehow bring my dad back. But eventually, I had to choose to say, "This is the present tense, and I want to learn to live healthy and whole." It was a journey and I still miss him daily, but I am grateful I learned to grieve well.

Growing through Grief

So many of us are afraid of leaving the past because our loss has left such a hole in our lives that we fear we will never be the same. That somehow the loss will make us less.

One of the very best books I read when I first started to do my own grief work many years ago was *A Grace Disguised* by Jerry Sittser. His entire family was hit by a drunk driver, and his wife, mother, and four-year-old daughter were killed. In an instant he became a widower and a single father to his three surviving children, ages eight, seven, and two. He says,

> It is therefore not true that we become less through loss—unless we allow the loss to make us less, grinding our soul down until there is nothing left but an external self entirely under the control of circumstances. Loss can also make us more. In the darkness we can still find the light. In death we can also find life. It depends on the choices we make.[2]

I began to see that grief can actually grow something in us. We will never be able to return to what was, but grief has the potential to grow good fruit. While we would not choose the loss, we can choose to do the work of grieving the loss, knowing it can bring growth in our lives. Grieving can be fruitful.

Ungrieved Loss Grows	Grieved Loss Grows
Chronic complaining. Loss needs someplace to go, and when it's not grieved it starts to come out in chronic complaining, often in a sarcastic or cynical way. Not working the grief through comes out in bitter and critical words.	*Peaceful appreciation.* This is not an appreciation for the loss but for the growth and transformation that results from it. There is a sense of reconciliation made with the mystery of loss.
A guarded heart. We become protected and closed off, not allowing ourselves to get close to others, because we fear being out of control with our grief or fear another loss will eventually come.	*An open heart.* We allow ourselves to be with the loss. To be as raw and undone as necessary. To stay open, soft, and pliable to the loss.
Resentment. When the loss remains a hole and we don't do the grief work, resentment grows in that hole. It produces irritation, defensiveness, and self-protection.	*Contentment.* There is a spirit of surrender and reconciliation that comes with knowing there are things in this world we will never have an answer for.
Isolation. This is a closing off from others. An internal determination that no one would ever understand, and therefore you don't share your pain with anyone.	*Connection.* Grief connects you to others. I will never forget walking into a grief recovery class and sitting with others who had unexpectedly lost a parent. I didn't want to be there, but I needed to be there, and those strangers became sojourners with me and helped me heal.
Repressed emotions. A person unwilling to grieve the loss holds their emotions in instead of finding a healthy way to release them. Repressed emotions always end up coming out in unhealthy behavior, causing pain to self and others.	*Expressed emotions.* This allows for a healthy movement of whatever emotions are present, knowing that emotions are not looking for answers—they are looking for space.

I remember getting ready for my dad's funeral, looking in the mirror, and saying to God, "I know that you use everything, even this, to grow more and more good in my life. But God, all I want is my dad back." I knew grief would grow me; I just didn't want any of that growth.

Our losses are not meant to leave a hole; loss can be used to make us more whole, if we are willing to grieve it. Good grief produces good fruit. Loss leaves a hole—it just does. There is no getting around that, but there are two possible paths when loss comes: ungrieved loss and grieved loss. Both grow something in us.

Grief can actually grow something in us.

We are not meant to get over our losses; instead, we are meant to allow our losses to permeate our present lives. Only good fruit grows when the stinky compost of loss is mixed into the soil of our souls, expanding our hearts into more of who God created us to be.

Maybe you are not currently in a season of grief but know someone who is. How we hold space and support one another in grief matters. Job has a challenging relationship with his friends as he walks through his loss. But when they first encounter Job, pay attention to what happens.

When Job's friends Eliphaz the Temanite, Bildad the Shuhite, and Zophar the Naamathite hear about all the troubles that have come upon him, they go to sympathize with Job and comfort him. They agree together, "Let's go and offer our presence and our comfort." But when they see Job from a distance, they can hardly recognize him. That is what grief often does—we become unrecognizable.

> They began to weep aloud, and they tore their robes and sprinkled dust on their heads. Then they sat on the ground with him for seven days and seven nights. No one said a word to him, because they saw how great his suffering was. (Job 2:11–13)

It is so beautiful that they just sat with him in the midst of his suffering. Later on, they forget how they started and end up causing Job more pain as they try to hurry his grief process along with insensitive and unkind words. But they started well. Often when someone is grieving, we don't know what to do and end up unintentionally causing them more pain.

One of the best ways we can be present to others in grief is to do the following.

1. *Show up.* You will never regret going. You will never regret bringing a meal. You will never regret meeting a tangible need.
2. *Speak up.* Say "I love you" and "I am aching with you." Instead of asking what they need, say, "I am going to take care of this need for you." A person in grief does not know what they need.
3. *Shut up.* They don't need your story in the midst of their grief. They don't need your advice. The "Everything happens for a reason" and "God needed another angel" platitudes are not helpful. When we are brokenhearted and crushed, we don't need prescriptions; we need presence.

Loss is never something we would choose. None of us goes looking to take a ride down a chute of pain, but grief has a way of enlarging our souls and, somehow, through it we experience even more of God.

4

Bitterness

She Let Go

Bitterness is cancer—it eats upon the host. It doesn't do anything to the object of its displeasure.

Maya Angelou, interview

My dear friend and the worship leader at our church, Patrick, is a fantastic songwriter. He has a way of taking lyrics and melodies and weaving them together into songs that declare the desires of my heart. I will never forget being on a staff retreat with him as he worked out a new song.

He sang through the first verse and then launched into the bold chorus, "It's time for letting go; I'm not in control, But *Jesus* you are, *Jesus* you are."[1]

I simultaneously felt understood and uncomfortable. I wanted to sing the words and be able to mean them, but so many of my days feel like the lyrics should read, "I'm not letting go; I am in control, *Jeanne* you are, *Jeanne* you are."

LETTING GO IS HARD. And yes, the bold, all caps, and underline are deserved. If I could have a whole page dedicated to only those four words, I would. Letting go is hard.

Letting go of things.

Letting go of plans.

Letting go of relational desires.

Letting go of money.

Letting go of time.

Letting go of people you love.

Letting go is hard.

Recently, a handful of people with whom I spent several years sharing meaningful moments of friendship decided they no longer wanted to be in a relationship with me. Part of their process of ending our relationship was to take to social media in a multiday smear campaign filled with hateful lies and defaming content about my character and leadership. I felt gutted. My heart seemed ripped in half, and I was filled with pain, tears, hurt, and anger. No part of me wanted to release what they had done. I felt justified in my hurt. My resentment felt righteous, and I wanted to retaliate and return their spite with spite—until I realized my quickly hardening heart was laying down a foundation for my own personal prison.

Debtor's Prison

Whenever you start rolling around in your own animosity, you are not only strengthening the steel of your own jail cell but also your future behavior toward more animosity. Growth always leads to letting go of a past that will never change, and I have come to believe that all of life is a lesson in letting go. Any lasting spiritual transformation will lead to surrender. It's what we are created to do, but I am here to make an announcement: letting go sucks. (Sorry,

Mom, I know you don't like it when I use that word.) Really. I hate it—every single time. Especially when I believe I'm right and justified in not letting go. It just feels so much easier to hold on than to let go when someone does what feels unforgivable.

It is not pleasant to compare holding grudges to hoarding, but that is exactly what we do when we hold on to false power and control while we withhold forgiveness. I think many of us fear that choosing to forgive will somehow justify the unthinkable injustice we've experienced, and the other person will forget all we chose to forgive.

Somehow my brain always tries to trick me into thinking that hoarding my grudge leaves me the winner, yet I am never left clutching the victory but instead only bitterness.

When I hold a grudge, I have make-believe conversations in my head with all I am going to say if I run into the person. And in my head the conversations are good. Really good. And for some reason there is always a gospel choir in the background giving me loud choruses of "Amen!" "Preach it, sister!" and "Hallelujah!" And somehow the conversation always ends with the person who hurt me confessing their wrongs and begging for my forgiveness.

Clearly these conversations are a figment of my imagination because I can go on record and say that never once has one of those scenarios come true. And it's probably for the best, because in my made-up fantasy I'm still the one holding the grudge.

When unforgiveness grips you, you will never have freedom in your life. The longer you hold a grudge, the longer the grudge has a hold on you. Bitterness is desperate for you to keep the past alive as resentment attacks your very life force, silently hurting you from the inside out. Hoarding past hurts and suffering is tricking yourself into stockpiling all those past words and actions into an oversized debt that can never be paid. Your mind busies itself replaying the offense over

> **The longer you hold a grudge, the longer the grudge has a hold on you.**

and over, racking up more interest, believing that one day you will force someone to settle the bill. But in the end bitterness always leaves you holding the check.

Bitterness keeps you locked up in a dull past, numbing yourself on a never-ending hamster wheel instead of pursuing the sharp but hopeful pain that comes through the courageous and healing journey of forgiveness. Whether you are in the middle of a relationship breakdown, breakup, or betrayal, inviting the question, *What's here now?* offers an opportunity to choose freedom through forgiveness.

Brothers in Bitterness

One of the most profound stories that has impacted my journey with bitterness is the biblical story of twin brothers Esau and Jacob. Their father, Isaac, didn't marry their mother, Rebekah, until he was forty, and then they struggled with infertility for twenty years. Eventually they got pregnant, but it was a difficult pregnancy. The Bible says that Rebekah described it as a great battle. She could tell the two brothers were fighting within her. Literally, when she gave birth, Esau was first but Jacob was grabbing on to his brother's heel. The parents named their second son Jacob because it meant "sneaky one" or "cheater."

Can you imagine meeting other parents at the playground and introducing your child like this? "Hi, this is our son, *the cheater*. How about a playdate?" The brothers were very different: Esau liked to hunt, and Jacob liked to cook. One time, when Esau came back from hunting famished, Jacob had made some stew Esau wanted. So Jacob convinced Esau to give up his birthright for some of his stew, and he did. I understand Esau; when I'm hangry, I often make unwise decisions.

Later in their lives, when Isaac was about to pass away, Jacob conspired with Rebekah to steal the blessing meant for the first-born son by pretending to be Esau. Jacob tricked his dad and stole his brother's blessing. When Esau found out, he was furious

76

and wanted to kill Jacob, and he easily could have. Jacob escaped and went to live in hiding. The brothers were separated for decades. They each married, started families, and experienced their own ups and downs. They never saw one another and essentially lived estranged, separated—and brooding with resentment and anger.

Eventually Jacob has some trouble with his father-in-law, Laban, and goes out on his own, and as he leaves the land where he had hidden for many years, he knows he is most likely going to see Esau again, so he makes preparations. Jacob pulls together a significant number of livestock as a peace offering and sends his herds and people ahead to greet Esau. Before going himself to meet his brother, after all the years of unforgiveness that have mounted up between them, Jacob decides to spend the night on his own.

> So Jacob was left alone, and a man wrestled with him till daybreak. When the man saw that he could not overpower him, he touched the socket of Jacob's hip so that his hip was wrenched as he wrestled with the man. Then the man said, "Let me go, for it is daybreak."
> But Jacob replied, "I will not let you go unless you bless me." (Gen. 32:24–26)

Jacob was still trying to get the same thing he stole from his brother, Esau, years earlier: a blessing.

> The man asked him, "What is your name?"
> "Jacob," he answered.
> Then the man said, "Your name will no longer be Jacob, but Israel, because you have struggled with God and with humans and have overcome." (vv. 26–28)

I know you're probably wondering two things. First, why did I insert a biblical wrestling match in a chapter on bitterness? And second, who is this mystery wrestler? Well, if you keep reading, you'll find Jacob eventually does the same thing the man he wrestled with did: he has a renaming ceremony right there. Just as he received a new name, *Israel*, he renamed the place where he wrestled *Peniel*, which means "the face of God."

Jacob knew how to hold on. He had been doing it since the womb. He began life by holding on to Esau's heel, and his life remained a grabbing for control until that moment at Peniel.

It wasn't until God touched his hip that Jacob let go of the struggle. He surrendered to God. The Bible says that he walked with a limp for the rest of his days. But he was finally free.

As the sun came up after that life-changing night in Jacob's life, "Jacob looked up and there was Esau, coming with his four hundred men" (33:1).

Can you imagine? Jacob literally wrestled with God all night. He received a whole new identity; from Jacob the Cheater to Israel, which means "one who struggled with God." He was made new, but Esau didn't know about his miraculous makeover moment with God. Jacob's last encounter with Esau was when he cheated, deceived, and stole from his brother.

What would you think at that moment? I would be like, *Um, God, can you come back here and let's do a tag team match against my brother?* "But Esau *ran* to meet Jacob and embraced him; he threw his arms around his neck and kissed him. And they wept" (v. 4, emphasis added).

I kept reading that verse over and over as I was writing this chapter, and I found myself weeping. Esau ran to his brother. He threw his arms around him. Kissed him. And they wept. We only know what was going on in Jacob's life all those years, until his wrestling with God, but clearly Esau had walked through his own forgiveness before he was even in Jacob's presence. He *let go*. He chose to forgive. When he saw his brother, instead of running to do battle against him and get revenge with his four hundred men, he ran to him seeking restoration.

Esau asked, "What's the meaning of all these flocks and herds I met?"

"To find favor in your eyes, my lord," he said.

But Esau said, "I already have plenty, my brother. Keep what you have for yourself."

"No, please!" said Jacob. "If I have found favor in your eyes, accept this gift from me. *For to see your face is like seeing the face of God.*" (vv. 8–10, emphasis added)

To see your face is like seeing the face of God.

Jacob knew what it was like to see God. He'd just wrestled with him the night before. And Jacob compared the forgiveness he experienced at that moment with Esau to experiencing the very presence of *God*. All those years of unforgiveness had kept Jacob chained to his pain, but forgiveness from God and then from Esau reframed his pain. That's what is so powerful about forgiveness.

Unforgiveness chains you to your pain. Forgiveness reframes your pain. That is what we see in the relationship between Jacob and Esau.

Sadly, the message of forgiveness is a messy one in faith circles. I have heard so many destructive messages.

- You just need to let go and let God.
- You need to lay down your right to avenge, because somewhere in the Bible it says that vengeance belongs to the Lord.
- The godliest thing you can do is to take the wrong that was done to you and turn the other cheek; remember "seventy times seven."

While there is some truth woven in those sentiments, they all lack the raw reality that we live in a world where absolutely horrific and painful things happen. So often the reason we hold on to past pain is because we are handed only

> Unforgiveness chains you to your pain. Forgiveness reframes your pain. That is what we see in the relationship between Jacob and Esau.

bandages for wounds that need the precision of a surgeon. Sadly, many of us forget we have 24/7 access to the very best surgeon: God. At any moment we can put ourselves on his surgery table, unlocking the power unforgiveness holds on our hearts.

Choose Freedom

The older I get, the more forgetful I become. I've had to create little systems to remember where I place all the important items I need on a daily basis, especially my car keys and phone. While I often find myself looking for these things, I never struggle with locating all the things said and done to me that have caused pain in my life. It's amazing what the brain decides to remember. Clearly my brain is very good at holding on to bitterness. But as Anne Lamott says, "Not forgiving is like drinking rat poison and then waiting for the rat to die."[2]

I have watched hundreds of people fall into the tricky territory of bitterness. The leftover acidity always dims their once bright light and turns them into sour and defensive people. They lock themselves up in the past and overlook the key to freedom in their own hands.

I have learned over time to detect the power of unforgiveness. It's easy to spot. If you shut your eyes for just a moment and bring to mind the face of someone who has locked themselves up in a prison of bitterness, I bet you can see the unforgiveness all over them. You see them clinging tightly to their resentment as a trophy worth protecting. As Elizabeth Gilbert says, "A bitter person looks like he/she is being dragged through hell alive, and dragging everyone else down to hell with him/her."[3]

While you may not think *you* are locked up in unforgiveness, are any of these common symptoms are present in your life?

Judgment

You still make up speeches of what you are going to say to the person, or what you should have said to them.

You judge their every little move and find something wrong with it.

Resentment

You leave the relationship in your mind.

You give the silent treatment.

You shut down, close up, and wall off.

Gossip

When you talk about the person, you also feel anxiety that causes you to say, "Don't tell them I said this," or "This is just between you and me."

You tell the same story over and over again, and each time you make sure to paint them as the guilty one, even if you say "I'm not totally innocent."

You say things about the person you would never say to them.

Vengeance

You find yourself railing against the person with harsh words, arguments, name-calling, sarcasm, and belittling.

You still think of ways to get even with them.

You struggle to sincerely pray for this person and bless them.

You don't feel any compassion or mercy for them.

Slander

You believe your story about the other person is true, and you tell it as if it's true.

You tear down their character in front of other people.

All these symptoms of bitterness lead to bondage. The irony is our minds tell us we are right. That our judgment and gossip and slander and everything else are justified. But somehow, we are the ones left in chains. As Lewis B. Smedes says, "To forgive is to set a prisoner free and discover that the prisoner was you."[4]

One of the many reasons I have found so much hope in a relationship with Jesus is because of some of the last words he said: "Father, forgive them; they don't know what they're doing" (Luke 23:34 MSG).

Jesus, in all his divinity and all his humanity, had a choice in what he would say in that moment. All of us have that choice. Somehow it took me to middle age to really understand that. I wish I would have gotten it much earlier, but it was not until this fourth decade, with my accumulation of battle scars and bruises, that I realized we can choose to be bitter or choose to be *better*.

The reality is horrible things happen. I bet some really horrible things have happened to you. You've probably been gossiped about, let down, or let go; you may have been lied to or betrayed; you were harmed physically, mentally, or sexually. You may have experienced injustice or inequality or been blamed for things that weren't your fault. At some point someone probably used you for what you could bring to the table, wasted your time, wanted your money, and maybe even wasted your heart. You may have been diagnosed with a disease you didn't deserve or had a loved one die too early. You may have wanted to sue someone or have been sued yourself.

But as Jesus hung on the cross and could have said any number of words, in his most vulnerable moment he strung together nine words that would change all of life.

Father,
forgive
them.
They
don't

know

what

they're

doing.

And in those few words, he not only offers us forgiveness but also the same choice.

We get to choose.

Who would you be if you chose to be free?

When you choose to stay bitter, you get to hold on to your pain and carry it around with you the rest of your life. Lots of people make this choice, and their badge of unforgiveness keeps them locked up all their days. Or you can choose to use the key in your hand to unlock the door. Be an honest and vulnerable version of someone who once was incarcerated to bitterness and chose to do what you could to get better.

I have seen that those who take this risk have the residue of both grit and grace all over their lives. They are cloaked in a stubborn steadfastness to search for light even when all signs point to the dark. They don't shy away from looking for hope, because they know without it life can't come forth. These are the people dripping with symptoms of forgiveness.

Instead of judgment, forgiving people offer LOVE.
Instead of resentment, forgiving people offer PEACE.
Instead of gossip, forgiving people offer GOODNESS.
Instead of vengeance, forgiving people offer MERCY.
Instead of slander, forgiving people offer KINDNESS.

What is perhaps most spectacular about a forgiving person is that they know they will never be the same once they unlock the door. They will no longer be bitter. They will finally be *better*.

I have been a Jesus follower for many decades. I have usually found that Christians are some of the most sincere, kind, and loving people. But when unforgiveness finds itself on the doorstep of a believer, I have noticed that they don't look much different from an unbeliever. The faith of the unforgiving believer tends to resemble an imitation version of the gospel that looks more like a spiritual drive-thru kind of faith. Over the years I have sat with so many different people chained up in unforgiveness. I have heard unthinkable stories. I have held space with people who don't believe they can forgive themselves. I've had my own moments when I kept myself in chains as I found out about things people said about me and ways I was slandered and gossiped about, and every time I saw the person I felt locked up, because I was holding on to my unforgiveness.

Nelson Mandela spent over twenty years in prison, accused of conspiring to overthrow the government. After he'd finally been set free, he said, "As I walked out the door toward the gate that would lead to my freedom, I knew if I didn't leave my bitterness and hatred behind, I'd still be in prison."[5]

One of the single greatest powers God gives us is the power to heal past pain that cannot be changed without forgiveness. By asking *What's here now?* we can take a past shadow and reframe it with the present light.

Letting go of past pain is not a suggestion to lay aside important boundaries or to excuse injustice, inequality, or inequity. When we let go, we don't forget the damage done, or say it doesn't matter. But we release the power that the past bitterness is bringing into the present moment. This has proven true in my own struggle to unlock my prison of self-righteous unforgiveness.

Asking *What's here now?* is a practice in opening our bodies, hearts, and minds to be able to freely give and receive love. Unforgiveness blocks vision. Forgiveness frees vision. Letting go somehow allows us to be able to see anew.

● ● ●

I will never forget when Gigi was around six or seven and was invited to a birthday party where she knew only the birthday girl. She wanted to go but was also apprehensive because she didn't know any of the other girls at the party. I assured her it would be fun, and if she wanted me to stay around so she felt comfortable, I would be happy to stay.

When we got to the party, the second we walked in I could see in Gigi's eyes she felt scared. She was quiet and shy. She didn't bring her outgoing self into the room, and every nonspeaking fiber in her body was communicating with me to not leave her alone. I helped the other moms with games and food while I also tried to hold back and not interfere with Gigi finding her confidence in the moment.

> Unforgiveness blocks vision. Forgiveness frees vision.

Then one of the moms announced a new game, explaining that all the girls would stand in a circle and toss a rope across the circle to another little girl until they'd formed a web between them. I watched as the birthday girl went first. I quietly prayed she would pick Gigi, because I knew it was likely none of the other little girls would either know her name or pick her. But the birthday girl threw the rope to someone else, and the web began to form from one girl to the next—and each time I watched my baby's eyes increase in sadness as she continued to go "unpicked." The game ended with no one picking Gigi until the mother stepped in to make sure she got the end of the rope.

Watching my little love's heart breaking across the room almost took me outside of myself. I desperately wanted to rescue her. To swoop in as her hero while I subsequently villainized every other little girl in the circle. Right after the game Gigi came to me, fighting tears. She pulled me down to her level, got right in my face, and whispered into my ear very firmly, "I want to go."

I read the situation and mentally fast-forwarded through both scenarios: leaving versus staying. I said, "Gigi, I am going to let you choose right now. Listen to your heart and your body. What are they telling you to do?"

Tears were now streaming down her face. "They both say *go*," she said.

I gathered up Gigi's things. I motioned to the host mom that we were taking off, and we walked out the door.

Gigi was sobbing as we walked across the front lawn toward our car. "They didn't even know I was there. No one picked me. I didn't know any of their songs they were singing from school. No one talked to me. I felt so left out."

I picked her up, held her, and started crying with her. We were both fully present to our feelings. There was an innocence to it. I didn't apply any "effort" to that moment. I did not solve her problem. Instead I chose to crawl into it with her from as healthy a place as I could.

On our drive home, I could tell Gigi was replaying the moment in her mind. Bitterness was mounting and making a play for her impressionable heart. As I looked at her in the rearview mirror, I invited the question to help her let go of the past and come into the power of the present moment. I simply said, "Gigi, what's here now?" Then we had a profound conversation about being with our feelings. How to honor what our hearts and bodies are telling us. How to be in moments when we feel uncomfortable. How to see others who feel left out and how to choose to let go when everything inside wants to *hold on*.

We both declared the things we wanted to let go of. Gigi wanted to let go of being scared, and I wanted to let go of control.

I don't know what you are holding on to, but I am here to tell you bitterness is a terrible friend. It will make secret deals with your heart, trying to convince you that being bitter is better—but letting go is better. Every. Single. Time.

5

Guilt

Backpacking

When you are guilty, it is not your sins you hate but yourself.

Anthony DeMello, *One Minute Wisdom*

How much weight are you looking to carry in your pack?" the woman in REI asked. It was a question I had never been asked, and one I had absolutely no idea how to answer. A friend had invited me to climb Mt. Kilimanjaro in Tanzania, Africa, and before I could pause and come up with reasons to say no, yes came tumbling out of my mouth. I have always preferred saying yes over no to new opportunities, but now I was reaping the ramifications. Mt. Kilimanjaro is 19,341 feet high, and I had never climbed any other mountains, so it was a foolhardy yes at best. I had never even been inside an REI store before, and I didn't own one necessary item for climbing anything, let alone a mountain.

The highly experienced woman in REI who asked me about the weight of my pack quickly discerned I had absolutely no idea what I was doing. Thankfully, she could tell I was already overflowing with novice nervous energy as I stood with my printed checklist entitled "Important items for first-time climbers," and she decided to fill me up with mountain climbing wisdom instead of more stress. "You're going to do great," she said in an optimistic tone. "But let me tell you, every ounce of weight you put in your pack is weight you carry up that mountain, so my advice is to travel light."

I tucked her advice away—and ignored it. On the first day of the climb, I decided I wanted to be prepared for all situations, so I loaded up with every possible item I might need for our eight-hour climb. I crammed extra shirts, socks, hats, and gloves into every little compartment in my fancy turquoise backpack. I filled every last water bottle and brought along all of my new mountain climbing gadgets. By the time we ended that first day of hiking, my back and shoulders were screaming at me. Oh, how I wish I had heeded the counsel of my REI friend. I lay in my tent on my state-of-the-art sleeping bag (that I did not know how to use) and resolved to only bring necessary items in my pack the next day. Each day I put less and less in my pack, and it began to serve as a living metaphor for the way I wanted to live my life: light and free.

What was true of my backpacking experience on the mountain was also true about how I lived my life. I realized my overloaded pack was a mere symbol of my overdeveloped gift for storing up yesterday's mistakes to carry into tomorrow's reality. And my consistent weight of choice was self-conscious guilt. While I know lots of guilt starts with *would* or *could*, my guilt almost always begins with *should*.

I should not have eaten that extra serving. I'm never going to get to my ideal weight if I can't control my portions.

I should call my family and friends more. I will do it another day, when I don't feel this way.

I should exercise way more than I do. That Peloton bike is certainly not going to ride itself.

I should drink more water. Even though coffee is mostly water, it does not substitute for water.

I should take my own advice and practice what I preach about self-care, get off of my productivity treadmill, and rest and sabbath this weekend.

I should not let the kids be at home alone this long in their online classes.

I should have better habits with my screen time.

I should have a menu in my kitchen, like my friend Tracy does.

I should recycle more.

I should post on social media more.

I should finish all those books I started that are piled up on my nightstand.

I shouldn't leave our dogs, Moses and Louie, in their crates so long. Better yet, I should stay consistent with the training plan for Moses and Louie, and then they might not need their crates.

That's what guilt does in our lives. Like an unwelcome burden, it entangles us in our past as we rehash all we could've, would've, or should've done. My *should* always keeps me from the present moment.

As we talk about guilt, let's pause for a quick reminder of the differences between shame and guilt we discussed in chapter 2: shame says I *am* wrong. Guilt says I *did* something wrong. If shame says you are wrong, guilt is committed to making sure that, even if you didn't do anything wrong, there is something hanging over your head that warrants an apology.

Guilt is a self-conscious emotion committed to rehashing past experiences that have not been repaired or released in our present reality.

Guilt turns us inward, revealing that our insides don't match our outsides. This is the self-conscious part of guilt. Like a persistent telemarketer, guilt doesn't give up until we pick up the phone and listen to it.

Guilt is felt in the heart, held in the body, and replayed in the mind.

Guilt hearkens us back to what *was* so that we cannot fully experience what *is*.

Regret from the past can have so much power over your present life. It is committed to holding you underwater while whispering lies that you will never catch your breath from your past mistakes. Like a terribly tacky millstone locked around your neck, guilt says you are the sum of your bad decisions and desperately tries to get you to stay submerged in the past, believing there is nothing good waiting in the present or future.

> **Guilt is felt in the heart, held in the body, and replayed in the mind.**

The more past weight we keep in our packs, the harder our daily journey to live in the present moment becomes. Like a straitjacket confining us from the present, guilt becomes our own personal, self-appointed lockup where our failures and flaws play on a 24/7 loop. Guilt's primary role is to keep us feeling weighed down and overwhelmed. David, who wrote many of the psalms in the Bible, was familiar with this kind of feeling. Psalm 69 says,

Save me, O God,
    for the waters have come up to my neck.
I sink in the miry depths,
    where there is no foothold.

I have come into the deep waters;
    the floods engulf me.
I am worn out calling for help;
    my throat is parched.
My eyes fail,
    looking for my God.
Those who hate me without reason
    outnumber the hairs of my head;
many are my enemies without cause,
    those who seek to destroy me.
I am forced to restore
    what I did not steal.
You, God, know my folly;
    my guilt is not hidden from you. (vv. 1–5)

You can hear the invisible weight wrapped around David's words. He legitimately fears the waters might go beyond his neck, and he may never catch a firm and secure place to stand again. You can hear his exhaustion and fatigue from crying out and seeking help but feeling like God is nowhere to be found.

Perhaps David's most vulnerable and honest words in this psalm are "my guilt is not hidden from you" (v. 5). One of the most elusive and yet dead-end lies of guilt is that no one knows what we are hiding, but deep within ourselves we know nothing is hidden from God.

My guilt and the guilt I have seen in so many others is committed to getting us to replay past poor behaviors that weigh us down with the limiting belief that we are unworthy of belonging. Any misstep is an automatic decree sending us to the back of the line, where we are doomed to spend our lives constantly trying to catch up to the rest of the pack.

Guilt has a predictable pattern, and it prides itself on getting you to believe that the pattern can't be broken. But this is not true.

Guilt's Pattern ·

GAFFE

THE GUTTER
(Rehash the Past)

THE GUIDE
(Receive the Present)

The Gaffe

Guilt always begins the same way, with a gaffe. This gaffe is either real or perceived. You did something you wish you wouldn't have or didn't do something you wish you would have. What is essential with guilt is learning to name the difference. The things we have done that require fixing can lead to great introspection and intentional relational repair. But often the things we wish we would have done are self-imposed expectations that will leave us insecure and doubting ourselves. Valorie Burton, in her fabulous book *Let Go of the Guilt*, says, "Your job is to accurately read the message of guilt so you can take the right next step to address it appropriately. Remember this: if you misread the message of guilt, you will react in ways that are unhealthy and counterproductive."[1]

Knowing whether the message of guilt is real or perceived is essential in understanding the impact guilt has on our lives. It's critical to ask questions in the present moment to determine if your guilt is real or perceived. Is it true you don't call home often enough? What would feel like "enough" in that situation? Is it true you should post on social media more? What would a healthy version of "more" posting look like?

The Gutter (Unproductive Guilt)

Once a real or perceived gaffe occurs, the brain wants to get you to take the easier step in guilt's dance. Guilt is more comfortable with condemnation and would always prefer to send your thoughts to the gutter—a place that's hard to climb out of. Guilt wants you to push the rewind button and repeatedly relive all your wrongdoings. When you live in a past loop of real or perceived mistakes, you let guilt run the show. Eventually, guilt rules all your decisions. From relationships to finances to how you spend your time and what your purpose in life is, guilt commits you to living a life of obligation and then resenting it.

The brain is conditioned to take the path of least resistance.[2] So the natural tendency is for your thoughts to steer toward this gutter, but it's a terrible place to live. Life in a gutter is not a life of freedom. Love, joy, peace, patience, kindness, goodness, faithfulness, gentleness, and self-control don't hang out there. When you keep your thoughts in the gutter, you give up living in flow with the Spirit. You feel like you are always doing something wrong, always needing to apologize for everything, always replaying past gaffes—always feeling like no matter how much you seek to atone for the past, you can never do enough to feel OK in the present. This is unproductive guilt. It does not lead to life, and it keeps us from the healing presence of God.

The Guide (Productive Guilt)

The gutter is where guilt wants you to live, but when you bring guilt into the present moment it can become a significant guide in your life. Transforming your guilt will mean learning from your mistakes. No growth happens without healthy learning. Unhealthy guilt gets you to spend all your energy in the present feeling upset about something that occurred in the past. It's not only unhealthy but also unproductive, because no amount of guilt can ever change the past. It's meditation in the wrong direction and nothing but an avoidance move. When you marinate in guilty feelings about something that has already happened or you wish would have happened, you don't have to be in the here and now. By shifting to the past, you get to avoid the transforming work that can only be done in the present.

It is always easier to cripple yourself with guilt than release yourself to grow. But if you allow yourself to sit in the now moment with God and ask yourself, *What's here now?* guilt can become a guide.

I experienced this gift of pulling guilt into the present even while writing this chapter. My family and I are in the midst of a whole lot of transitions in our lives. We've lived in Chicago for the past ten years. Jarrett and I moved into the hustle and bustle of this major metropolitan city with a two- and a four-year-old and started a church out of our living room. We went all in on our urban lives and watched God provide and guide us throughout the next decade. Our kids attended Chicago public schools, and we tried to do our best to be good neighbors and advocates for the best possible education not just for our own kids but for all the families in our community and city. Sadly, the city of Chicago still has an antiquated system for attending high school. Kids can't simply attend the school in their neighborhood; they have to apply, take all kinds of tests, and rank their order of desired schools. I think it would be easier to get into Harvard, Oxford, or Yale than a particular high school in the city of Chicago. Our son, Elijah, was in eighth grade when the COVID-19 pandemic hit, and as all of life shut down in March 2020, we still had to navigate through a crazy and complex system to figure out his high school for the following year. The wild thing about our situation was that Elijah's high school of choice was literally 250 feet from our front door. We lived three houses down from the high school he dreamed of attending, and our church was only another three blocks away. We had set up our lives to comfortably navigate the remaining middle school and high school years all within a few blocks' radius.

Due to reasons beyond his control, Elijah did not get into the school on the corner. And so we began to lift our eyes beyond our radius and try to figure out what we needed to do in the coming years as our son started high school and our daughter completed her remaining years of middle school. All of this occurred while we were leading our church through the pandemic and the housing market began to crumble in urban areas and boom in suburban areas. None of us wanted to move, but as we prayed and talked and navigated through all of our options, it became apparent our season of living in the city was coming to a close.

So, with a few weeks remaining before the school year began, we made an offer on one of the only available houses in a suburb just outside of Chicago. It needed lots of renovation and work but was affordable and available in our time frame. So, in the midst of a pandemic, our kids started their new schools online with people they had never met. We stepped into a major renovation and continued to lead our church through multiple unknowns. To say our leadership horsepower began to grow weary is an understatement, and I know that we are not the only ones. This season has unearthed so much fear and anxiety in all of us. We lost multiple loved ones. Walked through church transitions. Reimagined our entire church, renovated a whole house—oh, and I had heart surgery (more about that later) and wrote a book (a.k.a. *insanity*, and not the good kind).

When we realized that our new-old house would not be ready in time for us to move in before we had to leave our current home, we set out to find three months of temporary housing. Everything we looked at was either too expensive or not ideal for our family of four and two dogs. One day I was talking about our situation with my friend Susan, and she said, "Why don't you come and live in the house next to me up on the lake?"

Susan had just purchased the house next to hers, and it was sitting vacant. It was over an hour from the city but overlooked Lake Michigan. It felt like a gift from God yet almost too good to be true. After exhausting all other options, we decided to put our things in storage and move to the lake for three months. We knew we could commute into the city as needed, and it was such a short period of time that perhaps it might just be the exhale all of us were looking for.

After one week of living on Lake Michigan, I felt the kind of peace I had not felt in my body for almost eighteen months. Each time I looked at the water, absorbed the fresh, clean air, or gazed into the dark night with twinkling stars, I found myself overwhelmed with the goodness of God's provision.

While sitting on the dock one day, attending a counseling appointment on Zoom, I said to my counselor, "The goodness of this season feels too good to be true, and a part of me feels like it's too much." As I described the gift of our current living scenario, I said, "It's almost like everything is as good as it can be, but there is still a tiny pebble in my shoe that is keeping me from enjoying it fully." She pressed in like any good counselor, and asked, "Can you describe what the pebble represents?" Then I said, "I feel guilty for so much abundance." And as tears trickled out of my eyes, I realized I'd brought a past story into the present moment. I'd let that old story serve as a guide as I continued to pull the thread that ran through my life labeled "you do not deserve excessive abundance." From my upbringing to my still-unresolved stories around how a pastor "should" live, I couldn't allow myself to absorb all the goodness without the weight of guilt still showing up in my personal backpack.

What occurred in that moment was a great gift. It was such a reversal to the gutter my mind had learned to hang out in. Instead I chose to let it serve as a guide. I shared the story with Jarrett and my dear friend Sue, and then my friend Jeanne M and our staff team. I began to recognize that by bringing my perceived guilt into the present and into a community of belonging, I could start to see myself not as permanently blemished but just in need of the bright light of presence. The healing and hope from Jesus, myself, and others were able to dissolve my guilt.

Guilt's Gift ·

What I experienced is what happens when our guilt comes into the present moment. The guilt we are compelled to keep hidden prevents us from belonging. But the exact opposite is true. When we expose our guilt and let it serve as a guide, it becomes a gift. When we let others see us as we are, some of the greatest healing takes place.

Guilt's first play is always to direct us toward the gutter. To restrict and restrain us from the present moment and force us to swallow the lie that a life of silent suffering is the only way to pay for the gaffes we have made. Guilt's goal is to leave us feeling like garbage, wondering if others can smell our stench. Like the character Pigpen in *Peanuts*, guilt feels like a dust cloud impacting every relationship we have. But what if guilt could get redistributed in our lives, becoming compost to nurture our souls instead of burying them?

> **When we expose our guilt and let it serve as a guide, it becomes a gift.**

To become garbage that serves.

Garbage that reshapes.

Garbage that metabolizes into something beautiful.

One of the most redemptive parts of God is that our failures, mistakes, and regrets are what he builds our lives upon. It's the absolute audacious and ridiculous idea of grace that only God could come up with—that guilt would lead to a gift.

None of us get to God by doing everything right, and many of us only come back to him after doing it wrong. After we sleep in a pen of pigs and have our filth all over us, we come back expecting penance and instead are greeted with a party. Guilt wants to keep us in the pigpen; grace throws us a party. When we are at the bottom of our guilt, grace lies pooled and waiting for us.

I have found that love always beats guilt. Light always invades the dark, and grace is always on the other side of any and all guilt.

* * *

Perhaps the most transforming moment on my Mt. Kilimanjaro expedition was not the climb but rather the descent. After a long and arduous climbing day, a few of us were still a good way off from our camp. It was dark and cold, and we were exhausted. The air was thin, and many of us were struggling to breathe while also staying encouraged. Our guide that day was a Tanzanian man named Emmanuel. He seemed unaffected by the terrain, oxygen level, or cold air. He continued to sing and to assure us that we were almost there, even though his version of "almost there" was very different from mine. At one point, when I was at the point of exhaustion, Emmanuel took my pack from me and said, "I will carry it the rest of the way." I remember thinking, *I really should carry my own pack; this man has to be exhausted*, but I also knew I didn't have much left in my tank. So, pushing through my *should*, I gave up my pack to Emmanuel, and he carried it the rest of the way to camp.

Love always beats guilt.

As I lay in my tent later that night, dirty, exhausted, and just wanting a real bathroom and shower, the name of my guide who came to my rescue dawned on me: *Emmanuel*. God with us. The very presence of God met me on that mountain and carried my pack when it was too heavy. And the wise words from the lady at REI reverberated in my mind as I drifted off to sleep: *Keep it light*.

My friend, I don't know what's in your backpack, but if it feels heavy I offer these same words to you. Guilt is a heavy burden no one was meant to carry. Keep it light.

PART 2

Rehearsing the Future

6

Worry

Turn It Down

To pay attention, this is our endless and proper work.

Mary Oliver, "Yes! No!"

I always marvel at people with hidden talents and skills. We have a family group text, and the majority of our texts are funny memes and videos of people sharing their crazy or hidden talents. Like the video of a girl who can do the Siri voice perfectly. Really. It is so bizarre. Or a guy who can make his eyebrows dance with each other. You have to google it. And one of my personal favorites is a girl who can say every word backward the second she sees it. *What?* How does her brain have to work to be able to do that?

I don't really have any interesting hidden talents, though I always wished I did. Something I can do, however, is fall asleep anywhere, at any time, and stay asleep. When I say anywhere, I mean *anywhere*. The back of a bouncing jeep in Africa. The last row of the plane with seats that don't recline. A tent on the side of a mountain. On a couch in the middle of a conversation with friends. For some reason, sleep has never been an issue for me. If I can get into a somewhat comfortable position, give me five minutes and I'm out. On more than one occasion Jarrett and I have been in conversations with friends during which a movie or TV show comes up, and I'll say, "Oh, we need to watch that." And Jarrett always responds the same way: "We have; you fell asleep." Sleeping is one of my secret talents. I am good at it, and I am grateful.

That's why when I began waking up every night at 3:20 a.m., for multiple weeks, I was concerned. I found myself wide awake in a mental gymnastics routine that would have rivaled Simone Biles's. Fretting and fearing. Tossing and turning. The noise of my thoughts was deafening and had me swirling around both important and inconsequential things. My mind felt like it was stuck looking for a signal as it continued to recalibrate. Jumping from one worry to the next. Up. Down. Back. Forth. In. Out. Repeat.

I rehearsed our upcoming move to a different town, wondering if we'd made the right decision to start our son at a new high school in the middle of a pandemic. I exhausted all the nuances around a particularly difficult leadership decision I knew I needed to make at work. Then my mind started pestering me about my upcoming heart surgery. Would I feel normal living with a heart defibrillator? Isn't that what old people had to do? *Does this mean I'm old?* And then, with no warning, I jumped to worrying about how to get rid of the mildew smell in the washing machine. How did I get from moving to a new house to mildew in my washing machine? My mind was leading me down a haphazard road, pointing out unpredictable future issues I felt I couldn't do anything about.

It was unlike me to be awake and worried. Remember, my hidden talent is sleeping. And on top of that, I am an optimist. For me the glass is more than half full; it's usually overflowing. I truly believe the best possibility is always going to work out, but this time I wasn't buying my own hype. A silent and sneaky culprit had moved into my thoughts without any notice.

Worry is like that—an unexpected windstorm of fear carving a path through your mind while knocking down every other thought you have. It can be about something that will happen in a matter of minutes or something you fear will happen in ten years. The language of worry has a dialect that is easy to detect, especially for those fluent in speaking it.

"I don't have enough time to . . ."
"I don't know what to do about . . ."
"I can't stop thinking about . . ."
"I'm really nervous about . . ."
"I'm scared to death that . . ."
"My heart sinks when I think about . . ."
"I don't know what I will do if something happens to . . ."

I have heard every one of those phrases, and I'm pretty sure at some point I've said them too. The language of worry consumes itself in the *not yet* as it looks beyond the *now*. Worry sweeps away today's happiness by rehearsing tomorrow's headaches. It gets us stuck in possible problems. And when we are run-down and overwhelmed, it's rarely our hard work that causes our frustration and resentment—it's our worry.

Worry is simply living in a *not yet* that is worse than your *now*. A fictitious construct versus a factual reality. And the magical power of worry is that your mind blindly follows along its path. Worry interrupts our present with concerns about the future.

> **Worry is simply living in a not yet that is worse than your now.**

Interruptions

The good news? Interruptions can be irritating—or they can be intentional invitations. To interrupt is to cause or make a break in continuity. That's exactly what an interruption feels like: a break in continuity.

- You're all settled with a book and a cup of coffee, and the baby starts to cry.
- You have a plan for your day and all you need to get done, and the phone rings summoning you to come solve a problem.
- You're writing a book and have a very real deadline, and at the same time you have to have heart surgery, renovate a house, and reopen a church after a global pandemic. It all feels like too much, and to escape the worry of the deadline, you decide to clean out every closet and reorganize your pantry. (I don't know anything about this last example.)

Usually, the initial purpose of an interruption is to draw your mind to something that requires your performing, preparing, or preventing. Interruptions aren't always bad, and they are a part of life. We can't always choose the interruption, but we do always get to choose our response to it. When interruptions enter our lives, we decide what to do with the noise inside our minds. Especially the noise that leads to worry. In other words, we don't always get to decide the sound, but we do get to decide the volume. The sound of worry is often unavoidable, but its volume is adjustable.

Volume Up = Problem   Volume Down = Possibility
for Presence

Interruptions enter our lives with a purpose. When we turn the volume up that purpose can become a problem, and when we turn the volume down it becomes a prompt to practice being

104

in the present moment. Interruptions are inevitable, but worry is avoidable. Why, then, do many of us get hooked into worry's trance? No child grows up saying, "I hope to one day be chronically addicted to worry." In my own life, I know that I often turn the volume up because I don't want to be surprised by anything and prefer to feel safe, so I believe the lie that I am the sole solution to my problems. Perhaps you do the same thing. We are better at turning the volume up to try to drown out our fear than turning it down, but what we end up doing is creating more problems.

> Interruptions are inevitable, but worry is avoidable.

While none of us would choose an interruption, when interruptions come, we have the perfect opportunity to ask ourselves, *What's here now? What's going on in my heart, mind, body, and soul?*

Jesus regularly asked *What's here now?* He may not have used those exact words, but his desire was to draw people out of their *not yet* moments and into the *now* moment. Sometimes he was subtle when making his point, but there is zero chill in the following verses. (I imagine if he were writing it out himself, he would use all available formatting: bold, capitals, underline, and largest possible font size.)

> Therefore I tell you, do not worry about your life, what you will eat or drink; or about your body, what you will wear. Is not life more than food, and the body more than clothes? Look at the birds of the air; they do not sow or reap or store away in barns, and yet your heavenly Father feeds them. Are you not much more valuable than they? Can any one of you by worrying add a single hour to your life?
>
> And why do you worry about clothes? See how the flowers of the field grow. They do not labor or spin. Yet I tell you that not even Solomon in all his splendor was dressed like one of these. If that is how God clothes the grass of the field, which is here today and tomorrow is thrown into the fire, will he not much more clothe

you—you of little faith? So do not worry, saying, "What shall we eat?" or "What shall we drink?" or "What shall we wear?" For the pagans run after all these things, and your heavenly Father knows that you need them. But seek first his kingdom and his righteousness, and all these things will be given to you as well. Therefore, do not worry about tomorrow, for tomorrow will worry about itself. Each day has enough trouble of its own. (Matt. 6:25–34)

It would be easy to think of Jesus as a Bob Marley superfan, singing about how "every little thing is gonna be alright."[1] (I can picture his music video, with the dancing birds and the flowers of the field.) But that's not what Jesus is saying here. He calls out birds and flowers because the birds live higher and the flowers live lower, rising above and below the circumstances in life. They know where they are supposed to be at every given moment. They don't look around and wonder if there is something else they should be doing. In other words, the birds and the flowers don't have a problem with the volume dial. Jesus is clear: when worry comes into your life, turn the volume down. Don't even let the noise and confusion of worry enter your mind.

● ● ●

Living in downtown Chicago provides an ongoing soundtrack of "L" trains, buses, sirens, and other city clamor. It's beyond stimulating but also strident. I love any chance I can get to leave the concrete jungle and purposefully put myself in God's creation. My ability to turn the volume down on all the busy interruptions that bang around and bully my mind improves, and they seem to move into their proper place.

I will always pick the ocean over the mountains, but a few days staring at the majesty of a mountain range is not a bad runner-up. On a recent trip to Colorado, as I gazed at a wide expanse of the trees perfectly placed on snow-covered mountains, I noticed that each part of creation played its inspired role. I did not see a mountain looking as though it was trying to stand taller and prouder than the other mountains, and no tree seemed to be wondering if it was swaying more rhythmically in the wind than the tree beside it. Not a single bird looked worried about what it needed to get done that day.

Why did I struggle and worry so much about doing the same in life? While I can appreciate that Jesus is direct and clear in this passage, another part of me wants to say, "Yeah, but do birds and flowers and oceans and mountains have to cook meals, run meetings, put up the perfect response on social media, and earn a living, all while keeping up with the laundry?"

Thankfully, when I turn the volume down, I can answer my own question and recognize the silliness in it. What Jesus wants us to understand is that when we worry, we rearrange what should be first in our lives. I believe that's why he reminds us to "seek first his kingdom and his righteousness" (v. 33). Turning the volume down on worry quiets all the other noise and draws us back into awareness of the peace that is always present in Jesus. There is more than enough of whatever it is you fear you won't have. Jesus is the master conductor. The volume is perfect when he is in control. Our job is to root ourselves in the now and trust that God is in control of the not yet. I think this is why Jesus uses creation to call us back to presence. Living with the volume up always leads to anxiety in our lives. Learning to adjust the volume and turn it down creates clarity.

The interruptions in my life that usually turn into worries always seem to start out as innocent ideas. A simple thought—then the volume goes up, and that's when confusion and chaos create a reverberating pressure in my mind I don't know how to handle. Jesus is telling us the volume is too high, and we are not meant to live with this much noise.

I have noticed some patterns when it comes to the volume in my mind. Since we can't control the interruptions, I think it's critical we understand how we often unconsciously turn the volume up and how we can consciously turn it down.

Volume Up	Volume Down
Rapid Pace	Slowness
Unboundaried Relationships	Solitude
Excessive and Unfiltered Input	Silence

Rapid Pace

When my life is over, I want it to be said, "She was wide awake, fully alive, and always here." I don't want to have had just a handful of moments of practicing presence. I want a bold red stamp across my life that says FULLY PRESENT. But it's impossible for me to *be here* when my rapid pace has me everywhere but here. As John Mark Comer says, "Hurry is a form of violence on the soul."[2] Every time my pace of living has gotten out of control, I feel like I lose my soul.

Being able to do it all and do it faster is not helping us; it's hurting us. One of the most loving limits God gave us is that of time, but so many of us forget to find God in the limits. I know this is true in my own life. For years, limits were often the last place I would look for him. In all my planning and possibilities, I would try to find work-arounds to my limits. Deny them. Overpower them. Arrange my life around them so I wouldn't have to face them. But I began to see that in overlooking my limits I was ultimately overlooking *me*. While I was looking for a detour around my limits, God was wanting to meet me in the middle of them.

We all have limits. They are designed to help us live at a healthy pace and practice peace. They lead us to whole lives. At first glance they may seem like barriers, but God sees them as blessings. When we refuse to live within our limits, we eventually find ourselves broken down, sapped of energy, and drained and dry. And if I have learned anything about worry, it is that it feeds an out-of-control pace.

When we own our limits, God supplies us with strength. Think through some of the personal limitations in your life right now. Are you opposing them or owning them? Are you trying to answer your worry by doing more, running faster, and pushing a pace you can't sustain? These are five key areas in which we often turn the volume up in our lives:

- Financial limitations
- Relational limitations
- Physical limitations
- Time limitations
- Energy limitations

As you pause and ask yourself *What's here now?* with your limitations, can you allow yourself to be at peace with where you are today?

Slow

The way to turn the volume down on a rapid pace is to slow your life down. I think so many of us forget it's our own fingers that spin the dial. We also have the authority to pause, change the song, or even turn the power off. Jesus uses the birds of the air and the flowers of the field as the authority on worry because birds and flowers are never in a hurry.

I know I don't know everything about your life, but I'm pretty sure it's safe to say you and your people would be well served if you would slow down. *Fast* and *furious* are not compatible terms with the life Jesus offers. Always being in a rush doesn't make room for love. I used to think the problem was that I just needed more time. But we all have the same amount of time

> When we own our limits, God supplies us with strength.

that Jesus had. The solution is not more time. The solution is to simply slow down because slowing is what settles the soul. As Vincent de Paul says, "The one who hurries delays the things of God."[3]

Unboundaried Relationships

I am an introvert who loves people. I got this backward for many years. I used to think, *I love people, so that must make me an extrovert*. But after lots of significant seasons with little to no boundaries on the number of people in my life, I realized the opposite was true. Too many people left me feeling drained and dry, not because people are bad but because I had the "people" volume turned too high. You can be an extrovert and thrive with all kinds of people, or you can be an introvert and just need a few, but either way when our lives are too overloaded with people, the volume of worry gets turned up.

I think about how many times Jesus pulled away from the crowds to be alone. My work in this world is all about helping people wake up to God, themselves, and one another, but the people part of that mission is impossible to do when I have too many unboundaried relationships in my life. While boundaries feel at first like a limitation on your relationships, their purpose is liberation in your life. And one of the best ways to learn to practice boundaries is in the practice of solitude.

Solitude

The first time I ever hit a season of burnout from both a rapid pace and unboundaried relationships, I was blessed to walk through a season of spiritual direction with Ruth Hayley Barton. I remember driving to her home and sitting in her living room in the quiet with one another. Ruth lit a candle; neither of us said a word, and yet the tears started to flow. After a few moments of quiet, she asked if I knew what my tears were about. I simply said, "I keep giving myself away to everyone else and there is nothing left for me." I remember Ruth saying, "The only place you will be able to reverse that is in solitude with Jesus."

Solitude is the place where striving and straining cease. Where the knots of worry begin to detangle, and we can ground ourselves simply in the love of God. To live as God has invited us to live, we have to step out for a while so we can step further into living in the flow of God's love. Solitude and sabbath are the steady practices of trusting that intermissions always lead to a second act.

Excessive and Unfiltered Information

No other generation in human history has been able to carry around all the information they would ever need or want to know in their pocket. While the availability of knowledge has never been greater, our capacity to be available to God, our own souls, and one another is decreasing at accelerated speeds. Having all this data at our disposal without also having healthy barriers or boundaries decays our lives, leaving us drained and dull. The information comes from so many outlets and with so much weight and speed that most of us don't have time to process what we've seen, heard, or experienced before the next wave of information comes barreling into our lives.

I have a distinct memory seared into my mind from a weekend in May 2018. Prince Harry and Meghan Markle were married, and it was also the same weekend as a deadly school shooting in Santa Fe, Texas, that killed ten people. The headlines and news feed had me zoned out in a trance. I didn't know how to process all of it at the same time. I struggled to try to make sense of a world that falls asleep to the hollow hopelessness and broken hearts in Santa Fe, then awakes to horse-drawn carriages and ringing bells in a castle celebrating the love of a royal couple. All of it felt like so much. I had to turn it all off for a bit. To quiet everything so

I could process it all. So I could hold both the hurt in the world and the hope of new love.

I think so many of us feel conflicted and chaotic, skeptical and scared when we take in information. We don't know how to process it all or where to put it, and we end up feeling paralyzed, not knowing how to return to the present moment.

Silence

Perhaps you're having a hard time hearing your soul's voice because it's been a long time since you have been loving and kind to yourself and trusted your own voice. And to hear your voice, you must be willing to turn the noise down in every other area of your life. When I first started practicing silence, I was so afraid of what I might find. I was good at finding enough noise to drown out the quiet voice. I was good at overworking and pushing; I wasn't sure if I would be good at being silent and still.

> **Worry wants to trick you, over and over, into believing that its presence is necessary in your life.**

Worry wants to trick you, over and over, into believing that its presence is necessary in your life. When I began waking up at 3:20 a.m., it started because I had a full bladder, but the bigger problem was that I also had a full mind overcome by worry. I felt unsure and unclear. The decisions I was making felt heavy and big, and my mind was telling me that lots of important things hung on how I would proceed. I felt weighed down, and worry had bullied me into a corner with the belief that none of it would turn out.

After one too many times of waking up in the middle of the night, instead of letting the noise blare and the reverberations of all that could happen hold me hostage, I began to turn the volume down. I started by just paying attention to what was going on inside. I welcomed the question, *What's here now?* I chose to be open, kind, and loving with myself instead of condemning and harsh. I started to recognize that I didn't need to oppose the worry; I just needed to pay attention to the signal it was sending me. This simple action has helped me detangle the knots of worry that try to ravage my soul.

Worry likes to take up residence in our minds, and let me tell you, it is a troublesome tenant. It pays its rent in lies about the future. I am learning that turning the volume down on worry is the perfect eviction notice. It still comes around from time to time, looking for a lease, and instead of kicking it out in the cold I have learned to love it by telling it that its stories are just stories, and that something else is now occupying its old space. *Peace.* And that present peace is a much better resident.

7

Denial

The Elephant in the Room

There is no greater agony than bearing an untold story inside
of you.

Maya Angelou, *I Know Why the Caged Bird Sings*

The warthogs outside our tent were squawking like an old car
desperate for a new muffler. It was still dark when we woke
and rolled over under our canvas canopy in the Masai Mara, deep
within the dusty grasslands of Africa. Soon a kind man knocked
on the door of our tent and, with the most endearing Kenyan ac-
cent, said, "Good morning, friends, your tea is ready. Timothy,
your guide, will meet you at the jeep in thirty minutes." I was
giddy with excitement, knowing we would be spending the day
bopping up and down in the back of a jeep, roaming the dazzling
African landscape. After devouring the best Kenyan tea I have
ever tasted, we made our way to Timothy's jeep. I could write
a whole chapter on my adoration for Timothy, our safari guide.

Our entire family fell in love with him. He still sends us pictures from his adventures through WhatsApp. His most recent video was thousands of wildebeests leaping across the river during the great migration. It was just like in *The Lion King*, only better. Timothy is kind and fun, and I think he has more knowledge than Google when it comes to African animals. He curated three of the most magical days in our family's life.

As we climbed into the open-air jeep, Timothy threw out a question. "What animals do you most want to see on our safari?" We each jumped to answer. Lions, leopards, rhinos, buffalo, and giraffes all got a vote. With a big grin, Timothy said, "Now, why didn't any of you mention wanting to see our elephants? Does anyone want to see some elephants today?" We all nodded, realizing we had left out the largest of all the animals in Africa. "I think you are going to fall in love with our elephants here in Kenya." Timothy then offered up one of his many random facts about the animals in the Masai Mara. "Do you know they spend a third of their day eating?"

I was sold. A creature that loves eating as much as I do? That was my kind of animal.

We darted off into our day. A few minutes outside of camp, we spotted a tribe of lions hunting some gazelles. The circle of life was transpiring right in front of our eyes. We then drove through a tower of giraffes. We spotted a family of hippos taking a bath in the river. And we even interrupted a cheetah halfway up a tree in the middle of its midmorning nap. It was magical. Almost surreal. I wondered when *The Truman Show* would pull back the curtain, revealing we were on some sort of over-the-top movie set. But it never happened. It was all legit and beyond magnificent. When we pulled up over a ridge on our way to lunch, hundreds of elephants appeared. Our entire jeepload was speechless. I had never seen anything like it. I'd seen elephants at the zoo and circus, but this was different. They were mammoth. They were grazing all over the lush green grass. Rolling around in the mud. Cleaning their backs with their trunks. They were beyond impressive. Everything about them took my breath away. My favorite picture from our entire trip is of Gigi, jaw dropped, as a six-ton elephant fed her baby right next to our jeep.

The sheer magnitude and mass of the elephants could not be ignored. For the first time, I truly understood the phrase "the elephant in the room." Their stature and size were inconceivable. Being in a room with any one of these beautiful beasts would require everyone to take notice. Later, I did a little research to try to understand where the phrase "the elephant in the room" came from—because clearly, an elephant in a room would be hard to ignore. I found the origin story of Ivan Krylov (1769–1844), a poet who wrote a fable called "The Inquisitive Man," which tells of a man who goes to a museum and notices all sorts of tiny things but fails to notice an elephant. In the 1950s, the "elephant in the room" phrase came to mean what it does today: something so massive that people choose to ignore it because it is uncomfortable to deal with.

● ● ●

We all have things that feel too big. Things we would rather ignore. Some start small and inconsequential—like renewing my license at the DMV. I am 100 percent guilty of waiting until the last minute and then making it bigger and more complicated than it needs to be. Or taking care of my vehicle emissions test—no, thank you. Getting my teeth cleaned at the dentist. Do I have to? While these may not start out feeling like an elephant in the room, the more I deny their need to get done, the bigger they become.

There are just things in this life we don't like dealing with. It's part of the human experience. But it's the things we deny over and over again that keep us from experiencing the gift of presence with God. Denial is often like the elephant in the room. It's the thing we need to pay attention to, but the longer we ignore it, the harder it becomes to live with.

Denial begins to appear in our lives when we are rehearsing too much future and not experiencing enough *presence*. When we live inside of all the things that could happen to keep from having to face what *is* happening. When we deny the here and now, bury whatever unpleasant feeling is hanging around in our thoughts, and hold off on dealing with what we convince ourselves is beyond us.

Denial is a common practice for many of us; at the deepest and most intuitive parts of ourselves we somehow just know that once we name something out loud, it will become true in a way it wasn't before. But even though we wish and hope and act like it doesn't exist, most of us know that when we don't talk about something, it doesn't go away or get less real—it only burrows deeper into our beings and grows scarier. Denying the truth will never erase the truth. I have come to understand that denial delays what we fear will define us. I know this is true in my own life. I have experienced it in my relationships, and I have watched it play out with people I love.

Denial is simply a way to dodge transformation. A defense mechanism. By ignoring our pain, we separate the world into good and bad. Good thoughts and bad thoughts. Good feelings and bad feelings. And denial takes on the job of keeping all the bad out of our lives. The problem with living in denial is that it makes us unable to face our own "bad." To look at our flaws, failures, and shortcomings. Over the years, I have had the privilege of holding space with many people as they navigate their way through this sacred and often scary human experience. And I have offered this metaphor countless times to those using denial to distract themselves from the deeper work God is inviting them into. Every time we try to push a beach ball underwater, it eventually finds its way back to the surface—but it comes out sideways and with greater force. It always pops up.

Denial delays what we fear will define us.

The same is true when we use denial to push down our pain, hurt, and struggles. They always pop out somewhere else in our lives.

What is so tricky about denial is the longer we do it, the more power it gains in our lives. Denial defines the present as too difficult to deal with while selling us the false promise that the future will be better. I can always tell when I am wading in a sea of denial. My warning signs include ignoring emails or messages that feel hard, avoiding hard conversations, or not facing a decision that is looming in my mind. Denial is the worst kind of lie—it's the lie you tell yourself.

When we were a few years into starting Soul City Church, so much about our lives felt miraculous and exciting. People were finding community and connection. Week after week I witnessed people encountering healing and hope. Our whole world was within a five-block radius. We found a townhouse to rent under market price. Our kids were in one of the best public schools in the city. We walked everywhere we needed to go. The energy and electricity of living in a fast-growing neighborhood was mesmerizing, and I felt like I was smack-dab in the middle of a dream come true.

> **Denial is the worst kind of lie—it's the lie you tell yourself.**

The problem was there were two sides to my life. On the other side of all that excitement and momentum was an exhausted and drained woman. A gnawing ache lived in the pit of my stomach (remember our beach ball?). All my different roles felt harder and heavier than they once were: wife, mother, daughter, sister, friend, boss, pastor, neighbor. Everyone needed something from me, and I felt like I was only bringing leftovers to the table. The leadership decisions kept growing in complexity, and life felt heavy and hard. My mind felt distracted all the time. I was tired, dry, and overwhelmed. But when people asked me how everything was going, I regularly answered, "It's *fine*. I'm *fine*. The kids are *fine*. I mean, we're busy and moving fast, but we're all doing well. Everything is *fine.*"

I remember my inner flares of fear and wanting to make it all slow down, but I didn't know how to sound the alarm and let myself really be seen. I was better at the other side of my life. I felt accomplished on that side. I was good at those things. But those same things were what flattened and silenced all of the signals screaming that something was really wrong.

I wasn't sleeping well. My weight yo-yoed up and down. My self-care happened in fits and spurts. I was overwhelmed more than I was at peace. But *fine* was my answer on how everything was going. I didn't think I was lying to myself or anyone else—I just didn't want to face what I had been pushing down. The elephant in the room was evident, but I told myself it would eventually find its own way out once I solved whatever problem was in the current moment.

In short, I ignored all the evidence that I was far from fine. I silenced my intuition, swallowed my emotions, and described my symptoms as "It's just a busy season." My performance was Oscar-worthy. But I knew I was not fine.

With what little courage I could muster, I decided to go looking for my authentic voice. I shared some of my story with our board, and I offered just enough vulnerability to feel like I was still somewhat in control and could hold it together. I just told them I was tired but a week's vacation would most likely not provide me with enough rest. They lovingly listened and encouraged me to take whatever time I needed. I was too afraid to tell the whole truth: I was dangerously tired and unsure if I wanted to keep going. That was too much to say out loud.

I called a dear friend and asked if she knew of a place where our family could get away for a little bit to try to find some much-needed rest. She said she knew just the place, then said, "Get yourselves out here, and I will take care of the rest." Tears puddled in my eyes. She knew I was even too tired to handle figuring out where to go. We booked some tickets to Northern California and drove to the address my friend gave us. It was late at night, so everything was dark. We opened the door to a little cottage that resembled something my imagination labeled *Narnia*. I fell into bed and slept until the sun woke me up the next morning. As I walked out to the kitchen of our little getaway, I looked out at a field of green grass as a family of deer moved across it. I couldn't believe how beautiful it all was. How peaceful and serene. It was beyond quiet; the chirping birds were the only sounds filling the early morning hours. My eyes caught two wooden chairs on the other side of the lawn, and I felt a little nudge inviting me to go and sit there. I made some coffee, grabbed a journal and pen, and made my way. As I nestled into a chair, I peered over at the other empty chair. I felt God's loving Spirit whisper to me, *I know you feel like this chair. Empty and hollow. Here is where we will sit until you find yourself.*

We stayed at the little cottage in the northern hills of California for ten days. Each morning I walked across grass still dripping with dew and sat in the wooden chair. Some days there were no words. From me or from God. Just silence. Some days I feverishly poured my heart out on the pages of my journal. Other days I yelled and cried and stomped around like a toddler, making declarations that I would not return to how I was living if it was just going to be more of the same. And then one morning I felt the loving whisper again: *Are you willing to lose this life to find a new one?*

A Scripture came to mind: "What good will it be for someone to gain the whole world, yet forfeit their soul?" (Matt. 16:26). I wasn't sure I was gaining the world, but I knew I was losing my soul. I wanted a new life, but I was in denial over losing my current life.

I have now learned that when good things fall apart, better things can come together, but at that moment I couldn't see the better things, so I'd held on for dear life to what I had. And it was at those wooden chairs I began to open myself up to a different kind of life. Getting well meant facing what wasn't well in my life. It meant dying to the life that was keeping me from living.

Denial can take on many forms, but its basic need is to avoid, ignore, and flee from all potentially painful possibilities. It's a subtle but powerful weapon to escape the present and instead rehearse the future in your mind. While the consequences and impact of denial vary, its patterns are almost always the same. Whenever you are in denial, you will . . .

Dismiss the evidence,

Escape your emotions,

Neglect your body's signals, and say

Yes to limiting beliefs.

Dismiss the Evidence

Any unhealthy pattern has a root story. It didn't just appear out of thin air. All our patterns can be traced back, and the ones we deny always come from a place of pain. What we often don't realize is that it takes more energy to deny the need for healing than to lovingly bring it into the present moment with careful attention to begin healing.

The mind is skilled at wandering. Whenever I sing the line from the old hymn, "Prone to wander, Lord, I feel it, prone to leave the God I love,"[1] I feel like it may be the truest line ever written. My propensity to wander is an overly developed skill, and my impulse to be everywhere but the present moment is downright impressive. Wandering is one of the ways I'd learned to dismiss the evidence. To deny its existence by envisioning a different tomorrow. Dreaming about different possibilities. Living life in my mind that is anywhere but *here*. Through denial, I learned how to live in the future.

Hear me: in no way am I discounting the power of dreams. God fashioned me to be a visionary. Give me a minute, and I will give you an idea. I crave new possibilities. What I am saying is that so many of my dreams were ways to avoid my day-to-day life. From filling my calendar to planning trips to making lists—I love a good list with little boxes—these were all good things but also ways to dismiss the evidence that I was not present.

Escape Your Emotions

After dismissing the evidence, most people living in denial find a way to escape their emotions. Paying attention to my feelings was not something I was good at, and learning the language of my emotions was not something that came to me easily. I had also heard far too many destructive messages that feelings should not be trusted.

Unfortunately, many have learned to repress their emotions in the name of faith. None of that teaching holds up to good biblical interpretation or sound systematic theology. It also goes against a scientific physiological understanding of who we are as human beings. It breaks my heart that so many have left the church because of this kind of teaching and have even walked away from God because they couldn't reconcile why they were experiencing certain emotions they were told they should not have.

When you try to escape your emotions, you are trying to deny energy in motion. That's all an emotion is. E-motion = energy in motion. You try to harness what does not want to be harnessed and put resistance around something that isn't to be resisted. But what you resist will always persist. Your emotions aren't looking for restraints; they are looking to be released.

Neglect Your Body's Signals

Not only do we dismiss the evidence and escape our emotions, but whenever we are in denial, we learn to neglect the signals our bodies are looking to send. In the next section I am going to devote a whole chapter to both emotions and paying attention to our bodies, but one of the most powerful things I learned as I began to face my denial was that my body was one of my most trusted allies. She was unequivocally for me and supportive of me. But I had offered my body the opposite treatment: a gag order. I handled her messages like a headache—just take some Advil and keep going. When I numbed out through overeating or then undereating to counteract the previous behavior, I didn't pause to listen to what my body was trying to say to me. I just assumed my body would be reliable and do what I wanted her to do. Then I realized my body was incapable of lying to me. She always told the truth; I just wasn't listening.

Yes to Limiting Beliefs

While my body was telling truths I didn't always want to hear, I yielded instead to far too many limiting beliefs about myself. I believed them for far too long, impacting how I saw myself and how I showed up in my relationships with others. Some circled the cul-de-sac of my mind for many years. *I'm not smart enough* has made frequent recurring visits since my middle school years. *It's up to me* is another limiting belief that has had consistent airtime in my life, playing on my control issues and on my mental vice that the only person I could ultimately depend on was myself.

As so much about my life was changing, some new beliefs started showing up on my doorstep too, and I said yes to them without first peeping through the door to see if they were healthy and whole truths. Like any limiting belief, they started rearranging the furniture of my mind as soon as they came in. Some of these newer limiting beliefs were associated with my role as a pastor, such as "people want a spiritually secure leader, not a spiritually curious leader." I started believing people wanted my confidence more than they wanted my vulnerability. Secure in where we were headed instead of shaky. They wanted my answers more than they wanted me to sit in their questions with them. I began to build a moat around myself in my mind. Saying yes to these limiting beliefs built up more walls that would eventually need to come down.

As I sat in that wooden chair and inhaled the crisp Northern California air, I began to realize that a real life was not going to be found in rehearsing the future. It would only be found in learning to receive the here and now. As I welcomed my trusty question, *What's here now?*, I also welcomed what I had been trying to deny. Instead of tucking it away, I allowed it to have space with loving care. I started to

> **The life I wanted could not be found; it could only be lived.**

see for the first time that the life I wanted could not be found; it could only be lived. I needed to make finding God and finding myself in the *now* the focus of my life.

A part of me wanted to fix the patterns of denial I had spent a lifetime building quickly. But it would take a lifetime of learning to live in the moment to be able to fully restore them. Sometimes the best learning starts with unlearning. I needed to practice being HERE:

- Hold the evidence.
- Express your emotions.
- Receive your body's message.
- Edit the limiting belief.

I stopped dismissing the evidence and instead welcomed it. I unlocked my emotions and let them come up for air. Most of them had been pushed underwater for far too many years. I deliberately noticed the signals my body was sending me. I took naps. I read books. I went on long walks, and I ate nourishing food instead of numbing food. Instead of giving a blind yes to the limiting beliefs that had become primary driving voices in my life, I started to believe for the first time that losing my life might be the best thing I could do to find real life. So much of what I discovered in that chair and through the years since that trip boils down to this: there is no better place than here. In the present. Where you are, in the here and now, is where God is. The present is God's zip code. And God invites us to be with him in every moment.

Hold the Evidence

I have been learning to name the evidence. Face it. Acknowledge what happened. If I'm a participant in the experience, I recognize my collaboration in what occurred. Recently I worked through this step with some hurtful posts about me that were shared on social media. I wanted to push them away and power through the experience. I wanted to dismiss the evidence and put it under an easier-to-digest category like "the realities of being a leader." I could even hear myself starting to do that both in my head and with some trusted friends, saying things like, "This is what happens when you lead. People have opinions and they share them. There will always be small vocal minorities that disagree with you. I just need to get over it."

While such things may be good and helpful in dealing with unkind content online, I was also dismissing the evidence and trying to pretend it didn't affect me. I found myself leaving the present moment and made the choice to ground myself back in the here and now. I named what happened. I named the people who were involved and what they said. *On this date, this was said, and I acknowledge that it affects me.* The power of holding the evidence in the here and now allows you to embrace that you are human. You aren't made to power through. You are pliable and moldable, always capable of being shaped. Holding yourself and the evidence with care is a way to invite loving-kindness toward yourself.

Express Your Emotions

Instead of escaping my emotions, I learned to express them and offer them sacred space. (We'll talk about this more in chapter 11.) Learning to let go of denial meant letting my emotions out. In the social media storm that occurred, for example, I had to name in safe and loving circles that I was sad, hurt, and angry. And I had to learn how to not just talk about my emotions but to let them come out without words. The temptation is to talk about our emotions instead of feeling them. With my sadness, I needed to cry. With my anger, I needed to yell. With my hurt, I needed to place my hands over my heart and breathe. Your emotions aren't looking for comments, they just need some clearance.

Receive Your Body's Message

Instead of negating the signals my body was sending, I learned to receive the messages from my most trusted ally—my body. I started with small practices to help me pay attention to her again. Drinking water before coffee each morning. Shifting my sleep routine. Honoring sabbath days. Putting screen time limits on my phone. My body was craving rhythm, and I had been out of rhythm for so long. I had to look for what a mentor of mine calls a "whole-body yes." I was so used to autopilot hyperspeed that I often denied my body's limits.

Restoring rhythm took time—and still is. I still struggle when it comes to living in rhythm with my body. (In chapter 13 we'll discuss doing a deep dive on trusting your body.) But coming out of denial with my body meant a whole-body yes to rhythm and an emphatic no to erratic schedules. It meant a whole-body yes to deep rest and a no to more pushing and pulling to get one more thing done. It meant yes to enjoying food and seeing it as fuel and no to mindless and excessive eating.

Edit the Limiting Belief

Instead of blindly saying yes to my limiting beliefs, I learned to edit the fictions into facts, and I started by simply rewriting the phrases I would tell myself.

> Limiting belief: I'm not smart enough to lead us through a multimillion-dollar campaign.
>
> Edit: You have never led a multimillion-dollar fundraising campaign. You know lots of smart people who have; you can reach out and ask for help.

> Limiting belief: I guess the life of a leader is lonely.
>
> Edit: Parts of leadership can be lonely if you let them be lonely. There are people who love you, and they want to know you. It's up to you to take the vulnerable risk of letting them see you.

In order for us to move beyond denial, we have to receive the present moment. We have to feel it all the way through, as scary as it may seem. Denial always starts out as thoughts and feelings, and packed within every moment is the ability to tell your thoughts and feelings you are not going to push them out. Instead, you're going to welcome them *here*.

When I really started practicing this powerful question, *What's here now?* I realized I had spent so much of my life thinking I wasn't at the right place at the right time. That I needed to do more or be more to get there. I began to see I am *always* at the right place at the right time, and every time I begin to deny this I bury untold stories deep inside myself and forfeit my soul.

As Brené Brown says, "When we deny our stories, they define us. When we own our stories, we get to write a brave new ending."[2] God invites us to coauthor our stories. To write new chapters. To clear away the elephants in the room so that the fullness of who we are can shine bright.

One of the things I remember our safari guide, Timothy, telling us about the elephants was that their temporal lobe (the area of the brain associated with memory) is larger and denser than that of people—so an elephant never forgets. While an elephant in the room is hard to ignore, the elephant is incapable of ignoring anything. Elephants remember life instead of denying life. Oh, to live more like elephants.

8

Pretending

Hide and Seek

And tears came before he could stop them, boiling hot then instantly freezing on his face, and what was the point in wiping them off? Or pretending? He let them fall.

J. K. Rowling, *Harry Potter and the Half-Blood Prince*

I really wanted to make sure I was on time for the first group meeting, and early was my preference. Someone once told me early people are impressive people. Being impressive sounded better than being insignificant, so long ago I'd programmed my inner treadmill to the speed of perform, please, and perfect.

I set my alarm and also set two backup alarms. When my Uber driver pulled up forty minutes before the meeting was supposed to begin, I was ready and waiting, and I jumped in the car and headed across town. I wanted a good strong start with this new group. I found myself churning with both excitement and fear. I was not the leader; I was a member. "Leader" was the role I was used to. It is for sure my comfort zone and preferred seat in any circle. But in this group, I was intentionally choosing to just receive.

The way I'd been doing the work of God was quickly diminishing the work of God in me. I knew I needed to find a space and place where I could slow down and just be. My deeper hope was that I would hopefully uncover a new way of being. But another, more overdeveloped part of myself was also aware I feared letting myself truly be seen. Would I really be accepted? Could I really be myself? And a more dangerous question—Would I even let myself be seen? Would I allow this group of strangers to see the parts of me that felt raw, messy, and vulnerable?

> **The way I'd been doing the work of God was quickly diminishing the work of God in me.**

I didn't know any of the other members, and the leader was an acquaintance from many years ago. I felt conflicted about what I wanted from this group. One part of me wanted this group to continue to feed the automatic part of me that wanted to impress and inspire others. But my authentic self was craving *real* and wanted this group to enfold and hold me just as I was. I was hungry for a circle where there would be no charades, no masks, and no pretending. I wanted the scaffolding holding me together to come down, and I wanted to drink in the nourishment of being known. While I was hoping to experience this kind of vulnerability with a group, I was also aware of the risks and costs associated with it. The risk of not being impressive. The risk of being ordinary. The risk of not being received and loved for who I am. What if they really saw me and didn't want to keep seeing me? What if they thought I wasn't smart enough, hadn't accomplished enough, hadn't accrued enough wealth, and didn't offer enough value to the group?

I was certain joining a group was a crucial next step in my personal growth and transformation. I had devoted myself to creating these kinds of spaces for so many others, but somehow, I wasn't experiencing the same fruit in my own life. I knew I had been a part of creating a beautiful community in which people regularly told me they were growing and transforming—but I felt like the soil I tilled and cultivated for them was not the same soil in my own garden. The soil my soul was planted in felt dry and cracked; it had not been watered for far too long. And the sun had been under an eclipse.

When I arrived at the leader's home, some people were already there, standing around and talking. Some already knew each other but others did not. I put my things down and started to engage in small talk. I have always struggled with being good at chitchat, plus I knew that going through the normal topics of conversation would eventually bring us to our professions, and I was very aware I didn't want anyone to know what I did. I didn't want to lead with my occupation because I was certain it would taint how people viewed me. I worked hard to remain vague, representing myself as someone involved in nonprofit work.

Eventually the leader called us all into the circle, and he began by giving some introductory remarks about things like how long the group would last, how many breaks we would take, and where the bathroom was located. He then started the meeting by inviting us to observe our own breathing. He invited us to stop. To pause. To notice our inhales and our exhales. To place our attention on what was going on inside. Not just what was going on in our minds and our thoughts but also what was happening in our bodies, hearts, and souls. Tears formed in my eyes right away. I remember feeling a strong urge to make sure my tears were not noticeable. I didn't want to be the first person in the group to cry. I feared that a label would get slapped on me: "emotionally unstable, can't hold it together—even breathing is too much for her."

With each inhale and exhale, I could feel myself beginning to relax. To slow down. To stop bracing for another problem to solve. I felt my body, mind, and heart coming together in a divine dance, thanking one another for the gift of caring I'd given myself by joining this group that had hardly started. The only thing we had done was breathe together, and yet I sensed the Holy Spirit whispering, *You're safe here. It's OK. You can wake up here.*

I didn't consider myself as someone unaware or stumbling around in the dark when it came to the deeper movement of the soul. I had done a significant amount of counseling and spiritual soul work. But the container I had created that housed my life wasn't working anymore and I knew it—yet I was terrified about what it would mean to let go of that container when I didn't see a new one in sight. My hope was that I would find it here.

The leader of our group said, "I have a series of questions I want each of you to answer to get to know one another. But this is going to be a different kind of introduction. I want you to introduce us to your essence, not your ego. What you do, your relational status, what you own, and where you live are not necessary here. We want to know *you*." More tears started to puddle in my eyes. I felt the inner conflict. I wanted to run—and I wanted to dive all the way in. We went around the circle, answering four questions.

- If you knew me, you would know . . .
- If you really knew me, you would know . . .
- What I don't want you to know about me . . .
- What I really don't want you to know about me . . .

I can still picture the room and the people around the circle as I write this. I was sitting to the left of the leader, and thankfully he looked to his right to start. Each person vulnerably answered the questions. No one took a safe passageway. Each person allowed the others in. One by one the circle was connected through uncovered, bare, and honest answers. I felt like I was on holy ground. And then all eyes landed on me. I jumped in the deep end and tried to pull back all the layers I could.

"If you knew me, you would know that I purposefully lied to all of you in the entryway earlier today. I was afraid of letting you know what I do as a profession for fear it would ruin or stain our relationship before it ever started.

"If you really knew me, you would know I feel like the life I am living isn't working for me anymore. I feel like an imposter. Like I am pretending and it's exhausting.

"What I don't want you to know about me is that most days I don't believe I am enough. I don't believe I'm smart enough. Thin enough. Pretty enough. Wealthy enough. Wise enough. Spiritual enough.

"What I really don't want you to know about me is that I mask my lack of *enough* with silently judging everyone else around me as not enough."

It was a relief to say this out loud. These thoughts and feelings weren't new; my lack of *enough* had been slowly suffocating me. Now, for the first time I gave it what I feared would squelch me for good: oxygen. I let it breathe. And somehow what had always been so heavy instantly felt light.

The strangest thing occurred at that moment. The story I had always told myself was that baring my soul would be too much. Too damning to the position I held and too compromising to what I had built. All the things I thought would come with that kind of honesty were the exact opposite of what I experienced at that moment. I received no judgment. No advice. No superior glances from across the room.

No one backed away; they leaned in. They welcomed me. They saw me. Without knowing any real facts about me, they knew me and, more importantly, they loved me.

The Automatic Self versus the Authentic Self

How long had I been hiding? How long had I been playing hide-and-seek? When my daughter, Gigi, was young, she loved playing that game. Now that she is in her teenage years and has started babysitting, her hide-and-seek skills are a huge hit with the littles she watches. Gigi's specialty is in the hiding. She is quiet and patient as people prowl around trying to find her. She has been known to stay in a hiding spot, completely silent, for twenty minutes. Gigi is not the only master of hide-and-seek. Most adults are playing the game without even realizing it. And instead of looking for secret hiding spots, we play out in the open. We hide with closets full of masks at the ready for any situation that may arise. We are professional pretenders, hoping to trick everyone around us into believing those masks represent who we really are.

Hiding all the time is a terrible way to live. It keeps you from the present and from living as your true, authentic self. Hiding keeps you as sick as your secrets—reluctant to admit your weakness or flaws to others.

The ego (which every one of us has) has been dominating the game of hide-and-seek from the beginning of time, and it's always found in the last place any of us ever think to look: hiding within itself. The ego has lots of different names. Some call it the "false self," others the "pseudo" or "idealized self." I like to call it the "automatic self." Your automatic self is who you *think* you are—far from who you really are. The automatic self is where we start in life, but it's not where we're meant to stay.

Many people describe the automatic self as bad, but it's not that it's bad, it's that it's bogus and cannot carry us through life. It specializes in being a stand-in for the most sincere and substantial part of who we are. It may get us started but it is never meant to last for the whole of our lives. The automatic self begins to show its restrictions once it's exposed to authentic light. Letting go of the automatic self is necessary for transformation and growth, but this is often incredibly painful, and many people choose to stay trapped in what feels safe.

Your authentic self is who you are when you are no longer hiding and what we all crave in our lives and in our relationships—yet most of us are better at hiding. I'm sure you've had a moment with someone, perhaps in the early stages of a dating relationship, making a new friend at work, or meeting a new neighbor, and you experienced that inner discomfort as you wondered how and when to reveal something about yourself. You were looking for areas where you were similar or had commonalities, and you had a desire to let them in on a part of you to see how they would respond. To see if they would still want to hang out with you. But you were also terrified that if you let yourself be seen, they might not reciprocate, and then the relationship would change.

> Hiding all the time is a terrible way to live. It keeps you from the present and from living as your true, authentic self.

I remember early on when Jarrett and I were dating, and we were trying to figure one another out. He is from California, and I am from the Midwest. He grew up surfing and skateboarding, and I grew up with two brothers who played football, basketball, and baseball. He liked hip-hop and old-school rap, and I dominated at karaoke when it came to Broadway show tunes. He thought Chili's was an upscale restaurant and the perfect spot for a date night, and no disrespect to Chili's, but I did not hold the same opinion. We really liked each other but we were very different. I remember thinking, *I'm not sure I should tell him that the things he is into I am not really into.* So I held out for a while. I pretended I liked what he liked because I liked him. Then I remember being so happy once I told him that I didn't know what an ollie on a skateboard was. I also didn't know who a Tribe Called Quest was, and I didn't know what they were questing for. And if we were going to keep dating, getting chips and queso at Chili's did not count as a date. This was such a small step of vulnerability, but it felt so freeing. Obviously, I was taking only a minor risk. I wasn't putting myself in the deep end of vulnerability, but it still felt so good to offer my authentic self instead of my automatic self.

I imagine you've had many moments of wanting to let yourself be seen. Wanting to reveal your authentic self but feeling it was safer to pretend. To stay hiding. To play the part of someone else.

I've read countless books and studies on what people most desire in their relationships—and *vulnerability* shows up in the top five every single time. We all desire vulnerability, and yet so many of us are terrified to offer it. Or you have been vulnerable only to have it blow up a relationship, so you've decided to keep yourself safe and in hiding.

Camouflaging your deepest desires advances your ability to please and play a part, but it keeps you from who God created you to be. When you disguise yourself, it's often because you are seeking approval from everyone else instead of sourcing it from God and yourself. Pretending forces you to live life in the future, leaving you overwhelmed, empty, and disconnected from God, yourself, and others in the present.

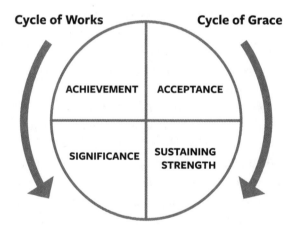

The Cycle of Grace versus the Cycle of Works

I began to realize that I was a card-carrying member of a cycle of works way of life. I preached grace but practiced works, and it was no longer working. I found confidence in moments of achievement, which fed my feelings of significance and sent me looking to sustain my strength and acceptance through what I did. I built a pattern of pretending in my life. I became good at pleasing and performing. I looked for acceptance in my achievements, and, along the way, I lost myself. The true essence of my being got covered up with trying to be someone I was not.

The cycle of grace starts on the other side. It starts with acceptance, which gives sustaining grace, and true significance with God, which leads to a different kind of achievement. But grace only works in the present moment when the masks are off. Grace has offered so much freedom in my relationship with God, and it has unleashed me to be my authentic self. Letting go of pretending offers each of us wholeness and freedom. When we welcome the question, *What's here now?* we get to pay attention to the way we are living. We can lay down our masks and return to the gift of the present moment.

So much of my life looked "spiritually mature." For goodness' sake, I was a pastor, but being in the present moment with God was not how I lived. I was good at rehashing the past and rehearsing the future, but receiving the present was so foreign to me. I wanted to live in the light, in the present with God, but I was unsure how to really do that.

> But everything exposed by the light becomes visible—and everything that is illuminated becomes a light. This is why it is said:
>   "Wake up, sleeper,
>   rise from the dead,
>   and Christ will shine on you." (Eph. 5:13–14)

I was a spiritual sleepwalker. I looked awake, but so many of my thoughts, words, and actions took place in the dark. This sleepwalking over many years had formed my automatic self: the things I wanted people to know about me and the things I didn't want them to know. When I started to expose my true self in that sacred circle, I began waking up. And I began to see that locating the automatic self is the birthplace of transformation.

I felt as if the Holy Spirit was hovering over all my control tactics, impressive facades, accolades, and achievements. Lingering around my hidden piles of shame and regret, aches and pains I had pushed down and away. He knew all the things I thought were safely locked away in closets. When I let myself be present with God and with myself, I recognized the room I was actually in and decided to tell the truth about who I was. As Teresa of Ávila says, "It would be absurd to suggest that someone go into a room she is already in!"[1]

We spend much of our lives unaware we are sleepwalking—burdened under the weight of choosing to be in the dark. We're trying to get to places we already are. I was more concerned about all of my what ifs as I rehearsed my future, but what I came to find is that God is more concerned with *what is* as I receive the gift of the present moment.

* * *

As I have already said, the present is God's zip code. The most important thing to do as humans is to get to that location. Location, location, location—I am reclaiming this real estate mantra as a *spiritual* mantra. The single most important thing we can do is surrender to what God is doing in the present moment. But do we know how to locate ourselves in the present moment? Addicted to the enticing elixir the future always offers, so many of us only know how to live in *what if* instead of *what is*.

> **The single most important thing we can do is surrender to what God is doing in the present moment.**

We need to start with figuring out where we are. Like finding the YOU ARE HERE dot on a shopping center directory, so many of us need to locate ourselves in the present moment, and we can do so by paying attention to our thoughts, words, and behavior.

The list on page 142 is a way to identify your behavior in the here and now. I often use this list to help me pay attention to if I'm living in my automatic self versus my authentic self. To begin, simply ask yourself if you are willing to do three things.

> **Acknowledge**—be willing to locate yourself. Are you willing to honestly acknowledge where you are?
>
> **Accept**—agree that there is no condemnation for those who are in Christ Jesus (Rom. 8:1).
>
> **Adjust**—determine if you're willing to shift into your authentic self.

You groped your way through that murk once, but no longer. You're out in the open now. The bright light of Christ makes your way plain. So no more stumbling around. Get on with it! The good, the right, the true—these are the actions appropriate for daylight hours. Figure out what will please Christ, and then do it. (Eph. 5:8–10 MSG)

We aren't doing anyone any favors when we pretend and delay our own agency over our lives. This only leads to more anxiety, pain, and drama. To stop pretending, we have to start telling the truth.

Coming out of pretending is never easy, but it's always worth it. "Fake it till you make it" requires energy, but it never requires courage. Pretenders are always scanning to get permission from someone else to be their true, full selves. Pretending is the fear of learning in public, but learning in public is the only learning that changes us. Confidence is being in alignment with your heart, soul, mind, and strength. When you fake it, you are living out of alignment.

Pretending looks for anyone other than God to validate you. Pretending forgets that God is *here*. Pretending tries to get you to think it's all up to you.

Real love doesn't need you to be different.

When we pretend, we abandon love. Instead of "fake it till you make it," let's embrace *facing* it till we make it.

Asleep / Works / Automatic Self	Awake / Grace / Authentic Self
Thoughts	**Thoughts**
• I'm right. • There is not enough. • There is a "they" and "they" did not give me what I needed, deserved, or wanted. • They didn't approve. • I'm in control. • I'm better than or less than. • There is a right way and a wrong way. • My way is the right way. • I don't have any options. • My story is true.	• Learning is better than winning and being right. • Approval, control, and security come from the Holy Spirit and dwell within. • Curiosity guides my thoughts, not judgment. • It's not as serious as I'm making it. • God can use anyone and anything to be a learning ally. • Revealing is better than hiding.
Actions	**Actions**
• Obsess over my opinion. • Find fault or blame. • Fight, flight, freeze, faint, or fix. • Argue and attack. • Rationalize and justify. • Gossip. • Stay overwhelmed. • Distract myself, numb out, or avoid. • Get others to agree with me.	• Listen with my whole self instead of just waiting to talk. • Make clean agreements. • Take responsibility. • Speak without arguing. • Appreciate others aloud. • Feel my feelings all the way through. • Be curious. • Take every thought captive.
Words	**Words**
• I should. • I can't. • I'm right. • It's hard. • It's not my fault. • I'm confused. • The "fact" is. • I'm sorry, but . . . • Always/never. • It's no use. • This is how it's done. • They don't get it.	• What can I learn? • How can I grow? • What's it like to be on the other side of me? • How is the pattern familiar? • I agree to . . . • What I hear you saying is . . . • I choose to . . . • I take responsibility for . . . • I appreciate you for . . .[2]

9

Obligation
Check Please

Expectations are resentments waiting to happen.

Anne Lamott, *Crooked Little Heart*

As the older sister of two younger brothers, I joyfully assumed the self-appointed responsibility of always looking out for them. In other words, I was the boss. My parents didn't enlist me in this role. My brothers were perfectly fine and would have preferred I stay out of their business, but what is an older sister to do? Boss I became. My brother Andy was first in line to deal with my amiable but annoying drill sergeant personality. We were sixteen months apart in age and one year separated us at school, so that meant each time we had the same teacher, he had to deal with the title of "Jeanne's little brother." Sometimes this worked in his favor, other times not so much. In our elementary years, I would regularly go to his classroom after school to pick him up for our walk home. As I stood in the doorway, I would ask his teacher how he was doing in school. How was he getting along with the other kids, and did he have any homework that night? My poor brother, seething with embarrassment, wanted to crawl out of his skin. I, on the other hand, probably glowed like a summer lightning bug, proud as could be. This and many other "older sister" duties ignited a repeated phrase I heard regularly from Andy, and eventually, my youngest brother, Eddie, followed suit: "You're not the boss of me, Jeanne."

When I recall my childhood memories, I can still hear them saying it. "You're not the boss of me." But since I was the oldest, I adhered to all the unspoken rules that I *should* be the boss. I *should* look out for my brothers. I *should* tell them what to do. It just made sense. While this is a normal thing firstborns feel toward younger siblings, what started out as innocent behavior became a foundational pattern for how I lived. I absorbed enough unconscious jargon to encourage my overly responsible and always-in-charge mindset. I fell for all the subtle marketing floating throughout the world that told me doing all the right things was superior to learning to live the right way. And I decided obeying all the *shoulds* was the best way to live. I paid little attention to what *could* be done and listened attentively to what should be done. Believe me, I have spent many years and many pennies with counselors peeling back the layers of living far too many years with *should* at the helm of my life, and let me tell you not much good comes from that little word.

Should is almost always based on someone's perceived expectations. Should wheels and deals a promising future if you're willing to let obligation lead the way. When the squeeze to do something big or small rises within you, and you don't want to do it but follow along anyway, you can be certain that feeling is coming from obligation. Shoulds are everywhere. Like harmless and helpful prompts, they almost always start out as a small suggestion. An innocent promise of something better.

I should floss more.

I should drink less coffee.

I should drink more water.

I should return my library books.

I should send them a card.

These shoulds seem innocuous, like the sticky notes I write for myself when I think I might forget to do something or pick up something from the store. They aren't trying to sabotage you from living in the present moment. But such little reminders are very different from *obligated shoulds*. Like a never-ending tornado spinning with frenetic energy, obligated shoulds are always sending messages that your future won't work out unless you obey all their unspoken rules. They are single-minded in their attempt to pluck you out of the present moment and force you to rehearse a future filled with an endless checklist of unspoken and unrealistic expectations. Obligated shoulds are like squatters taking up free room and board in your mind with the resolute ambition to always be the boss of you. Regardless of their specific message, they almost always fall under the same category: *you should do better/be better*. Who you are in the present moment is not good enough . . . but if you do everything the subtle messages instruct you to do, then in the future you will finally be who you *should* be.

I should really lose weight.

I should lead a certain way.

I should parent the same way she parents.

I should be making more money.

My dance with all my unspoken shoulds didn't seem to leave any noticeable marks at first. But the longer the dance continued, the more obvious my shoulds became.

I tried to ignore their impact. I hoped if they were unrecognizable to everyone else, maybe they would eventually be unrecognizable to me. Up until that point, I just followed all the hidden rules. Most people probably never detected my inclination to follow the unspoken rules of obligation. I was outspoken, confident, and decisive on many things. My battle was with the inner whispers. What I really wanted and how I wanted to live was like a hidden pea under a pile of mattresses. I remember Sue Monk Kidd wrote in *The Secret Life of Bees*, "The hardest thing on earth is choosing what matters."[1] I was unsure if I really knew how to choose what mattered most because I was so good at doing what I thought *should* matter most.

• • •

Early on in our marriage, Jarrett and I were invited over to a friend's house for dinner. After determining a date that would work, I asked if we could bring anything. Our friends knew I was in a busy season and said, "Grab a bottle of wine and just bring yourselves." But something in me refused to take this path, even though it would be best for my schedule and most likely keep me present and enjoying the moment. I insisted that we (and when I say we, I mean *me*) would be happy to bring a homemade appetizer. I could not bring myself to go without bringing something. I'm sure my behavior sprung in part from a desire to contribute to the meal, but a deeper part of me, tied up in all my *shoulds*, felt like I had to bring something. And not just anything but a beautifully curated appetizer that looked like it had just fallen off a Pinterest page. I remember hustling to pull this showstopping starter together. I was stressed and separated from myself. All that evening, I struggled to be present and in the moment with our friends. I remember sitting at dinner that night wondering what had held me back from just bringing a bottle of wine. Why was I so compelled to follow the bossy demands that I should always go above and beyond?

As we drove home that night, Jarrett commented on how quiet and almost removed I'd been during dinner. In a burst of emotion, I erupted, "Why can't I just bring a simple bottle of wine? Why do I always have to do more and be more and give more?" Hot, steamy tears started flowing from my eyes. I was done. Tired. Exhausted from letting obligation boss me around for so many years. My heart was no longer interested in the game it had me playing. I was ready for the deep soul work of returning to the part of myself that had committed to over-responsibility and had hidden in a life of obligated shoulds.

Obligated shoulds keep you from being in the present moment. By ricocheting you into your tomorrows, they leave you overthinking decisions that aren't within your today. Just about anything can trigger an unhealthy obligated should.

- How to parent. Should I do public school, private school, or homeschool?
- How to be a good employee. Should I just fit in to the already created culture? Should I offer up feedback to my supervisors? Should I speak up about the issues or keep my thoughts to myself?
- How to respond on social media. Should I post about the issues that everyone else seems to post about? Should I comment, share, save, or repost? Should I make myself the brand or highlight someone else?
- How to navigate the grief of others. Should I say something? Should I send something? Should I do something?

Lots of "should-ers" feel obliged to do all sorts of things no one expects them to do, leaving them with an inner burden that results in burnout. Should finds a way into every little crevice of our lives, especially in our relationships with God and one another. I remember talking with a dear friend who shared that she wasn't sure her marriage was going to make it. I asked her if there was ever a moment before they got married when she had doubts or wondered if the relationship had the right ingredients to go the distance, and she recounted a moment weeks before their wedding when her fiancé, during a disagreement, asked her, "Are you sure you want to marry me?" She said every fiber in her body screamed *No, I don't think we should get married!* but the voice of obligation took over, and she said, "Of course I want to marry you." With tears streaming down her face, she asked me, "What if I had listened to myself? What if I didn't do what I thought I should do?" She said yes even when everything in her was telling her to say no.

Letting *should* be the boss will never lead you to the life God longs for you to live. If there is one thing I have learned from letting far too many should storms blow through my life, it's that should says yes even when yes is not best.

Whether you've put a should on yourself or someone else has put a should on you, should *never* leads to freedom. Living under the weight of unhealthy obligations is like carrying an emotional debt made up of a million unspoken assumptions. The debt stealthily piles up over time and slowly silences your voice, leaving you wondering if you are just meant to grin and bear it through this life.

> **Should says yes even when yes is not best.**

The Predictable Pattern

A life of obligation always follows a predictable pattern of unhealthy behavior, and humans have been following the pattern from the beginning of time. It goes like this:

Obligation → Resentment → Entitlement → Escape

Resentment

Doing something because of an unhealthy and obligated should leads to some form of resentment: *I didn't want to do this, but I*

148

felt like I had to. Resentment is a complex and multilayered emotion. It's also known as *bitterness*, and it always affects the person with the resentment more than the person or thing being resented. Resentment feels like a tightness in the chest as your mind rides around a carousel of doubts.

Why did I do that?

How much more do I need to do?

Why don't they value and appreciate me?

Is anything ever going to change around here?

Whenever resentment circles your thoughts, your authentic needs have not been met. I love how Elizabeth Gilbert describes resentment: "As smoking is to the lungs, so is resentment to the soul; even one puff is bad for you."[2]

Resentment happens in two directions, but it always starts as an inside job. When you resent yourself, you abandon the most authentic part of yourself to gain affirmation and acceptance from someone or something outside of you. In your unconscious dance with resentment, you eventually feel overwhelmed by all your uncomfortable and irritating thoughts, and in that aggravation you move resentment to an outside job by blaming and projecting it onto others.

Resentment is a sign that all the unnamed, unowned, and unfelt expectations in your life have now broken the camel's back. Sadly, resentment leads you to desert your authentic self, and a deserted self often leads to feelings of entitlement.

Entitlement

Resentment always leads to a feeling of entitlement because resentment's basic belief is that there is a debt to be paid. Entitlement wants to settle the score and is usually looking for a nice tip too. Your entire focus becomes "me" and what "I need." Entitlement is a wounded state where you cannot look outside of yourself because you are obsessively preoccupied with having your needs met.

Escape

When such a debt has not been paid or maybe can't be paid, it leads to escape. No longer able to bear the burden of expectation, resentment, and unmet needs, you decide to check out and escape in some way in your life.

When I was talking with a friend of mine a few weeks ago, she shared with me about her parents, who had been married for a couple decades. Her mom had given up her career when the kids were born, and her dad overworked for many years. Her mom kept the family running while her dad was often traveling for work. Their marriage became more like a contractual agreement than a loving covenant, and as time passed her mom grew resentful. Eventually, once the kids moved out of the house, her mom felt entitled to the life she'd given up all those years ago, and she began to escape into another relationship.

Another friend shared with me how they had been so faithful and consistent at work. They were always the first one in, last one out. They went above and beyond and became the person everyone went to when they needed a problem solved. However, their supervisor never really gave them any recognition or shift in responsibility. They started to grow resentful and frustrated. Eventually, during a reorganization in the company, they were overlooked for a job they felt entitled to. They grew angry and frustrated and eventually turned in their resignation.

You can see how the pattern works.

Obligation → Resentment → Entitlement → Escape

The only way to stop the pattern is to start noticing it and ask *What's here now?* Healing from obligation, resentment, entitlement, and escape requires becoming conscious of the present moment. The journey is often uncomfortable in the beginning because you often discover that what's hiding under obligation is fear. Fear of rejection. Fear of failure. Fear of people no longer loving you if you live with healthy boundaries. Fear of what others will think about you if you aren't in control of how you want them to think of you.

A New Pattern

Should says you have no choice, but by sitting in the present moment—breathing in what is true and exhaling what is not—you can begin to realize that love is stronger than obligation and always leaves you with a choice. Love never operates out of obligation. Love offers options. Love is the overwhelming reality of a God who enables us to choose what we otherwise would not choose. So instead of should, love offers a new pattern.

**Radical Grace → Personal Responsibility →
Healthy Boundaries → Sacrificial Love**

Jesus did not come and offer his life out of some obligation to God. He never resented the Father or the Holy Spirit. He never said, "Listen, I'm entitled to the best throne or I am peacing out of this Trinity gig altogether." There was no heavenly should involved.

It was a choice. Jesus gives us another way: the way of radical grace. Grace is the opposite of obligation. It's the opposite of should. Jesus didn't heal people because he had to. He didn't feed people because it was the right thing to do.

He did it because of love.

Jesus made a choice and left us with a choice too. He didn't even tell us we were obligated to love him or follow him. The radical grace of Jesus says we *can* choose a different path. While obligation feels heavy and forced on

Love never operates out of obligation

us, grace feels light and free. It offers a choice. You get to decide if you want to take personal responsibility in this life or feel like you *should* be responsible. It's an entirely different motivation.

Personal Responsibility

Taking personal responsibility reminds us that even though we are not in control of all of life's circumstances, we always have a choice in how we respond to every circumstance.

While it may not sound like rocket science, knowing we always have a choice is life-altering. I know reading that makes it sound too easy, and some of you are thinking, *But what about the things I didn't get to choose in this life? What about the confusing and hard and heartbreaking things in my story?* While there are circumstances that come into our lives we would never choose, we always have a choice in how we respond to those circumstances.

I certainly have had moments I would have never written into the plotline of my story if I were its sole author. Moments where every part of me wanted to reverse the clock. To change the circumstances. But that is beyond my power. A couple of weeks after my brother suddenly died—the same brother who used to tell me that I was not the boss of him—I felt out of control and overwhelmed. I knew the choice was mine in how I would respond. Everything in me wanted to get back into bed and stay there. Feeling my emotions seemed overwhelming; numbing looked like an easier path. So did eating all the food that had been put in my house over the past two weeks. Telling Jarrett I must go shopping and get whatever I want to help me feel better. Taking more than my share of responsibility to power through and just take care of everything. All so I wouldn't have to sit in the deep grief and pain.

My dear friend Juliet flew in to be with me the night after my brother's funeral. I sat in her room and just wept, and she said, "Jeanne . . . you know this, but you have a choice. Everything is a choice. Even though you feel out of control. You have a choice in how you move forward."

That is perhaps one of the most loving and empowering gifts God has given to us. He gives us a choice to take personal responsibility in our lives.

Healthy Boundaries

In order for us to love well as we take personal responsibility, we need to practice creating healthy boundaries. Having healthy boundaries in our relationships prevents obligation and resentment that lead to entitlement. I think so many of us get stuck in obligation because we have simply forgotten that "No" is a complete sentence.

"No" is a complete sentence.

No is a perfectly acceptable answer. Maybe you just need to put this book down for a moment and practice saying it as loud as you can. *No.* Didn't that feel good? (I would not recommend walking into your boss's office tomorrow and saying, "I'm working on my *no* muscle.")

Every time you say yes under obligation, it's not a healthy yes. A lack of boundaries always invites a lack of respect. Either a lack of self-respect or a lack of respect from others. But the gift of healthy boundaries leads us to be able to offer the very thing to others that Jesus offers to us.

When we receive radical grace and choose personal responsibility that leads to healthy boundaries, we are able to offer sacrificial love.

Sacrificial Love

Sacrificial love is the opposite of should. It's the opposite of obligation. It's the fulfillment of everything Jesus first offers us—and then we get to offer it to one another.

This is the way of Jesus. A life of obligation is empty, and it eventually runs out and dries up. A life of radical grace is full of freedom and never runs out. I have been a follower of Jesus for decades. Never once has he asked me to do something and then followed it up with an obligated should. When I first started practicing *What's here now?* every time I noticed a *should* I replaced it with the word *can*. *What should I do?* became *What can I do?*

You can do the same things in your life from two different motivations: from *should* or from *can*.

- I should do the laundry *or* I can do the laundry.
- I should call this person *or* I can call this person.
- I should take care of all the details *or* I can take care of all the details.

Are you working *for* love, or are you working *from* love? There's a big difference. Living under obligated shoulds that have us working for love feels like an unpredictable thunderstorm, and the aftermath on the soul is easy to spot. Should is a master at masquerading itself in the cloak of extreme responsibility. Remember: you can say no and still love. Love doesn't mean saying yes to everything. Saying no to everything is selfishness. That's not love. But there is a difference between everything and something. There is always something that love is inviting you toward. And love will never try to be the boss of you.

10

Waiting and Control
Waiting Rooms

> When you're waiting, you're not doing nothing. You're doing the most important something there is. You're allowing your soul to grow up. If you can't be still and wait, you can't become what God created you to be.
>
> Sue Monk Kidd, *When the Heart Waits*

I have never liked waiting rooms. Especially the ones with the extra small TVs that only get four channels, and every time you're in there the Montel Williams talk show seems to be on. Of course, there are four-month-old magazines scattered all around, and for some reason, there always seems to be a copy of *Highlights for Children*. I don't know if it's the extra-uncomfortable chairs or the cheery pastel wallpaper that clearly hopes to put you in a good mood, but most waiting rooms seek to distract you from the reason you're there. I have yet to meet a person who loves waiting rooms, because I have yet to meet a person who loves waiting.

I've done my fair share of waiting, and I confess I'm not good at it. I try right away to figure out just how long it will be before my name is called. Not feeling great in a waiting room is the worst. I will never forget several years ago, while we were in Florida visiting some friends over New Year's, I had some sort of strange allergic reaction to a lotion I put on. Most of my body broke out in bright-red, itchy hives. I called my doctor, and she told me I was going to need to go to the ER. We figured out where the closest ER was and went. Instantly, when I walked in, I scanned the room to assess the situation. It was overflowing with people, and the basic look on everyone's face was, *If I could be anywhere else in the world, I would be.* The prognosis on how long I would need to wait was not looking good. I registered at the front desk and kindly asked how long the wait was going to be. I was pregnant at the time, so I tried to let the nurse behind the counter see my pregnant belly and my horrible discomfort with the hope she would show some compassion and somehow push me up on the list. She, of course, did not give me a clear answer and told me to take a seat. So I did. I sat and waited. And waited. And waited. And waited.

There is one common activity we engage in while we're waiting: we try to figure out who is still in front of us and gauge how long we will have to wait. I created an internal countdown as to when I thought my name would be called. I confess, I prayed that no one would walk in with a broken arm or some other sort of open wound that would require immediate attention.

I was not doing well with the waiting. Or with all the sick people around me. The crying baby. The young girl who kept running to the bathroom to throw up and multiple times left the door open so we all could hear. At one point I looked at Jarrett (trying to look as miserable as I possibly could) and said, "Jarrett, do you love me?" He smiled, knowing where the conversation was headed, and said yes. He knew I was about to set him up to prove it.

"If you love me, then you will go right up to that desk and ask where we are on the list, and then let the nurse know that your very pregnant wife is in a ton of pain and it would help if we could see a doctor quickly."

Jarrett smiled again and said, "Let me go see about the wait."

Right as he was about to talk with the receptionist, I was called. I think Jarrett was happier than I was. The entire waiting room experience had taken about three and a half hours, and every second was a reminder to me of how much I despised waiting.

I hate to wait because I do not like being out of control. Being out of control feels like God has plopped me into a big, bland, spiritual waiting room where all I can do is read old magazines, sit in horribly uncomfortable chairs, and wait for my name to be called. I don't know anyone who likes feeling stuck and out of control. Most people I know prefer a plan, a time line, an order of events—and if we must wait, we at least want to know for how long.

* * *

Every time I've found myself in a spiritual waiting room, the same questions always surface.

- Am I willing to loosen my tight grip of control?
- Am I willing to surrender to the unknown?
- Am I willing to trust that God is for me? That he is guiding and protecting me?
- Am I willing to have faith that God's plans are higher and better than my plans?
- Am I willing to let God do the job of God, or will I keep applying for a job that isn't open?

It seems every time God invites me to wait is the moment I tighten the grip of control. My mind thinks I'm just helping God out. Stepping up to take something off God's extra-long to-do list. But ultimately the message I send every time I clench for control is, *I don't know if I trust your plan, so I'll take mine.* I have done it countless times, and I've watched so many other people do the same. And sadly, for many of us, when God invites us to wait, we quietly say, "No, thanks," and end up settling for less. We choose a future that is still unknown but one we tell ourselves will be better if we are at the helm of all our decisions. The elusive sense of control we desire becomes a self-sufficient settling.

Self-Sufficient Settling

Initially, it doesn't seem like we're settling. In fact, it feels the exact opposite. It feels kind of good. Like taking the bull by the horns and reclaiming control of our lives. But over time, self-sufficient settling builds up, slowly leading us toward a calloused and calculated way of moving through life.

- All your decisions run through an autocratic funnel. Thoughtful reflection and waiting on inner peace and spiritual confirmation no longer play a part in your choices.
- Personal preference and desire win out over discernment in your decision-making process.
- Opinions outweigh obedience.
- Anger and bitterness increase when plans fall apart, and you blame everyone else for why things didn't come together.
- Jealousy creeps in when life works out for others while your life seems to stay stuck in neutral. People all around you are getting raises, making close friends, getting engaged or married, having babies, or buying homes, and life seems to be going as planned for them. It all feels like more fuel on the fire that God is obviously not in control of your life and is not worthy of trusting, let alone waiting on—another reminder why it's better when you are in control.

158

But waiting and surrendering control go hand in hand. They cannot be separated. Just look at every person in Scripture who was invited to wait on God.

- Noah had absolutely no control over when the flood would be over.
- Daniel had no way to know if and when he would get out of that lions' den.
- Joseph sat in a prison due to a crime he didn't commit, and he had no control over if and when he would ever get out.
- Sarah and Abraham could not get pregnant, and they had no control over if they would ever have a child.
- Jacob waited and worked for years for the true love of his life, Rachel, and then had no control over the fact he was given a different wife, Leah.
- The Israelites waited in Egypt for hundreds of years as slaves, with no control over ever having a better future. They were finally freed and then had to wait another forty years to enter the promised land.
- David hid in a cave while he was being hunted by Saul, and he had no control over if he would be found.
- Jonah sat in the belly of a whale and could not know if he would ever get out.
- Mary was engaged to be married, her life in front of her, and suddenly an angel showed up and told her she would become pregnant. She did not ask for the visit nor to be given the task of raising the Son of God.
- Simeon waited his entire life to see the Messiah and had no control over when it would happen.
- Mary and Martha watched their brother, Lazarus, die and could not know whether Jesus would come and raise him from the dead.

- The sick and crippled and diseased waited and hoped Jesus would come to their town to heal them, but they had no control over if and when he would come.
- Jesus waited in the garden and pled with God for another way, and in that moment Jesus gave up all of his power and control to the will of his Father.
- Saul was blinded on the road to Damascus and had no control over if he would ever see again.

When God invites you to wait, that invitation always includes surrendering control. While waiting sounds sluggish and sedentary, surrendering control is anything but neutral. To take your hands off your personal steering wheel is an active spiritual experience, one that can only happen while practicing the power of the present moment.

Deep Work

I know most of us hope that letting go will be as simple as letting a balloon float away. It sounds sweet and tender, just watching that control waft away into the bright blue sky. But in my experience, control is more like the kudzu that wrapped itself over every part of my backyard, choking every possible item it could get its vines on. Control touches every part of you. God wants to open every part of you that is tightly wrapped up in control. Your overprotective and watchful heart. Your self-righteous and dogmatic thinking. Your resistant and defensive body, and any soul tie that has taken emotional authority in your life. Surrender is deep work, and it happens in the heart, mind, body, and soul.

Deep patterns take time to form, so we should expect it to also take time for us to learn to surrender. At first it feels almost impossible to let go. And yet I have found allowing myself to be present with God in the middle of surrender is one of the most

160

holy places I can be. Waiting in the present can mean deep forward progress. Learning to let life happen—instead of controlling how life happens—always produces more growth and peace. Facing pain is not nearly as terrible as avoiding it.

Active waiting is just that: active. In fact, the different seasons of my life where God has invited me into active waiting have been some of the richest, most growth-producing moments of my life. But they didn't always feel that way while I was going through them.

The story told in Exodus of Moses and the Israelites as they journeyed from Egypt to the promised land reminds me of the ongoing relationship between waiting and control. The Israelites never got to take the shortest route anywhere. They were regularly asked to let go of control through the spiritual process of waiting. After they crossed the Red Sea, they found themselves in a desert for many years. They were in a situation they didn't think was a part of the plan. But God was faithful to provide for them in their waiting, and each morning a food called manna would appear so the people could collect it and have enough to eat for the day. Manna was a breadlike cuisine, which is for sure a bonus point for God. Who doesn't want to worship a deity who loves bread? The only instruction that came with the manna was that they could not store it up; they were to let God provide for them each day. They needed to wait and allow God to take care of them daily. But in Exodus 16 we see the Israelites wanted to be in control of their food supply, and the Scripture says, "However, some of them paid no attention to Moses; they kept part of it until morning, but it was full of maggots and began to smell" (v. 20).

They wanted to be in control and could not release control to a God who promised to take care of them daily. They struggled to wait and therefore were unable to surrender to God in the present moment. Releasing our concrete conclusions on how life should be is always part of surrender.

Releasing

When God invites us to wait, he also invites us to release our will. To move from the internal messages of "my will" to "your will." It sounds so simple, yet I have found it to be one of the most difficult things I have spiritually done. So much of who I am joyfully longs to be all of who God created me to be, and yet the truth is I am a patchwork of both light and dark and am torn between what I want and what God desires. When we hold so tightly to our wants, they can often become decayed and smelly, like day-old manna.

Choosing God's will is not about gritting our teeth and forcing ourselves into something we hope to like one day. Releasing in the present moment is wonderfully healing and happens through prayer, specifically the Lord's Prayer. I grew up praying the Lord's Prayer over and over. I had no idea how someone's name could be hallowed, which was the one part of the prayer as a child I didn't totally understand. But I memorized the prayer regardless, and am grateful; I had no idea how much I would need it as an adult. When I am in the midst of releasing control of how I want the future to play out, I always begin with Jesus's prayer.

> **When God invites us to wait, he also invites us to release our will.**

> Our Father in heaven,
> hallowed be your name,
> your kingdom come,
> your will be done,
> on earth as it is in heaven.
> Give us today our daily bread.
> And forgive us our debts,
> as we also have forgiven our debtors.
> And lead us not into temptation
> but deliver us from the evil one. (Matt. 6:9–13)

To actively wait will require you to release your will. The Israelites needed to learn to release control and to respond to God each day. You will know you need to pray the releasing prayer if there is something coming up in your future you are trying to control. When I pray this prayer, I often imagine myself holding my will tightly in my clenched fists. I picture what I want being held in my hands, and as I pray, I open my hands. It is a physical way of inviting my body to lead the way for my heart, mind, and soul to follow. Releasing is the first step in trusting that God will provide daily bread. The next step is actively responding.

Responding

Active waiting will change how you view your purpose. When we just want our waiting to come to an end and for God to give us what we're waiting for, we're not actively waiting on God or for God. We're waiting with a sense of entitlement. To receive what we believe we deserve. But when we actively wait, our true purpose starts to take shape, and we begin to see that God is transforming us more into the image of Jesus *in the waiting*. We can move throughout our lives in a posture of responding to the movement of the Spirit instead of just reacting to our life circumstances. As Eugene Peterson says,

> The assumption of spirituality is that always God is doing something before I know it. So the task is not to get God to do something I think needs to be done, but to become aware of what God is doing so that I can respond to it and participate and take delight in it.[1]

I have watched countless friends and family members walk through unthinkable circumstances. The kind in which you would go looking for the exit door the second you entered. And what I have learned along the way is that people who can weather storms and walk through unthinkable circumstances live with deeply rooted faith. To walk in faith and put your trust in God is not about getting God to give you what you want. It is about trusting that God is always at work bringing you what you most need.

People who learn how to respond to God also learn to look beyond the circumstance. They don't put their hope in circumstances changing or in the belief that God will make the circumstances better. When you grow in trust, you are becoming the kind of person who knows you are deeply and desperately loved by God even when you find yourself sucking the rust at the bottom of the barrel of life.

When we actively wait and release our control over the future, and when we invite the sacred question *What's here now?*, we invite ourselves into a posture of openness for God to root us even deeper into our purpose. Actively waiting and responding to how God is at work in the present is a way to trust that what God has planned is always better than what we have planned. I have noticed when I learn to move from reacting to responding, the very thing I am waiting on is often replaced with a deeper purpose. A deep reminder that we are called to be men and women who trust God—not try to control God. As God helps us release and respond in the midst of our waiting, he then begins to renew who we are.

Renewing

The place where I have seen God renew me the most is in raw and authentic vulnerability. When God invites us into waiting, one of the most active things we can do while we wait is to practice raw renewal prayers. Not formulaic, going-through-the-motion prayers but rather the kinds we see throughout the psalms. The gutsy, real prayers like this one:

> I yell out to my God, I yell with all my might,
> I yell at the top of my lungs. He listens.
> I found myself in trouble and went looking for my Lord;
> my life was an open wound that wouldn't heal.

When friends said, "Everything will turn out all right,"
  I didn't believe a word they said.
I remember God—and shake my head.
  I bow my head—then wring my hands.
I'm awake all night—not a wink of sleep;
  I can't even say what's bothering me.
I go over the days one by one,
  I ponder the years gone by.
I strum my lute all through the night,
  wondering how to get my life together. (Ps. 77:1–6 MSG)

What is amazing about vulnerability is that it renews every part of who we are. Learning to wait and surrender control will feel better in body, mind, heart, and soul. There are so many things that still confuse me in the Bible. But one of the things I am most grateful for is the vulnerability I find from cover to cover. Raw, real, and honest confessions are the only path to renewal. When we are in the middle of waiting, God wants us to actively engage with him. He can handle our yell-

> **Raw, real, and honest confessions are the only path to renewal.**

ing. He can handle our fear. He can handle our honest questions. Apparently, he can even handle our lute-playing all through the night.

Honest and active prayers give us the ability to remember the truth about who God is and what God is doing in the waiting, and this begins to renew our perspective. Just a few verses later, this psalm says,

O, God! Your way is holy!
  No god is great like God!
You're the God who makes things happen;
  you showed everyone what you can do. (vv. 13–14 MSG)

Active waiting is dynamic. It must include vulnerability. It's a conversation that is active and moving—even though we feel like our circumstances are standing still. Somehow, in the darkest moments of openness to God, we are also opened to new thoughts, new hopes, new desires, and new perspectives. God literally renews what we are waiting on.

* * *

As a recovering control freak, I have had lots of practice in releasing, responding, and allowing God to renew me. I can always trace back that desire to control with rehearsing a future I am convinced needs to happen a certain way. But when I trust that no matter what circumstances come into my life, God is doing just fine holding the universe together, I can begin to open myself up to possibilities that I can't see when I'm attached to one "right" path. And I come to realize it takes so much more energy to control life than to surrender.

When I'm controlling, my vision becomes limited and narrow, but when I am surrendered and at peace, living in the here and now, my hopes become abundant and wide. The twist in seeking to control everything is that it leaves us feeling less in control.

Surrender literally means to stop fighting.

Stop fighting God.

Stop fighting yourself.

Stop fighting others.

FULL STOP.

Surrender lets go of what if and welcomes what is. Surrender finds a way to accept that somehow all is well and will be well, even without your input. It's not about inaction. It's about taking action from a posture of surrender.

God has found multiple ways throughout my years on this planet to invite me into new spiritual waiting rooms. I remember when our son, Elijah, was little, he always loved taking a toy to bed with him and had a nightly ritual to decide what toy he was going to take. Clearly there were size and safety limits on what we allowed him to pick. But each night we would go through the choosing ceremony, and I used to imagine all of his toys having a *Toy Story* moment of crying out, "Pick me! Pick me!"

He would usually play with the toy until he fell asleep, and once I knew he was out I would come into his room, grab it from his bed, and turn out the night-light. One such night, while I was walking through a particularly difficult season of waiting and all I wanted was to be done with the waiting and move on, I went to take the toy out of his bed as usual. Elijah had a tight grip on his green John Deere tractor. I quietly and carefully loosened his fingers and removed the tractor from his hand, then knelt down to add it to the basket of other toy tractors. I felt God whisper, *What if this waiting room is the room I want you to be in? What if this is the only place where I can do what I most want to do in your life?* Tears puddled in my eyes as I hunched over the toys.

The waiting room is the real room where God transforms us. There is not another door to go through. There is not another place to get to. God is not beyond the door . . . God is in the waiting room.

I don't mean to sound bossy or controlling. (OK, maybe a little bit; old habits don't die quickly.) Friend, if I could pull you close and shoot the breeze with you over coffee until we got to the real conversation at hand, I would say, "It's not worth it." That thing you are holding on to so tightly. That job. That person. That idea of how you thought life was going to go. That

> **God is not beyond the door . . . God is in the waiting room.**

desire you think you can't live without. That old wound. That loss. Whatever you are still holding in your hand. The waiting room is the room where God transforms. I know you are smack-dab in the middle of the *no more* and the *not yet*. But it's between those two places where God is. God lives in the waiting room.

So, *stay*. I see you checking your watch, wondering how much longer you will need to wait. Don't leave the place God has put you. Actively wait on him. Allow him to transform you actively through releasing, responding, and renewing. What feels like our ending is always God's beginning.

> Meanwhile, the moment we get tired in the waiting, God's Spirit is right alongside helping us along. If we don't know how or what to pray, it doesn't matter. He does our praying in and for us, making prayer out of our wordless sighs, our aching groans. He knows us far better than we know ourselves, knows our pregnant condition, and keeps us present before God. That's why we can be so sure that every detail in our lives of love for God is worked into something good. (Rom. 8:26–28 MSG)

PART 3

Receiving the Present

11

Emotions

All the Feels

Emotions are given to us by God so that we can fully experience
our experiences.

Richard Rohr, *Radical Grace*

The fluorescent bulb flickered above me like a lightning bug
dancing through a sweltering summer night. Never fully on
or off. Just flickering. I was in another hospital waiting room. This
time, though I was physically alone, I felt emotionally crowded.
Fear. Worry. Hope. Confusion. They all held vigil with me as
my seven-year-old daughter was wheeled away to have her body
scanned in the hopes they could figure out how to remove her rare
and life-threatening infection. Like the blinking light, my emotions popped around in my body. It is one of the clearest memories
in my life of feeling emotionally out of control. Flooded with
feelings. I was, in fact, emotion-full. Thank God, only hours after
that scan Gigi was rushed into surgery, and after a week in the
ICU, we celebrated Thanksgiving in a stale but sacred pediatric

waiting room. It was the most delicious turkey and pumpkin pie I've ever had. We eventually brought our daughter home, and Gigi regularly reminds us that she truly is one in a million because she survived bacterial tracheitis, a rare infectious disease.

That night is seared into my emotional anatomy. I will never forget it. I imagine you've had similar emotion-full experiences in your life, when the feelings within you felt like electrical currents zinging erratically around the container of your being. These emotions have everything to do with being present and whole, but feelings are one of the most complex and confusing parts of life and relationships.

My best friend has the same name as me, with the exact same spelling. "Jeanne M" and "Jeanne S" are how we differentiate ourselves. I love whenever we go somewhere together and have to share our names. We are, in fact, double the trouble. Our lives are wildly different, and seventeen years separate us in age. She is stepping into a sweet season of grandparenting while I navigate hormonal teenagers. Everyone needs a best friend like Jeanne M. I have called her literally in the middle of the night. She has sat with me on my darkest nights, and we have laughed so hard we cried. She gets me, and I get her. I regularly tell her she is one of God's purest and kindest gifts in my life.

There are a million things I love about Jeanne M, but one of my favorite things about her is that she understands feelings like an emotional ninja warrior. Years ago, Jeanne M was the first person to teach me about the acronym for the six basic emotions: SASHET stands for Sad, Angry, Scared, Happy, Excited, and Tender. I still tease her that someone really messed this one up, because it's not the correct spelling of the word *sachet*.

SASHET is like a six-pack of crayons. While understanding the basic feelings is necessary and critical to emotional health, what fun is six crayons when you know there is a jumbo set available? What fun is *red* when you can use *razzmatazz*? Several years ago, I came across what is known as the Feeling Wheel, which is like the jumbo set of seventy-eight colors for your emotions.[1]

The Feeling Wheel

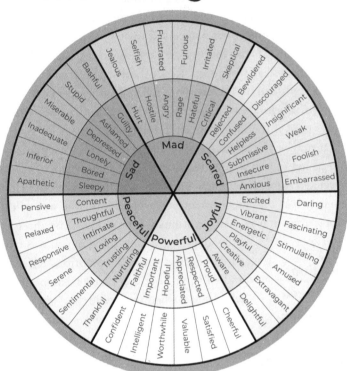

The Gottman Institute
Developed by Dr. Gloria Willcox

When I look at it, I think it's no wonder feelings can be confusing, and no surprise so many of us have developed patterns to fight, flight, or freeze when we experience any kind of stress or tension emotionally. This wheel reveals that there is *a lot* going on inside of us.

Because of the complexity of all seventy-eight of these feelings and all their possible combinations, when we experience any feeling we are uncomfortable with, most of us add something else into the mix before we fight, flight, or freeze. We try to *fix it*. It's an absurd idea to think we can fix emotions, but humans have been trying to do it from the beginning of time.

I'm sure you have been with someone who has been sad, and you have wanted to make them not feel sad anymore. Maybe you offered them a tissue. Maybe you've even said something like, "It's OK, don't cry. It will all work out." We see the discomfort someone else is in, and instead of holding space for that emotion, we try to fix it. It's usually for good reason. We don't want them to feel sorrow.

But what if the sorrow wasn't looking to be fixed?

Or maybe you've been around someone who was mad, and everything in you wanted to fix their anger, especially if it was directed toward you. Or here's another that may hit a nerve: Have you ever had a moment when you saw someone who was wildly happy, almost as if their emotions were having the brightest of shiny days—and everything in you was triggered because your own emotions felt dark and stormy? I bet there have been moments when you wished you could "fix" their happiness to match your sorrow.

Humans want to fix what feels complicated. I also think we've identified some feelings as *good* and other feelings as *bad*. But what if our emotions are neutral and don't require "fixing"? What if, instead, all seventy-eight of them just need some healthy space to be felt? Emotions don't need to be given answers; they need to be given space.

> Emotions don't need to be given answers; they need to be given space.

For far too long there has been a disconnect between faith and feelings. When it comes to how Christians need to handle their emotions, some destructive and poor theology has been taught. I have heard . . .

- "Facts are greater than feelings. Facts are the only reliable source to guide our faith."

- "Following our emotions will lead us to sin."
- "To live a godly life, we must get our emotions under control."

Somehow, some parts of the church have sent the message that emotions are unreliable, dangerous, and bad. That logic and reason are superior, and feelings are trivial and should be suppressed or ignored. I want to say, again, that this is simply not true and does not hold up to solid biblical interpretation nor to a scientific physiological understanding of who we are as human beings. Sadly, many people have bought the lie that faith is simply believing in the Word of God and acting upon it no matter how they feel, repressing their emotions in the name of faith.

I am here to say that my life has taught me that walking by faith is the exact opposite. Faith has led me to all the feels. From excitement to fear to sadness to joy to so much more. I am tired of people describing one another as "emotional" in a derogatory way. Many years ago, I decided I was no longer going to allow myself or anyone with me to say "I'm sorry" about feeling emotions deeply. Tears do not require an apology.

The last thing I want to do is to be critical or throw shade. I simply want to pull the curtain back in the most loving way I know how. It is impossible to be spiritually mature and emotionally immature. To be healthy and whole requires you to be emotionally aware. A transforming relationship with God, yourself, and others requires all of you. Heart, mind, body, and soul.

There are so many incredible examples of men and women throughout the Scriptures who found a way to be emotion-full.

You can see it in

- the deep desperation of Sarah
- the grieving pain of Ruth and Naomi

To be healthy and whole requires you to be emotionally aware.

- the excitement and calling in Peter
- the guilty sadness of the rich young ruler

One of the most powerful stories that seems to touch every quadrant of the feeling wheel is the Old Testament story of Joseph. It's filled with all kinds of troubling twists. One of Jacob's twelve sons, Joseph was his father's favorite. His ten older brothers were filled with envy and jealousy. Instead of dealing with their emotions in a healthy way, they conspired together to kill Joseph. If only Joseph's brothers would have pulled out the trusty feeling wheel and identified their emotions. If only one of them could have asked, *What's here now?* But instead of facing their anger and jealousy and giving their emotions space to be felt, they made their emotions supreme. They elevated their emotions above wisdom. As they were about to go through with their plan, there was a last-minute plot twist. Instead of killing him, they decided to make some extra coin by selling him into slavery. So Joseph was purchased, taken to a foreign land, and eventually thrown into prison.

Perhaps you've heard this story, or maybe you've seen *Joseph and the Amazing Technicolor Dreamcoat*. (Fun fact: this was the first musical I was in, while in high school, and ever since I've loved this story.) Whether you've heard it multiple times or this is the first time you're hearing it, I imagine you can feel the emotions in this story. Jealousy, hatred, envy, isolation, confusion—all the feels are here.

Joseph's story is a roller coaster from being a spoiled son to being sold into slavery to finding favor with his master to being falsely imprisoned to wielding nationwide power. He consistently overcomes each obstacle in his path and eventually begins to interpret dreams for the king. He gains notoriety, and that leads to his eventual freedom. He rises through the ranks in Egypt, and the pharaoh grants him favor and gives him a position of power. And Joseph's story could have ended there. The painful events from his past could have been overshadowed by his later successes. He could have tried to bury all that pain. Pushed it down and repressed it until it no longer lived on the top of his heart. But in the goodness of God, Joseph has an opportunity to reveal his emotions instead of concealing them.

Joseph's brothers eventually travel to Egypt in search of food, forcing the emotional plot of Joseph's life to the surface. When he is finally reunited with his brothers, Genesis 45:1–2 says,

> Then Joseph could no longer control himself before all his attendants, and he cried out, "Have everyone leave my presence!" So there was no one with Joseph when he made himself known to his brothers. And he wept so loudly that the Egyptians heard him, and Pharaoh's household heard about it.

Joseph could not contain his emotion. In fact, if you jump down a few more verses it says,

> Then he threw his arms around his brother Benjamin and wept, and Benjamin embraced him, weeping. And he kissed all his brothers and wept over them. (vv. 14–15)

The emotion continues and carries through the remainder of the story. In the ultimate reunion, between Joseph and his father,

> As soon as Joseph appeared before him, he threw his arms around his father and wept for a long time. (46:29)

What I love about Joseph's story is that it does not leave us wondering about the emotional impact of the experiences he faced throughout his life. His tears weave together his past pain with his present emotional posture. His weeping is an acknowledgment of the torment he endured and reveals that something profound happened. Joseph's story shows us what happens when emotions are released in a healthy way instead of repressed in unhealthy ways. Joseph allowed his emotions to have motion: *e-motion.*

As I mentioned earlier, e-motion is "energy in motion." That's what all our emotions are looking for. Healthy motion. They want to move and be felt and be given healthy space. When emotional buttons are pushed, a surge of energy starts coursing through the body. That emotional energy is looking to be moved. You've seen this, and I bet you've experienced it.

- Our son is a basketball player and an NBA junkie, so we go to lots of games. And there is nothing like a down-to-the-last-second basketball game. Each team battling for the win. Every person in the arena screaming and shouting, their internal emotional buttons flashing as the energy in their bodies comes out externally with wild and raucous chanting and cheering.
- When someone is shocked by something, their energy in motion causes them to put their hands over their face, widen their eyes, and maybe even brace their whole body in a frozen stance.
- When someone experiences a painful loss, their internal e-motion produces tears to release the sadness. Their body feels the ache and pain and can't contain it within, so it releases the energy by crying.

What is important to understand about our emotions is that every time an emotional button is pushed, the only thing that emotion is looking for is to be released in a healthy way. The problem is that many of us have learned to do the opposite. Instead of releasing emotions, we repress them.

Repressing Emotions

When we repress our emotion, two things happen: we deny it, and we stuff it.

1. Deny It

When you deny e-motion, you harness what does not want to be harnessed. You put resistance around something that isn't looking to be resisted. I bet you've seen this before. Someone walks into a room, and you can feel their anger. Every part of their facial expression and body language is screaming, ANGER IS PRESENT. But if you ask them, "Hey, is everything OK?" with a clenched jaw, they'll answer, "Of course, why?"

That is denying the emotion.

I have a faint memory of being at my grandma's house as a young girl. My grandma always had a bowl of candy out, and she was clear that we could only have three pieces. Three pieces were never enough for this sweet-tooth girl. I remember always wanting more. I don't know why I didn't feel free to ask for another piece, but instead of just asking for more, I started to sneak it. When no one was looking I filled my pockets with candy. I unconsciously taught myself to deny my desire instead of naming it. So many of us are good at denying emotions. Remember, emotions are just energy in motion, and so a denied emotion needs somewhere to go. And lots of times, when we deny our emotions, the next thing we learn to do is stuff them.

2. Stuff It

When you stuff your emotion, you push it down. Cover it up. Bury it beneath all kinds of other activities. The problem with stuffing emotions, as we talked about in chapter 7, is that it is often like trying to push a beach ball underwater; it only pops out somewhere else.

I bet you've experienced this. Perhaps you've experienced loneliness in your life. That feeling is sad, scary, and overwhelming. So, instead of allowing yourself to feel that loneliness and invite God to be with you in it, you stuff it away. You start filling that loneliness with all kinds of counterfeit imitations of what you are really longing for in your life. You long for community and connection, and instead of seeking it with others, you watch people live it out online in what you perceive to be connected lives on social media. Instead of asking for what you want, you hint at it and drop passive-aggressive emotional breadcrumbs with the people in your life, because saying you want connection feels too vulnerable. Stuffing emotions is a way many of us protect ourselves. We fear the emotion is bigger than we are, and if we can safely stuff it away, we won't have to deal with it. But denying and stuffing emotions often gets us stuck in an ongoing mental and emotional loop, and many times this causes us to grow numb.

I have a friend who, when he was young, was told by his grandmother that men don't cry, and he has spent the better part of his adult life trying to figure out why he runs away from sadness and from expressing himself through tears. This friend is working hard to break the mental and emotional loop that has told him sadness is not allowed. For the majority of his life, his emotions were not given healthy space and motion, so he is learning for the first time to trust that his emotions aren't here to hurt him, they are here to heal him.

I have another friend who grew up with a mom who was emotionally overbearing and overwhelming. To self-protect, my friend began to numb out with lots of little escapes to keep from having to feel so much. Now she has a very hard time accessing her emotions.

What I know to be true about repressing our emotions is that what you resist will always persist. When you resist emotion, it secures itself to you, and over time it stops being an emotion and becomes a mood.

- Unfelt sadness leads to apathy.
- Unfelt anger leads to bitterness.
- Unfelt fear leads to anxiety.
- Unfelt delight leads to depression.

- Unfelt excitement leads to gluttony.
- Unfelt tenderness leads to living detached.

Moods can last for years. All from e-motion just looking to be released.

Releasing Emotions

I am so grateful that God doesn't just invite us to release our emotions. He gives us an example to imitate: Jesus, in all his divinity and humanity, allowed his own e-motion to move in healthy ways. In the garden of Gethsemane, before he was arrested, tried, and eventually sentenced to death, Jesus said to his friends, "My soul is overwhelmed with sorrow to the point of death. Stay here and keep watch with me" (Matt. 26:38). With these two sentences, Jesus models how to release emotion.

1. Name It

Jesus named his emotions. His soul was *overwhelmed* with sorrow. Jesus was about to face death, and he chose to name what he was feeling. Can you just imagine for a moment if people everywhere would start naming their fear instead of acting out their fear? Or naming their anger instead of acting out their anger?

Oh, how our world would change.

Jesus was not ashamed of his e-motions. He didn't try to cover them up. He didn't use a socially acceptable way of describing his fear. He didn't say, "You know, I'd like you to sit here with me because I have an unspoken prayer request. I'm just struggling with a few minor things." Jesus was authentic and vulnerable. He named that he was overwhelmed.

When was the last time you took a risk like this and named what was really going on inside of you? When was the last time you allowed someone to see your emotions?

Even as I was writing this chapter, all the feels were swirling for me. All my doubts decided to double down. The nasty old stories of comparison and condemnation were clawing at my emotional ankles, trying to pull me straight back to my grandma's living room and whispering lies that it was better to avert my feelings instead of accepting what's here now. But instead of repressing, denying, and stuffing, I took out the extra big feeling wheel and named what emotions were present.

> *I feel fear.* Who am I to write a book on the presence of God? What qualifications make me worthy of helping people live in the present moment?
>
> *I feel tender.* How will I really be received? This all feels vulnerable and raw, and what if people would just prefer a feel-good, "three simple steps to find freedom in your life" kind of book?
>
> *I feel happy.* I'm doing it. I am actually writing this book. I'm stepping deeper into a calling that has been on my life for decades.
>
> *I feel excited.* What if people really start living with this question? What if they really start practicing *What's here now?*

I named all the emotions that were present. I named how I was experiencing them in my body, and I even sent a text to Jeanne M so she could be a witness to the present moment of my writing this chapter.

So many of us resist, judge, apologize for, avoid, look for answers in, or withhold our feelings. I wonder if you would be willing this week to just start with naming your emotions. One of the things I have shifted in my life is that I name my emotions by saying "I feel" instead of "I am."

Instead of "I'm sad," I say "I'm feeling sad."

Instead of "I'm angry," I say "I'm feeling angry."

Instead of "I'm excited," I say "I'm feeling excited."

Doing this is a reminder to me that I am experiencing e-motion. Energy in motion. I am not that emotion. That emotion is just looking for a healthy space to be named and felt.

2. Feel It

Once you name what you're feeling (I know; this is profound), FEEL IT.

That's what Joseph did with his brothers, and also what Jesus did in the garden. I would encourage you to read the whole chapter of Matthew 26. Jesus prays and names his emotions to God, and three different times he allows himself to feel what he is feeling in a healthy way. Jesus experiences the depth of his emotions and brings it all to God. So many of us tend to not take the fullness of our emotions to God because we fear we might freak him out.

There has never been a feeling that has freaked God out. We have a God who feels and invites us to do the same. Even when the emotion feels raw and messy. Even when we can't find words to describe it, the emotion still deserves the space to be felt in a healthy and productive way.

I will never forget the summer of 2020, when I saw the video of George Floyd being pinned down on the pavement as his arms were handcuffed behind his back. As he lay there, the officer who has since been convicted of murder held a knee on his throat as three other officers stood by, and George struggled to breathe and eventually suffocated and died. I felt rage, anger, and absolute horror pulse through my body.

I screamed in horror and then wept in grief. My body needed to name and feel the emotions all the way through. There was no neutrality in my feelings; they were fierce and ferocious and needed space. My emotions begged me to grieve, mourn, lament, and activate myself and others in the direction of justice. To speak up and speak out. To extend our table and widen our door. To confess my own broken bias and march for peace.

Feelings give us a way to respond. When we name them and feel them, God gives us a healthy release and resolution to know what to do with them.

I know that to name and feel our feelings means we will have to face some of the pain in our lives. "I am just looking to feel some more pain," said *no one ever*. But I have come to understand that pain is necessary to becoming who God created us to become. Suffering is what happens when we avoid pain.

I have prayed with and held space with many people who are afraid to feel their feelings. They worry that if they feel what they have learned to repress, it will rip the lid off the box of neatly stored emotions within them. They don't trust their fear, rage, hatred, bitterness, sadness, or self-doubt. They worry their emotion will erupt in all kinds of messy ways. This worry makes so much sense to me. I have anguished over the same thing, concerned that once I named and felt my emotions, I would only find myself in a darker well of despair. But I have found the opposite to be true. You can't heal what you don't feel.

> Suffering is what happens when we avoid pain.

Naming and feeling my emotions has transformed my marriage and parenting. It has repaired broken relationships. It has given me compassion for others and the feelings they are experiencing. It has helped me walk away from self-destructive behaviors. It has led me to have mercy for the different puzzle pieces in my past, and it has given me the ability to draw upon the power of the present moment. It has helped me ask for what I need, want, and prefer, clearly, directly, and respectfully. It has helped me resolve conflict maturely with the ability to hold all the perspectives of the argument. It has helped me distinguish between sexual desire and lustful desire. It has helped me to grieve the losses in my life. It has helped me to work through forgiveness toward those who have hurt me.

What the world needs is more emotion-full people, not emotional ones.

12

···

Thoughts
Crowded Runways

Your brain is involved in everything you do.

Daniel G. Amen, *Change Your Brain,*
Change Your Body

I sat down in my middle seat, overly annoyed. I'm a window seat kind of girl. I like the feeling of being safely tucked inside my row, and if I decide to take a nap, I have the window as a potential pillow. In the middle seat, if a nap was going to happen, I would have to use the stranger to my left or right as my pillow. And you know how everyone loves a total stranger falling asleep on their shoulder.

How did I forget to check in early for my flight—*again*? While I love Southwest and so many of their amazing benefits, I tend to be thrifty when buying airline tickets and often refuse to pay the extra money to get an early check-in. I always promise myself that I will set an alarm on my calendar and check in exactly twenty-four hours before my flight. But I forgot and was now sentenced to four hours of middle seat purgatory.

As if my seat sentencing was not enough, my flight mates were totally unaware of the unspoken but well-known rule that the person in the middle seat always gets the armrests. I was smashed in like a burrito, arms folded against my body. I endured the flight home, but I'm pretty sure I dozed off for a bit on the sweet lady to my left, because she awkwardly smiled when we made eye contact toward the end of the trip.

When we finally landed in Chicago and began to taxi to our gate, I couldn't wait to get off the plane and, more importantly, couldn't wait to get home to see Jarrett and our kids. But when I was only minutes away from being released from my middle seat prison, the pilot came over the loudspeaker to let us know the airport was overcrowded. We would need to pull off to the side of the runway and wait for a gate to open.

My feelings about the lack of an available gate made my feelings about the middle seat look saintlike. How could there not be a gate? I could see an open one right out the window. How could runways and gates get overcrowded? Wasn't there a whole matrix system created by really smart people directing when all the flights come and go? Why wouldn't they just let us all off, or at least release all the miserable middle seat travelers? But of course, the overcrowded airport won that fight. We sat there for thirty extra minutes until a gate opened for us.

This is not the first time this has happened to me, and I imagine it's not the last. A congested airport is something I have grown to expect. Especially living in Chicago with two major airports that are known as some of the busiest in the world. It's a fast-moving place with lots of people coming and going. Anyone who has ever spent more than an hour in a major airport in a large and rapid city knows that even with all the strategic master planning it is often chaotic and stressful.

The same can be said for my mind. Even though there is a strategic master plan that makes up the structure of my brain, sometimes it feels chaotic, congested, and stressful. Like the overcrowded airport, my mind often feels like there are thousands of thought planes looking to be cleared for landing on its runway. Experts estimate that the mind thinks between sixty and eighty thousand thoughts a day. That's an average of about three thousand thoughts per hour. I think we can agree that we are all doing *a lot* of thinking.

See the Scripts

The incidental and irregular thoughts that fly through my mind very rarely bother me. But the repeat offenders that show up at the worst moment and hijack my ability to be present—I don't always know what to do with those. For years, instead of slowing down and observing my thoughts and asking myself if I should clear the thought plane for landing, I came up with unconscious scripts to try to push the thought away.

The Overtired Script

Thought: *I can't keep going like this. This is an unsustainable pace, and no human is meant to function at this speed.*

Thought: *You're just overtired. Once you slow down, get a good night's sleep, and cut back on the caffeine, it will all get back into order again.*

Thought: *You know we are not cutting back on the caffeine.*

Thought: *Suck it up, Jeanne. This is what it takes. Don't you think Oprah gets tired? If she keeps going, surely you can too.*

The Unqualified Script

Thought: *You are nowhere near qualified to do what you're doing. You've never had this many employees or led a budget this large, you didn't get an MBA, and sooner or later someone is going to figure out you are underqualified.*

Thought: *Just keep pretending. Act like you know what you're doing. Fake it till you make it. It's what has gotten you this far.*

The Not Smart Enough Script

Thought: *You were a decent student but never the best student. Sooner or later your inability to understand a complex spreadsheet is going to catch up to you.*

Thought: *You know you don't know what they are talking about, and yet you nodded your head.*

The Comparison Script

Thought: *You can't write like she can. It's like she opens her mouth and words fall out that resemble rubies, emeralds, and diamonds.*

Thought: *You don't have as many followers as that person. Your platform is not as expansive, and you don't have the same interest in your content as they do.*

Thought: *You're not interesting or special. Your life is bland and boring. You're just a wife and a mom who started a church.*

All of my thought scripts were consistent in one thing: they were almost always unhelpful and untrue. They crowded up the runway of my mind, and even though I was trying to push the thoughts out, I was still thinking about them. Still reading the same deafening script and clearing thoughts for landing that were not bringing peace into my life.

I had no one else to look to but me. They were my thoughts. What I began to realize is that when I clear a thought for landing, that's the moment I start to believe the thought is true. Instead of just acknowledging I was having a thought, I welcomed the thought in and started believing it was true. My own unconscious thought scripts were often the cause of so much of my fear, pain, and anxiety. It wasn't something in my past that I was mulling over, or something out in the future that I was overanalyzing. While I desperately wanted to blame someone or something else, it was *me*. I was the one believing everything I thought was true. I was the one keeping me from the peace I was craving. It was me who chose to be everywhere else in my thoughts other than the here and now.

Asking *What's here now?* was like flipping a light switch on the dark and cluttered runway of my mind. I started to pay attention to what I was thinking, and I began to realize that when I unconsciously believed my thoughts were true, I was the one inviting the mindless suffering in. I started seeing what Byron Katie says: "a thought is harmless until we believe it."[1]

I began to realize that I was the one taking my thoughts and turning them into beliefs before I ever gave myself a moment to ask, *What's here now? Is this thought even true?* It wasn't the thought that was causing so much angst in my life, it was my attachment to that thought being true.

Flip the Scripts

Your thoughts are powerful—but more importantly, your thoughts have the power to change your mind. What you do with all the thoughts that fly through your mind will determine the way you live your life. The good news is that *you* are in control of what you allow in and out of your mind. If you get control of your thoughts, you will get control of your life.

When you get this . . . everything changes.

You don't have to believe everything you think. But most of us believe our thoughts are true because we have been doing so

> **If you get control of your thoughts, you will get control of your life.**

longer than we even knew we were having a thought. It happens in big and small ways every day of your life.

I just had this happen with a coworker and friend, Patrick. This past week I sent him a text on a Wednesday at 10:11 a.m:

> Hey, Pat—if you have an open second today, I would love to clear something with you.

He responded at 10:12 a.m. (a very impressive text turnaround):

> Totally.

His next text came at 10:14.

> I will swing by your office when I'm out of my meeting.

When Pat was done with his meeting, he came into my office, plopped down on my couch, and said, "OK, what did I do wrong?"

I instantly started laughing and said, "Why do you think you did something wrong?" He said, "I don't know, I just usually do." We both laughed. I said, "You didn't do anything wrong. I wanted to clarify something with you from the conversation we had the other day."

We had a great conversation about something he had said that I didn't quite understand. We talked it through, and in a matter of minutes, we were finished.

But can you imagine if Patrick started to believe the thoughts running through his mind just from the text message I sent him?

Mind you (yes, pun intended), all I said to Pat was, "I would love to clear something with you." But from the moment I sent that text to the moment we were together, all kinds of thoughts began to form in his mind.

I didn't ask him what he started thinking, but I imagine he could have thought any one of these things.

- *Oh no. What did I do? Did I say something? Did I make a mistake? I need to get better at covering up my mistakes.*
- *Why does Jeanne always see my mistakes? She must have eagle eyes. She is really a tough boss. I mean honestly, she has unreasonable standards. Does she "clear" with anyone else like this?*
- *It must be me. I mean, I have been getting in trouble since I was a kid. I guess I just do everything wrong.*

If any of those thoughts started landing on the runway of Patrick's mind, and he began to believe them, can you see how that would impact our friendship? One of the things I appreciate about my friend Pat is that instead of letting all those thoughts land, he just said, out loud, "OK, what did I do wrong?"

Let's remember the facts.

FACT: I sent Pat a text.

FACT: Pat responded to the text.

That is all. But those two facts had the potential to form all kinds of thoughts, stories, and experiences and become something else in both of our minds. We all do this. We start with facts or experiences, then all kinds of thoughts about those facts or experiences start flying through our minds.

The world we live in preys on unconscious, invisible, toxic beliefs. It can be unfair, unprincipled, and undisciplined especially when it comes to our thoughts. Turn on the news for five minutes, and you will get that. The world wages war all day long with opinions and stories and toxic thoughts and beliefs. There are oodles of interpretations of all that is going wrong in the world, and every opinion and story told is hoping to land on the runway of your mind.

But we don't have to live like that. We're invited into a different way of living. A different way of being. A different way of thinking. God has given everyone the same ability to decide if we want to succumb to the temptation to believe everything we think is true. It's an invisible weapon, but one that brings peace and offers freedom.

So many of us have silent strongholds in our lives. Things we've believed about ourselves. Thoughts we've had about who we are, or who we are not. The power God has given us can demolish those strongholds. So many of us have experienced so much pain in our relationships, not from the arguments we have had but from all the thoughts that flooded our minds about the arguments we've had.

Do you know most of the arguments you and I have are not based on facts? They are based on the thoughts and stories we make up about the facts. This power from God can put an end to those kinds of arguments. This power can catch the untrue thoughts that fly through your mind. Thoughts about yourself. Thoughts about the people in your life. Thoughts about the experiences in your life.

This weapon that God has given you has the potential to be the single greatest protection in your life. Here it is: "take captive every thought to make it obedient to Christ" (2 Cor. 10:5).

● ● ●

If you want to use this weapon God has given you, if you want to take captive your thoughts, you need to know your thoughts. Most of us don't pause long enough to pay attention to our thoughts. To notice them and recognize them and then name them as thoughts. You are not your thoughts. Your thoughts are just that—your thoughts—but they are not *you*.

I wish I could grab you by the shoulders and make you go back and read that previous sentence over and over and over again until you believe it. That is some of the best news in the world. I don't know about you, but I have had some pretty crazy thoughts in my life, and knowing I am not my thoughts makes me want to jump up and down and run around saying, "Hallelujah!"

The power God has given us is to become a noticer of our thoughts, not a believer of our thoughts. To pause when we see a thought plane coming across the horizon of our minds. To notice it. To wonder where this thought is coming from and pay attention long enough to know what it is. To truly invite the question, *What's here now?*

Jarrett and I have been practicing this for many years now, and I will tell you it has radically shifted our relationship. Most of our strongly worded conversations (a.k.a. our fights) are almost always because we have believed our thoughts about ourselves or one another.

Recently Jarrett was prepping all kinds of podcasts, videos, and messages for a book release. He was recording something Friday afternoon, and we hadn't seen each other all day. He walked in the house a little after 3:30, and the first words out of his mouth were, "Aren't you going to pick up the kids?"

I instantly had the thought, *Well, hello to you too. Yes, I have been holding down our lives most of the week while you have been recording. Yes, I did just make all of the kids' doctor's appointments, filled out their testing forms, got them in their test prep classes, and mailed that package back to Amazon. HELLO TO YOU TOO.*

I quietly grabbed my keys. Very subtly smiled to make sure he knew I was having some thoughts.

I drove to pick up the kids and decided to catch my thoughts before they landed on the runway of my mind. I got quiet. I took four deep breaths and chose to notice my thoughts before I believed they were true. I asked myself, *What's here now?*

- *We are running too fast.*
- *It's been a nonstop month.*
- *I want to be seen.*

- *I'm feeling tender with the holidays approaching. I know
  I'll be walking through them this year while grieving my
  brother, and I just need to share that with Jarrett.*

Once the kids and I got home, I said to Jarrett, "Hey, I am
having some thoughts." He said, "I noticed." We both smiled.
I said, "When you said, 'Aren't you going to pick up the kids?' I
started thinking and believing all kinds of crazy thoughts, and
here's what's really going on. We are running too fast. It's been
a nonstop month. I want to be seen, and I'm feeling tender with
the holidays coming."

We embraced. He said, "Thank you for letting me see you and
for sharing what's going on in your mind."

Now, I wish I did this all the time. I'm far from perfect. And lots
of times crazy thoughts come and land on the runway of my mind.

But this is a phrase we say to one another regularly: "I am having the thought." Do you see the difference?

I am not the thought; I am having the thought.

This has led to so much freedom in our lives.

This is what it looks like to take thoughts captive. You are having a thought; the thought does not have you. God has empowered
you with the ability to notice your thoughts, but you have to be
able to catch your thoughts before they become beliefs.

Catching Thoughts

So, how on earth do you catch a thought? It's invisible and starts
to form sometimes before you even notice. Almost all thoughts
fall into one of two categories: a familiar thought or a freedom
thought.

A Familiar Thought Is an Invisible Toxic Belief

We all have familiar thoughts. They are often the thoughts you
think without even knowing it.

- *I have so much to do. No one gets it. No one ever asks if I need help.*
- *I know my boss doesn't like me. There's no way I'm going to get that raise.*
- *My spouse only thinks about themself. They never even think to ask what's going on in my life.*

You can see how easily these types of thoughts can form and how toxic they can be. Also notice that these thoughts almost instantly form as beliefs instead of thoughts. We very rarely say them out loud. They're automatic. We usually think them without even knowing it. The problem with a familiar thought is that we often don't take enough time to notice it and decide, *Should I believe this thought? Is it true?*

It's familiar. We've thought about it and believed it a million times before—so we decide to believe it again. And that invisible toxic belief continues to control our lives.

Thought: I have so much to do. No one gets it. No one ever asks if I need help.

Belief: My to-do list is longer than everyone else's. I'm all alone and a victim, with no one ever asking if I need help.

Thought: I know my boss doesn't like me. There's no way I'm going to get that raise.

Belief: I'm one down in the organization. My boss is not generous. I never get the raises I deserve.

Thought: My spouse only thinks about themself. They never even think to ask what's going on in my life.

Belief: I am married to someone selfish, and what's going on in their life is more important to them than what's going on in my life.

These kinds of invisible toxic beliefs have the power to sour and eventually sink relationships. They keep us from being in the moment. They are all either based on the past or the future. They also keep us from being true to ourselves, and they limit our potential for belonging.

A Freedom Thought Is an Invisible Truthful Belief

Freedom thoughts are the thoughts you make obedient to Christ and are filled with truth. Let's look at those three thoughts again:

- My calendar feels full, and I don't want to try and take this all on myself. Instead of growing resentful, I am going to ask for some help.
- I have not had much connection with my boss recently. I am going to reach out and see if we can schedule some time, because I would really like to talk about that raise.
- My spouse and I have been running fast with lots going on. I am going to ask if we can schedule a date night with no phones allowed and catch up on one another's lives.

Here is what I have learned about the difference between freedom thoughts and familiar thoughts: freedom thoughts are more powerful than familiar thoughts. But most of us are only allowing familiar thoughts to land on the runway of our minds. Having up to eighty thousand thoughts a day means there are lots of planes flying overhead. All kinds of planes too, which represent all kinds of thoughts

- to-do list planes
- relationship planes
- hobby planes
- social media planes
- past memory planes

- future possibility planes
- vacation planes (Hawaiian airlines planes, yes please)
- worry planes
- fearful planes
- secret sexual thought planes
- anxiety planes
- shameful planes

At any given time, the airspace of your life is filled with thought planes flying overhead, wanting to be cleared for landing.

Guess what . . . you are the air traffic controller of your mind.

You get to choose which planes land on the runway of your mind. You get to decide:

- What am I going to think about that person I'm jealous of?
- What am I going to think about that situation in my past?
- What am I going to think about that thing I fear in my future?

Not every thought plane needs to be cleared for landing. You get to take captive your thoughts. You get to lay them out in front of yourself and God and ask, *Is this true? Should I clear this thought for landing? Is this going to help my life or harm my life?*

. . .

But so many of us already have overcrowded runways. Planes are backed up, taking precious space, and looking for a gate. What do you do if your mind is already overcrowded?

So many of us have caught a thought as though we were catching a cold. Often it's more than just one thought. If you're like me, you've caught lots of thoughts. Your mind may feel overwhelmed. Stressed. Anxious. Weary. You've caught too many thoughts and

Thoughtful Subtractions −	Thoughtful Additions +
No phones in your sleeping space. Do not start your day on email or social media.	Stop and start your day at the same time. Begin your day with worship, Scripture, and meditation.
Limit relationships that revolve around gossip and drama.	Increase relationships that revolve around growth and love.
Reduce social media and screen time.	Listen to soundtracks, instrumentals, or classical music. Limit music with words. Read a book.
Avoid sitting all day.	Move your body. Go for a walk. Take an exercise class.
Catch familiar thoughts and redirect them.	Clear freedom thoughts for landing.

need to make space on the runway. This happens through thoughtful additions or thoughtful subtractions.

Some of us need to take some things out of our lives. Others need to welcome some thoughtful additions. Here are a few things that have helped me with cleaning up the runway of my mind.

Sometimes we get on some thought planes and like the ride—but don't like the final destination that thought has taken us to.

Before you clear a thought for landing, ask yourself, *Where is this thought coming from? Where is this thought going?* Pain and heartache in your life come when you allow a thought that does not belong on the runway of your mind to land.

However, the Bible says there are certain thought planes that, if you get on them, no matter what circumstances come your way, will always arrive at a good destination.

Finally, brothers and sisters, whatever is true, whatever is noble, whatever is right, whatever is pure, whatever is lovely, whatever is admirable—if anything is excellent or praiseworthy—think about such things. (Phil. 4:8)

- Do you think about who you are, or who you are not?
- Do you meditate on who God says you are, or do you meditate on who someone no longer in your life once said you were?

Much of the pain and heartache in my life have come because I started to believe something about me that God never said about me. I caught a thought. I let the wrong thoughts land.

That's how *What's here now?* began to save my life. I got to inch my way into my thoughts and see that they were often not true. I got to see that even though I let a lot of unconscious thought planes get crowded on the runway of my mind, I could consciously put myself on a new thought plane because there is always another thought taking off.

- If I caught a thought of shame, it was usually attached to me trying to live in the past. Instead I could catch a thought of grace.
- If I caught a thought of blame, trying to make my fears or problems someone else's fault, I could instead catch a thought of love.
- If I caught a thought of anxiety or stress, I could recognize that stress and anxiety were not in the now and I was usually worrying about something in the future. Instead I could catch a thought of hope.
- If I caught a thought that had me swirling around in the dark, beating myself up with beliefs that were unkind to myself, I could instead discipline myself to catch a thought of light.

- If I caught a thought of defeat that caused me to hide and play small, I could instead catch a thought of discipline and determination.

I began to see that the thoughts crowded on the runway of my mind could be thinned out if I was willing to really live in the *here and now*. To trust that because of the undeniable, present love of God, there is always a new plane taking off.

Every day we get to change the structure of our lives and brains by catching our thoughts and confidently choosing to be the air traffic controller of our minds. It's impossible to take hold of *What's here now* if our minds are wrapped up in what was or what is to come. Let's clear up the runway so our here and now has space to land.

13

. . . .

Body
Thank-You Notes

Your body hears everything your mind says.

Naomi Judd, interview

I need to start this chapter with a confession: this is the last chapter I wrote because it is the most "in process" one for me. Clearly, I am a save-the-hardest-for-last kind of girl. Guess what: it is still hard. I feel like an amateur when it comes to body intelligence. And being an amateur makes me feel squishy and insecure. I could probably write a perfect chapter on what *not* to do—all the ways not to be present to your body—because I am a professional in that area.

How to ignore your body for years? Got it.

How to punish your body? Let me count the ways.

How to expect your body to do things for you even though you do nothing for it? Done.

I am well equipped to write about all these topics. The irony in it all is this was one of the first chapters I knew needed to be in this book, as I have learned that if we don't understand how to live well in our bodies, we eventually have nowhere to live. I know it's impossible to be fully present to God, ourselves, and others if we are not secure in our bodies, but I don't know if writing any chapter could make me feel more vulnerable. I legit googled "how to hire a ghostwriter" when I sat down to write it. But, alas, I decided to drink my own medicine and check in with myself.

> **If we don't understand how to live well in our bodies, we eventually have nowhere to live.**

> *What's here now in my thoughts?* Look at you, Jeanne, writing a chapter on your body. If only you could find that guy in college who noticed how small your wrists were and then asked you why the rest of your body didn't match your wrists. Maybe you need to send him a personal copy.
> *What's here now in my feelings?* Fear, sadness, and hope.
> *What's here now in my body?* Butterflies in my belly, tightness in my chest, and tension in my neck and shoulders.

I am now checked in.

● ● ●

I was raised by a mother who taught us the fine art of writing thank-you notes. After every birthday, holiday, or special gift we received, the expectation was clear. Writing a thank-you note was not optional. My mother, Peggy Pieczysnki, taught me many good lessons in this life, but one of her best was the art of saying thank-you when someone chooses to bestow their generosity on me. Another confession: I hated writing thank-you notes as a kid.

I just wanted to play with whatever I received or go out and spend the money I got on something I wanted; I didn't want to have to pause and say thank-you for it.

But my mom did more than a few things right, and I have carried the art of the thank-you note into my adulthood. I have taught it to my kids too, and it's part of our culture at Soul City Church. And I say this with loads of humility: I now write hundreds of notes of thanks or encouragement every year. My mom is to be blessed for this behavior in my life. Now I thoroughly enjoy encouraging, appreciating, or showing gratitude to others.

But despite all the notes I have written over the years, I realized I'd never written a thank-you note to myself, specifically to the most reliable part of myself: my body. I think part of the reason I never offered gratitude to my body was because I often treated her like the furnace in our first home. As a new homeowner, I didn't know anything about furnaces other than I wanted them to work. I expected the furnace to do what it was meant to do: keep me warm. After a few months of living there, it became frustrating when I continued to turn up the thermostat but the heat would not increase. I eventually realized the furnace had not been serviced in many years. It still had the original filter from when we moved in. When I pulled out the filter, I am not exaggerating when I say the lint inside had become a whole universe unto itself. The fan belt had never been maintained, and the ducts had never been swept out. The reason we were freezing in our house was due to routine maintenance that had been ignored for many years. We could have invested $99 into an ongoing routine, but now we were looking to spend much more on either a repair or replacement.

I treated my body in similar ways. I just expected it to keep running without any consistent routine or maintenance. But our bodies crave a healthy rhythm. They long for dependable care. Without it, they will require repair—and the truth is, just like my furnace, the repair usually costs much more than ongoing maintenance.

My body has been only constant and faithful to me. It is incapable of telling a lie. Incapable of manipulating me or tricking me into thinking anything other than the truth. My body is perhaps the most reliable gift God has given me. If I care for it, my body is dependable to tell me the truth of what is going on in all my other parts—heart, mind, and soul.

> If I care for it, my body is dependable to tell me the truth of what is going on in all my other parts—heart, mind, and soul.

While our minds and hearts often hang out in the past or the future, our bodies are always and only in the present. Your body is always *here*. One of the best indicators that you are not here is if you don't feel present in your body. Learning to ground and anchor yourself through the awareness of physical sensation is one of the best ways to learn how to practice the presence of God.

We only refer to our *souls* as needing saving, but the truth is my body needed saving from how I'd treated her for years. I tended to only pay attention to my body through my thoughts and feelings—somehow sending messages that the sensations of my body couldn't be trusted. That arousal, pleasure, pain, hunger, butterflies in the belly, or chills up and down the spine, need only be silenced and never given the right to speak. Perhaps you can relate? So many of us have separated our bodies from our souls without even knowing it. We sent them to separate corners as if they were enemies.

And yet Jesus chose to have a physical body. Complete deity put himself inside the form of fleshy humanity. He decided to become an embryo, grow inside Mary's belly, come through a dark birth canal, and make a home in a human body for thirty-three years. Jesus was utterly physical, yet I don't know if anyone has made being in a physical body more confusing than Christians.

It wasn't until I started shifting my relationship with my body (reminder: I am still claiming amateur status) that I was able to understand the truth in these words by Pierre Teilhard de Chardin: "We are not physical beings having a spiritual experience; we are spiritual beings having a physical experience."[1]

You and I are meant to have a full and complete physical experience on this planet. We are not meant to hold our breath and keep ourselves at a safe distance from all physical enjoyment. The exact opposite is true. To be fully alive spiritually, we need to learn how to be fully alive physically. For me, the problem was that my relationship with my body didn't resemble abundant life; it resembled the behaviors of the thief Jesus talked about: "The thief comes only to steal and kill and destroy; I have come that they may have life, and have it to the full" (John 10:10).

I had learned to listen to the lies of the thief when it came to my body.

Steal

Stealing begins when we are young. The break-in starts in our minds. I can still remember, in fifth grade, three of my best girlfriends got the same pin-striped jeans and navy sweaters with pink hearts on them. They told me I should get the same outfit so we could all match. I begged my mom until she gave in. And then, at a sleepover, we all brought our matching clothes. The next morning, when we got dressed, we somehow mixed up the jeans. I tried on another pair accidentally, and they didn't fit. I instantly felt embarrassment and shame. I allowed that experience and the thoughts formed from it to follow me around for years. Here I am, forty years later, and I can still feel how that moment stole years I spent obsessing and comparing and believing there was something wrong with the shape of my body.

This situation is, in fact, the designed outcome of an industry created to steal your thoughts so that you feel bad about yourself in the hopes that you will buy any and all products to get back what was stolen. If you have ever had your thoughts stolen about your body, hear me—you are not the only one.

Kill ·

I will never forget listening to a podcast interview with Sonya Renee Taylor, author of *The Body Is Not an Apology*. Brené Brown interviewed her, and I kid you not, I had to pull the car into a Trader Joe's parking lot to avoid being distracted while driving. It was that good. I bought her book that day and finished it by the end of the week. Sonya says, "Body terrorism is a hideous tower whose primary support beam is the belief that there is a hierarchy of bodies. We uphold the system by internalizing this hierarchy and using it to situate our own value and worth in the world."[2]

Body terrorism. What? I had never heard it said that way, but I had, in fact, felt the effects of body terrorism for years. I had bumped into the support beam and thought that the hierarchy of bodies was natural, and my body type was nowhere near the top of the list. I don't think there is a person on the planet who does not believe there are unrealistic standards for a beautiful, healthy body. We are aware these standards cause depression, anxiety, and body dysmorphia in all ages—yet the killing continues. We know about it but keep putting money in the system that keeps it alive. Sadly, female beauty is good business. Advertisers have found it is one of the most effective ways to sell anything. There are no regulations against it, so we freely allow the terrorism of seeing unrealistic standards of beauty everywhere we look to continue. This killing happening in our bodies ultimately can be traced back to millions of businesses that know unrealistic female beauty sells.

Destroy ·

I invested lots of money into trying to change my body and then more money into trying to understand why I wanted to change my body. I have taken more online quizzes and body type profiles than one human should be allowed to take. (Really, there should be a quota.) I have gone along for the ride with so many different diet movements. The Master Cleanse should include a special warning about never going anywhere without knowing exactly where the bathrooms are located. The Atkins Protein Diet—really, I can have bacon for breakfast, lunch, and dinner; are you sure? Whole 30—or in my case, Whole 19. Body for Life—I followed it all the way down to the mantra. Each time I lifted my weights in the gym, I would say, "I'm building my body for life." While I may have developed a temporary discipline during each season as I followed the different plans, I slowly, over time, destroyed my ability to be present to what my body needed.

Even after so many plans and programs, I don't know if I have ever had a day where I felt thin enough. *Enough* being the most critical word in that sentence. As a grown middle-aged woman who still sometimes wishes she was skinny but never has been, I'm learning that the heaviest thing to carry around is the burden of shame. It is most certainly bigger than my thighs. For far too many years, I believed my body could never feel perfect until it became a certain size. What was so ironic about all the stealing, killing, and destroying going on in my body is that I could look at my daughter or any other woman and feel admiration, awe, and respect for her body. The rules I applied to myself never applied to anyone else.

My quiet agreement with the thief all those years kept me from the abundantly full and completely alive body I was living in. We cannot ignore the bodies we live in and expect an abundant life. I needed to learn how to feel my body again. I needed to love her and thank her for all she offered me. I hadn't listened to my body for years; I just expected her to do what I wanted her to do without making an issue.

> We cannot ignore the bodies we live in and expect an abundant life.

So, I started simply asking my body, *What's here now?* My mind and heart always try to cut in line and speak first, but I am learning to clear enough space to scan through my body and pay attention to the truth she is always offering me.

She regularly wants the same things.

Care

My body wants more sleep, more water, and more movement. She does not want to give up one minute of sleep; if anything, she wants more. She has spent too many years trying to get more done by stealing from the very fuel that would make her—me—more productive. So, I've radically shifted my sleep routine. (Remember, my superpower is I can sleep anywhere; I just wasn't sleeping long enough.) My preferred nighttime routine is to head for bed no later than nine and be asleep by ten. I love waking up early. It is my favorite time of day. So being asleep no later than 10:00 p.m. is a way to love my body for the next day.

My body craves movement. And not just the strenuous, intense cardio movement I was doing, hoping I would melt away a few pounds. My body craves dancing, walking, playing, and riding a bike just for the fun of it.

My body also craves a new relationship with food, and she doesn't want to always start the day with caffeine. She wants water first. She also doesn't want to eat mindlessly. A bottomless basket of chips and salsa will not help me be present. Food used to have two purposes in my life: numbing or entertainment. The very reason I needed it—to fuel my body—was not something I was well versed in.

I am still actively rearranging my relationship with food. It's still an easy numbing agent, but when I catch myself doing this, I can now ask myself, *What are you trying to ignore or not feel? What about the past or the future is keeping you from being in the present moment?*

My cravings were pleas for attention. My body wanted to know she was being cared for. She also wanted me to get curious about my body's sensations.

Curiosity ·

One of the best books I've read on understanding all our bodies hold is *The Body Keeps the Score* by Bessel A. Van Der Kolk. He says, "In order to change, people need to become aware of their sensations and the way that their bodies interact with the world around them. Physical self-awareness is the first step in releasing the tyranny of the past."[3]

I rarely practiced curiosity with my body. I anesthetized so many of my body's sensations. If I had a headache, I just took Advil instead of getting curious about why I had developed a headache. I also rarely brought a mindful wonder to the miracle happening at every moment through my ability to inhale and exhale. Practicing curiosity and learning to scan what is going on inside of us is a powerful way to develop appreciation and gratitude for the millions of things working together at every moment to keep our bodies going. Bringing curiosity and awareness to the body is also a fabulous way to get grounded in the present moment. Because the body has weight, it offers a counterbalance to our often flighty and sporadic thoughts and feelings that can race as fast as a gazelle running from a hungry pack of lions. Practicing curiosity with our sensations brings us back to the center of God's love and presence.

Courage ·

Paying attention to my body's sensations has also given me physical courage. When I set my sights on climbing Mt. Kilimanjaro, my body offered me the gumption, over and over, to stay the course and persevere when I wanted to give up. When I was first told by different specialists and doctors that it would be wise to get a heart defibrillator, it was my body's courage that led me to say yes.

I remember waking up in the hospital after my heart surgery. My doctor came in and said, "The surgery went beautifully. Your body welcomed the ICD perfectly as we tested it in the operating room." I said, "Wait a minute—how did you test it?" My doctor proceeded to tell me that they slowed the speed of my heart down enough to activate my new defibrillator. He said my body jumped six inches off the operating table. (I am happy I did not know ahead of time that this test was going to happen.) I remember thinking, lying there in that bed, *How courageous my body is!* Every little part of my body chose to lovingly work together to welcome this foreign new object that was coming to make sure she would be safe and strong for many years to come.

In the same way, all my cells naturally collaborate to keep all my organs working together in unison. I had a choice to join in with my cells to do my part in healing my body. When I learned that recovery from heart surgery could last from a week to six weeks, I decided I would order the one-week recovery plan. But my body decided to order a three-week recovery plan. As hard as it was, I courageously chose to rest and slow down as my body learned how to live with my new Tony Stark heart.

> **If the body never tells a lie, I wonder why we try to keep so many secrets when it comes to our bodies.**

The body is wildly capable of so much more than we believe is possible, but so many of us have detached ourselves from the courage the body has to offer.

My body has been telling me we try to control what we don't trust. Clearly, I had been trying to control my body, which is perhaps the biggest irony of them all, as she is my most trustworthy part. If the body never tells a lie, I wonder why we try to keep so many secrets when it comes to our bodies.

How much we really weigh.
How much we really eat.
How much sleep we really get.
How much time we really spend exercising.

I, for one, think it's time to stop all this madness. To not just trust our bodies but start thanking them. So, here is my thank-you note to my body.

Dear body,

This note is long overdue. I imagine you wondered if this day would ever come. If I would truly pause and appreciate you for all you've done. Tears are puddling in my eyes just three sentences in. You have been so faithful to me. Your resolute and relentless presence has never let me down.

When I needed you to help me run faster than Nathan Price at third grade field day, you mustered up all the energy I needed to leave it all on the field. I am so glad we won that day.

When I needed you to help me memorize all those scripts, songs, and speeches for our plays, piano recitals, and speech team meets, you made sure every part of my brain was firing in just the right way to store all of those words and notes in my head.

When I needed you to protect me from that senior boy who pretended to care about me but cared more about making out with an inexperienced freshman girl, thank you for giving me the courage to get out of the car.

When I fell in love with Jarrett and no part of my heart or mind was functioning rationally, you gave me the courage to take a risk and throw all of my belongings into that little red Honda Prelude and move across the country for the greatest love of our lives.

When I got the phone call about Dad, and then years later about Andy, you held me up. You released all your secret compartments of strength to walk me through the storms of grief I would have never chosen.

When we put our legs up into those stirrups and let go of every superlative to push two beautiful babies out into the world, you offered up power and presence that were speechless.

When betrayal and hatred found their way into your story, your perseverance and commitment to keep going inspired me.

I don't know how I went so many years without realizing all you do for me. I am sorry for all the ways I have neglected and ignored you. I know we are on the same team, and I am officially only going to wear the same jersey as you. I am committed to living like we belong to each other.

For every program and plan that caused me to starve or deprive you of the nutrients and vitamins you needed to be healthy and prosper, please forgive me. You didn't ask for much. Your needs have been simple and steadfast: consistent care, watering, healthy sleep, and exercise. I often made those simple things so complex!

For the times when I didn't take care of my skin or intentionally let it burn for the next day's glow that would follow, I promise to take better care of our largest organ from now on.

For the times when I pushed past healthy limits, and you ended up broken, dizzy, drained, and fatigued, I promise to pay better attention to your limits. To listen to your joints and muscles and, when you are craving rest, to slow down.

For the times I fed you garbage. OK—not actual garbage, but food loaded with preservatives and absolutely no nutritional value—and mindlessly ate so I didn't have to feel, please forgive me. I promise to continue the healing work to restore my relationship with food.

I often don't stop and compliment you. But you need to know that what's here now is I think you are beautiful. From your dark brown eyes to your short stubby toes, you are a masterpiece, and this thank-you note is my way of starting to live as if I believe it.

Love,
Jeanne

14

Gratitude

Squeezed

It is not joy that makes us grateful; it is gratitude that makes us joyful.

Brother David Steindl-Rast, *Gratefulness, the Heart of Prayer*

When our kids were itty-bitty, Jarrett and I decided we didn't want to refer to ourselves as "The Stevens Family." It felt too fancy and formal for us. We wanted to intentionally create a culture of fun and belonging in our home and wanted our kids to know they were part of something special and one-of-a-kind. We had some friends, Billy and Joy Phenix, who referred to themselves as "Team Phenix," so we decided to borrow the title and become "Team Stevens." This was right around the time hashtags were born, and so #WeAreTeamStevens was officially established, circa 2008.

I have always loved being on a team. I grew up in a sports house. My brothers played competitive sports all the way through college. My brother Eddie even had a short run on a MLB farm team. I dabbled with softball, volleyball, and track but eventually hung up my jerseys for music and performing arts. While Jarrett and I love being active, we both tapped out of competitive sports by high school. But what we didn't surrender was our competitive natures. We have many winsome and endearing qualities about us, but bring out a deck of cards or a board game and you are going to experience our dark sides. And sadly, the apple didn't fall far from our tree. Elijah and Gigi are already cold and ruthless sharks whenever they play a game. Thank God they are also warm, kind, and incredible young people away from the game table. We are counting on the latter qualities to take them further in life.

Our family loves games. The problem when we play games is that every member of Team Stevens is a savage. I don't know how it's possible, but we even turn easygoing games like Uno into cut-throat competitions. We love to retell the story in our family of when we were first teaching our kids how to play Monopoly. Jarrett and Gigi formed a team, so Elijah and I became the other team. Jarrett and Gigi named themselves "Team Tender Heart" to coach themselves toward good sportsmanship. Elijah and I went straight for what we wanted: "Team Victors." Many minutes into the game, it became obvious Team Victors was going to be victorious. Team Tender Heart's own obsession to win combined with no money in the bank and paying rent on all our properties did not bring out their tender hearts. Elijah and I beat them badly, and their tender hearts were now contested and contaminated as they sulked over their loss the rest of the night. We always laugh at how their idealistic name couldn't change their ingrained competitive nature.

* * *

While our family may be slightly more aggressive than others when it comes to games, I don't think we are alone in our dislike of losing. Winning always feels better. We would probably all pick winning over losing, but winning doesn't reveal what we're really made of. Losing has a way of divulging who we really are.

When life is hard. When the plotlines of our personal lives twist. When we feel squeezed and pressed, that's where we see what we're made of.

I hope you are reading this on the other side of the COVID-19 pandemic, but this book was written within it. A season when the whole world was unexpectedly squeezed. So much loss occurred. Many people endured the loss of

- simple freedoms
- income and stability
- physical connection
- routine and rituals
- loved ones

I could keep listing, but you already know. It was a global pressing. As life pressed in on you, what came out of you?

When Life Presses

I started the pandemic with almost a serene sense of motivation. I had been handed some life lemons before, so thankfully I had stored up a few recipes for lemonade. Even though none of us knew much about this deadly virus back in March 2020, I remember thinking it would be a temporary adjustment and then life would get back to normal. We canceled our in-person weekend services and pivoted to being an online church. We got the call from school that the kids would be off for two weeks. They celebrated because it felt like they'd scored an extended spring break. In the beginning, it felt like an inconvenient interruption. My intuition was that once the scientists and doctors figured out how to proceed, life would resume, and we would all return to normal. My limited view saw it as the two-week break I'd always wanted. I'd get to stay home, slow down, organize my closets, and downshift my life to a more manageable speed. I typed up our family values and a schedule for how we would shelter in place together and taped them to the fridge. We made it past the first week.

In the second week the wheels started falling off. We all began to sense this two-week pause would turn into so much more. As we all now know, the pandemic did not go away in a couple of weeks. The squeeze only intensified as all of life changed. The whole world has been wrung out during COVID like a wet rag, compressed and constricted in ways we would never choose on our own.

Though being squeezed is not known for its upsides, it is one of the best ways to see what you are really made of. When life puts a squeeze on your circumstances, it can serve as an unexpected spotlight on all you have to be grateful for. Darkness has a way of helping us notice the light in our lives. And one of the most profound gifts I received during the pandemic was a new understanding that gratitude and grief don't have to be separated. It's possible to feel both at the same time. One does not cancel the other out. Our binary world wants to force what first appear as opposites into separate corners. But I am finding that grief and gratitude are two sides of the same coin.

While most of the overly ambitious items on our early COVID-19 values and schedule fell to the wayside, one of the practices that shifted for us, which we still do to this day, is our "griefs and gratitude" dinner conversation. For years we always checked in with one another around the dinner table by sharing our highs and lows of the day. I still love that exercise. But during COVID we shifted to sharing one thing we were grieving and one thing we were grateful for. It was such a stabilizing way to keep us practicing the present moment as we waded through the global pandemic as a family.

One of the things I love most about Jesus is his ability to flatten the landscape on our finely developed opinions and limiting beliefs. He does this throughout the New Testament, but one of my favorite encounters is the one he had with the ten lepers. Knowing it was a highly contagious disease, the lepers practiced safe social distancing and stood off to the side as Jesus walked by. Once they realized who was coming down the path, they called out and asked him for healing. Jesus chose to show mercy and healed them. Immediately they went off to revel in their new miracle, but one of the men came back and began to praise, worship, and offer gratitude to Jesus. Noting the other nine did not come back, Jesus told the one who returned, "Rise and go; your faith has made you well" (Luke 17:19).

While it's easy to pay attention to Jesus's consistent and compassionate response to this group of lepers, I am more drawn to pay attention to their response to Jesus.

- All of them were healed. Only one of them returned.
- All of them had been given a fresh start. Only one of them thought to say "Thanks."

This one who only moments earlier had stood at a distance now threw himself at Jesus's feet. He may not have even fully known who Jesus was. He just knew he'd been given a gift, and he was compelled to come back and say THANK YOU. While all ten remained healed, it was the one who practiced gratitude who Jesus said was well.

What I am learning about the practice of gratitude is that, without it, you cannot be well.

- You can be healed but not be well.
- You can have resources but not be well.
- You can have people around you but not be well.
- You can gain the world but lose your soul and not be well.
- What makes you well is the practice of gratitude.

All the other lepers were healed, but they missed the blessing of being *well*. Clearly, it's not within Jesus's character to rescind his healing. But I wonder how many of us fail or forget to say thank you for the big and small blessings in our lives. For the highs and lows. For the triumphs and the trials. For the grief and the gratitude.

So often, gratitude gets lost in our lives because we aren't fully present. We aren't *here*. It's so easy to rehash the past and think about all the things we wish were different. Or to rehearse the future and focus on the things we're worried might happen. Receiving the present allows us to live in the here and now and accept it all as a gift.

Viewing right where we are through the lens of gratitude helps us see a bigger and better picture. We can lift our heads and shift our focus to what's really going on. To be grateful for the good things in our lives is easy, but to be grateful for all of life takes deep spiritual work. The good as well as the bad. The moments of joy as well as the moments of sorrow. The successes as well as the failures. The rewards as well as the rejections. This requires us to practice the present moment. Because presence is what makes us well.

We become truly grateful people when we can say thank you to all that has brought us to the present moment. If we keep dividing our lives between events and people we would like to remember and those we would rather forget, we cannot claim the fullness of our beings as a gift of God to be grateful for. When we throw our circumstances into categories like "keep" or "get rid of," we miss out on any potential redemption still waiting to come from the experiences we wish had never happened. To practice gratitude is to ground ourselves in the present and change the frame for how we view all of life.

● ● ●

Several years ago, Jarrett and I decided to get a juicer. I still can't remember whose idea it was, but we were both all in on our new liquid life. (Please don't ask me if we are still juicing. This is a judgment-free book.) I'm sure it will come as no surprise that we made our purchase the week between Christmas and New Year's, after a month of overindulging at holiday parties had left its mark on our bodies. Jarrett loves to go down rabbit holes of research, so he did all the exploration on figuring out the best juicer to purchase. We landed on a cold press juicer because it would protect and preserve the nutrients of the fruits and vegetables. Since no heat was involved, we'd get 100 percent of the vitamins, minerals, enzymes, and nutrients from all the juicing.

When we squeezed fruits and vegetables, we got their pure substance. Once we knew what we were doing, we loved coming up with all kinds of juice concoctions. But what was true every single time, no matter what combination of fruits and vegetables we juiced, was we always got the pure and authentic substance of whatever we put into the machine.

No human has ever been squeezed and had only one kind of juice come out of them. We are a holy concoction of unique preferences and diverse experiences, not a singular entity. A wild and flavorful mixed drink, far from one pure element. And what comes out of us when we are being squeezed reveals what is already within us.

So much research has been done that reveals gratitude is the missing element many of us are craving in our lives. I am firmly convinced that the practice of gratitude is an essential key to living in the present moment with new peace, perspective, and perseverance. And I wonder if the reason so many people are hungry for hope is that they are starving from a lack of gratitude in their lives.

The practice of gratitude in the present moment will start to squeeze out a new level of peace in your life.

Peace

Gratitude is central to living a life of peace. So many of us scurry toward achievement and skip over the deep and profound work of appreciation. Until we can learn to value what we have and what God is doing in the here and now, we will constantly be looking to attain a different life.

One of my favorite things to do before going out to dinner is to pull up the menu of the restaurant we are going to. I love looking through the options and picking what I think my taste buds will most enjoy. While there is nothing wrong with preselecting a meal, it is an example of living outside the present moment. While there are little to no consequences to preparing one's taste buds for the future, the reality is that when I think about what I want to eat in the future, I forgo being present to what is happening in the here and now.

The practice of gratitude helps us live in the present moment. Without this awareness, our peace is quickly stolen from us. Rehearsing a challenging conversation, stressing out about the number of tasks on a to-do list, or worrying about a future problem can keep us living off-balance in a world that seeks achievement over appreciation.

> **Peaceful circumstances do not create gratitude. Gratitude creates peaceful circumstances.**

One of the best ways to develop appreciation in the present moment is to pause. Slow your breath and meditate on all you have to be grateful for. We say it all the time at Soul City Church: God is faithful—people are forgetful. Pausing to remember and receive all you have to be grateful for right now is one of the quickest ways to experience peace. Peaceful circumstances do not create gratitude. Gratitude creates peaceful circumstances.

Perspective ·

One of the most holy aspects of being a pastor is that I have held spiritual space for literally thousands of people over the years. I have been a witness to unspeakable loss and uncontainable joy.

One theme has been consistent in every such conversation I've had: the direction of our gaze is what determines our perspective. It's hard to see hope when all we look at feels hopeless. It's hard to be calm when all we see is concern. It's challenging to feel peace when we see so much panic around us. When we are desperate to be anywhere but *here and now*, we will most certainly rehash our past or rehearse our future. To shift our perspective, we have to remember that gratitude is our personal responsibility.

No one else can make you grateful. It is your responsibility to shift your focus. It is your responsibility to redirect what you are looking at. This may sound ominous, but what often starts as a discipline eventually becomes a joyful practice. I shift my perspective through three simple ways of changing what I look at; try these, and see how they work for you.

1. *Look up.* This has to do with provision. What is something that God provided in this moment? Oxygen in your lungs. A warm sweater on your back. A roof over your head. There is always something to be grateful for when you're willing to look up.

2. *Look out.* This has to do with people. Who is someone God has put in your life who has been a gift to you today? Maybe it's the barista who served your coffee. The co-worker who took a few extra minutes to ask you about your weekend. The neighbor who helped you shovel your sidewalk last week. There is always someone we can look at to help us change our perspective.

3. *Look in.* This has to do with personal responsibility. What is something you can do to root yourself in the here and now? Are you rehashing the past in some way? Look for blame, shame, grief, bitterness, or guilt. Are you rehearsing the future in some way? Look for worry, denial, pretending, obligation, or control. All of these are tells that you are

looking away from the present moment. You must ask yourself, *Am I willing to look in to change my perspective?*

Perseverance

We all walk through storms that feel like they might destroy our lives, but I have grown to realize that not all storms come to rattle our lives; some come to redirect our lives.

While I don't know your specific story, I know you have been hurt. And you fear that the more you open yourself up to the possibility of that hurt being healed, the more you realize how much deeper your hurt goes than you knew. It is so enticing to give up or give in. To keep yourself stuck in a cycle of discouragement. But as Henri Nouwen says in *The Inner Voice of Love*, "Your search for true healing will be a suffering search. Many tears still need to be shed."[1]

Recently a person I would have called a friend chose to hurt me in a public and painful way. The person never reached out to me personally to share their feelings or their experience. I had absolutely no idea how much they hated me until they let me and everyone else know about it. It stung so deeply. My mind went all kinds of crazy. What did I do to them to deserve such contempt? What story were they telling themselves to justify such hateful behavior?

And, of course, this new wound resurfaced older wounds in me that needed new levels of healing. The part of me that still looks for acceptance and affirmation from others floated to the surface. The part that wants to be a friend to all and an enemy to none was triggered. The part that fears being misunderstood, so she idles until everyone agrees, felt so much fear. All of that old suffering was now hanging out with my present suffering.

This was the moment God reminded me that somehow suffering is a necessary tool for squeezing perseverance out of us.

Not only so, but we also glory in our sufferings, because we know that suffering produces perseverance; perseverance, character; and bibliographic essay at the back of the book. We include the major sources for each chapter as well as references for some (but not all) of the data used. Our intent is to provide the principal sources, so that anyone interested in reconstructing our discussion can do so from the original material.

We take this opportunity to thank two anonymous reviewers and Andrew Scott, each of whom made insightful and helpful comments about the initial manuscript. We are grateful to Robert Repetto, who improved our discussion of economic matters, and to our editor at Yale University Press, Jean Thomson Black, for her help and support as we wrote; her enthusiasm made a great difference to us.

Abbreviations

AIDS	acquired immunodeficiency syndrome
BP	before the present *or* British Petroleum
CBD	community-based distribution
CEDPA	Centre for Development and Population Activities
CEFPA	Centre for Population Activities
CFC	chlorofluorocarbon
COP	Conference of Parties
COWAN	Country's Women's Association of Nigeria
FCCC	Framework Convention on Climate Change
FGC	female genital cutting
GHON	Grassroots Health Organization of Nigeria
GNP	Gross National Product
HIV	human immunodeficiency virus
ICPD	International Conference on Population and Development
IPCC	Intergovernmental Panel on Climate Change
IWHC	International Women's Health Coalition
NCAR	National Center for Atmospheric Research
NCWS	National Council of Women's Societies
NGO	nongovernment organization
OPEC	Organization of Petroleum-Exporting Countries
RTI	reproductive tract infection
STD	sexually transmitted disease

TAR	Third Assessment Report
U.N.	United Nations
UNCED	United Nations Conference on Environment and Development
USAID	U.S. Agency for International Development
UWA	United Women's Association
WHO	World Health Organization
ZPG	Zero Population Growth

1

One Vision of the Year 2050

The biggest human temptation is to settle for too little.

—Thomas Merton

T he year is 2050, and the
world is a very different place than it was fifty years ago.

A couple of decades into the new century, both citizens and leaders recognized that the natural world of
unmanaged forests, other ecosystems, and diverse species is not one amenity among others, to be respected
only when budget surpluses allow, but is the very playing
field on which our economies and livelihoods unfold. It
became clear that our economic success, and in some
cases our survival, depend on the health of the natural
world.

No longer could our economies set at zero the dollar

value of nature's ability to cleanse wastes from the air, soil, and water. No longer could we consume trees, fish, and agricultural lands without regard for the pace of their regeneration. No longer could we mine petroleum and minerals without planning for future substitutes.

No longer could we take over complex ecosystems—forests, grasslands, oceans, lakes, rivers—as if our meager knowledge of parts of them could substitute for the vast unknown complexity of their natural functioning. We lost our surprise when a single predator or exotic plant introduced into an ecosystem wiped out all other species or blanketed the landscape. We realized that we had to back off and let ecosystems carry on under their own rules. We also realized that because we were altering the very chemistry of the air around us, almost nowhere on Earth was really untouched and had the option of carrying on under its own rules.

The crucial implication was this: the human species had to reduce its overall imprint on the natural world, pulling back from the contaminated air and waters, the simplified forests and grasslands. The world understood that we could not continue to grow in our human numbers, our material wealth, or our wastes if we were to lessen our impact. Yet accomplishing this was easier than anyone had predicted in the twentieth century.

On the population side—even with poor health, little education, and low incomes—most people in the world wanted fewer children than they were having in 2000. Better health, more education, and more reliable incomes, especially for women, brought fertility even lower and slowed global population growth to zero. In the fifty years after 2000, it became evident that human beings simply did not want to have so many children that populations would grow indefinitely. Improving people's lives so that they had a measure of mastery over them brought population stability, where exhortations and pleas to consider the environment and future generations had failed.

A parallel revolution unfolded on the material side of the ledger. Soon after the turn of the twenty-first century, it became clear that the reservoir of industrial innovation was vastly more powerful than had appeared from the resistance of business leaders to environmental problems facing the world in 2000. It became obvious, in fact, that in business, manufacturing, and industry literally lay the salvation of the world. Only those had the power, through technology, to bring about the revolution in resource use and waste production required for the world's people to have decent lives while reducing their imprint on the natural world.

Unfortunately, it took a disaster to spark the revolution in thinking about the environment.

In the years 2010 and 2011, a sudden acceleration of global warming and the natural variability of the climate combined to produce a year with no winter in the United States. In the summer, sixty days exceeded 90 degrees throughout most of the country, and Washington, D.C., saw thirty days with temperatures over 100 degrees— all while Congress was in session. Serious droughts occurred in the midwestern and western United States, in northeastern Brazil, and elsewhere. The U.S. wheat crop was small, and the corn crop failed completely. The Mississippi River dried up. The Colorado River had dwindled to a trickle years before, despite policies designed to maintain some flow to Mexico.

Four moderate-sized hurricanes came ashore along the southeastern and Gulf coasts of the United States. One struck Wilmington, North Carolina; another hit Jacksonville, Florida; Miami took a blow; and one, repeating the path of the 1969 storm Camille, struck the rapidly growing area around Bay Saint Louis, Mississippi. These storms took advantage of the higher sea level to send surges farther inland than had previous storms. This greater reach, combined with accurate aim at populous areas, caused many deaths and extensive damage to regions previously free from direct flooding by hurricanes. Similar storms plagued southern Japan and coastal China, as well as the west coast of Mexico and Darwin, Australia.

These dramatic events galvanized the United States into action. The federal government instituted a phased tax on all fossil fuels according to carbon content, thereby reflecting in the price of petroleum and coal some of the costs to the environment and the economy of global warming. With higher fossil-fuel prices, energy alternatives such as photovoltaics, wind power, and other sources became ever more economical. Research into solar-produced hydrogen for use in fuel cells, superefficient engines, vehicles, and other machines led to those renewable sources becoming economical as well. Use of fossil fuel plummeted, and efficient and environmentally benign alternatives replaced it.

U.S. businesses, whose traditional resistance to the carbon tax was overcome by the severity and clarity of the crisis, responded with ingenuity, inventiveness, and energy. They surpassed all expectations of how much and how fast the economy could convert from fossil-fuel–based to renewables-based fuel in efficient machinery. Whether or not they were environmentalists, whether or not they believed in the primacy of human ingenuity or the inviolability of nature, Americans used less energy. American industry, regardless of its beliefs, retooled in response to altered incentives and made it possible for Americans to "do the right thing."

Success with energy, and the link of energy to materials, led to a new, comprehensive materials policy. The government expanded its fossil-fuel tax to include natural resources, so that products made in the United States were either durable, reusable, or eventually composted.

Revenues from the carbon tax made it possible to reduce payroll, income, and capital-gains taxes. This tax shift, long proposed by environmental groups and progressive economists, proved to rejuvenate rather than check the national economy, as had been feared by some economists and businesspeople. Combined with other market-based strategies such as tradable permits in carbon emissions, the carbon tax made it possible for the United States to reduce its carbon emissions dramatically.

In fact, in 2015 the U.S. government announced its commitment to reducing carbon emissions by 3 percent a year until it reached a level 65 percent below the 1990 value. In doing so, the country revitalized international negotiations on global climate change, stalled since the turn of the century over the reluctance of developing countries to take action when the industrialized world, originator of most of the climate problem, held back.

As the largest economy and the most powerful nation in the world, the United States had an enormous influence on the rest of the globe. As the U.S. economic success became apparent and the international negotiations provided a forum for exchange of experience and policy alternatives, other countries (several of which had experimented with tax shifts in a desultory and incomplete fashion) followed the U.S. lead. They found that indeed such shifts provided the incentives needed to reduce carbon emissions at minimum cost. Also, trade negotiations began to include the notion that fair trade requires countries to have carbon taxes or other equivalent policies in place.

A problem that could not be addressed by these measures was an unavoidable commitment to future climate change, driven by the behavior of carbon dioxide in the atmosphere. Carbon dioxide and some other greenhouse gases, once emitted, remain in the air for a century or more, continually trapping heat. The emission reductions therefore did nothing to reduce the climate change already built into the climate system, nor to slow the additional warming that resulted from emissions during the decades-long phasedown of fossil-fuel use. Countries had to expect that the shorter, warmer winters, hot summers, damaging storm surges, and other climate-change impacts would continue and in fact worsen until they stabilized near the end of the twenty-first century. By 2050 a vigorous technological effort to devise means of removing the offending gases from the air had not produced any useful systems, so it was necessary for countries to take adaptive steps, some quite expensive, to live agreeably in the hotter, higher-sea-level world.

The most obvious adaptation tested in developed countries was moving homes and valuable structures out of river floodplains and away from exposed coastal areas. Such policies met with great resistance from residents and developers, who continued to maintain that the storms occurred only once every hundred or five hundred years and hence were a tolerable risk. Considerable experimentation was therefore required. The construction of new towns, and offers to move families on favorable economic terms, produced a few takers. Little more transpired, however, until another damaging storm occurred. Then government officials realized that canceling all of the insurance, mortgage, and other programs that subsidized living in hazardous places would be effective and a bit more acceptable—in part because most people did not recognize that they were being subsidized.

The Netherlands, in a farsighted action almost a century ago, had raised its dikes during reconstruction after a major storm. The Dutch were therefore somewhat protected against sea-level rise, but they found that the higher water caused more infiltration of saltwater through and under the dikes, forcing the abandonment of some farm areas. This problem of saltwater intrusion prevented several low-lying island nations from attempting to build dikes against the rising sea.

Tropical countries experienced less temperature increase than countries in other latitudes. But their rain fell in larger storms and was concentrated in different seasons than formerly. These shifts required modification of long-established agricultural practices, with glitches in food production—and consequent hunger—during the adjustment period.

This persistence of climate change and its damage while emission reductions were in progress had a parallel in the population arena. Population "momentum" means that populations continue to grow for some time after reaching replacement-level fertility, as disproportionately large age groups of young people, the legacy of past high fertility, move into their childbearing years. These large childbearing generations, even if they average two-child families, mean that the population as a whole experiences more births than deaths and populations continue to grow. Even with this momentum, the world succeeded in the fifty years after the turn of the twenty-first century in bringing about the social conditions that made slowing—and halting—global population growth possible.

The world's population in 2050, at 8 billion people, is healthier, better educated, and enjoys more equity between races, sexes, and classes than at any time in history. Incomes are not as high everywhere as analysts fifty years ago thought necessary for successful economies. But they supply an adequate diet, decent housing, clean water, and modest transportation for the world's 6 billion "middle-class," people in the middle of the global economic scale. Families average two children—the "replacement level" required to achieve population stability—and population growth is essentially zero.

Another billion people live in wealthy countries, where material conditions are generous, though less wasteful than at the turn of the twenty-first century. The populations of these countries are shrinking in size by an average of nearly 1 percent annually, as fertility is well below two children per family.

The world's other billion people live in countries still dominated by material deprivation. They are expected to experience positive population growth for another few decades, as families are still larger than two children, but at increasingly slower rates as health, education, women's status, and incomes continue to improve. These countries started so far behind the others in the social revolution that brings fertility and population growth down that they still have some years to go before they see real equity and zero growth.

On average, the world's population of 8 billion people neither grows nor shrinks, but is stable.

The world's most populous country in 2050 is India, with 1.2 billion people. But this giant has several hundred million fewer people than expected in projections made in 2000. Fertility reached two children per couple on average some twenty years ahead of expectations and fell below replacement level in about 2020. A new government elected in 2005 absorbed the lessons of Kerala. This very poor Indian state had low fertility before 2000, principally because women there enjoyed much higher status and better health than elsewhere in India. The result was a strong national government commitment—and funding—for girls' education and high-quality reproductive health care for all women, including adolescents, coupled with a countrywide microenterprise program that enabled women to finance small businesses and raise their incomes.

The United Nations held its 2024 population conference in India to highlight the country's achievements. These successes in turn demonstrated the power of the social development agenda set thirty years before at the U.N. International Conference on Population and Development (ICPD) in Cairo. India now has a small but significant industry that provides advice and technical assistance to other countries on investing scarce dollars in highly leveraged population and social-development programs.

Material development in China has proceeded continuously, though less rapidly than the government had hoped, in the fifty years since 2000. Social development there looks fine on paper: China's people enjoy educational equity and satisfactory basic health care. Its population reached 1.3 billion in 2005 and then began to decline. In 2050 the country's population is less than 1 billion and still shrinking, by nearly 1 percent a year. A combination of very low fertility and a sex ratio reflecting decades of selecting for male children drove the change. Women are scarce in China—though not necessarily highly prized. Indeed, in 2050 China illustrates the principle that when you force fertility levels and population growth rates according to a formula without taking the underlying culture into account, you sometimes get more than you bargained for.

The rest of Asia is dominated by Japan, Pakistan, Bangladesh, and Indonesia. Japan, resistant to large flows of in-migration, is clearly in population decline in 2050. Pakistan and Bangladesh had roughly the same population size in the early 1980s. But vastly different social development and fertility paths meant that in 2050, Pakistanis outnumbered Bangladeshis by more than 100 million.

A family planning program deeply imbedded in maternal and child health—and, after 2000, increasingly surrounded by broader reproductive health care—meant that fertility in Bangladesh, once the quintessential "basket case" of international development, reached levels like those in wealthy countries in 2010, and by 2050 overall population growth was negative. Many deeply involved with Bangladesh still worry that desperate economic and environmental conditions pushed people to low fertility for the wrong reasons, since the status of women appeared low in conservative Bangladesh long after fertility fell. But subtle ways of measuring women's status—less by outward indicators such as education level and income, and more by the extent of networking with other women and access to resources outside the mainstream—showed that in fact women's status in Bangladesh was better than the statistics suggested.

Corruption, political infighting, and conflicts with the international community over nuclear weapons isolated Pakistan from development assistance for many years. Health, education, and economic development programs that would have encouraged lower fertility fell behind those elsewhere in the Indian subcontinent. Also, Pakistan never focused on women as powerful forces for development, both social and economic, and women continued to live second-class lives in Pakistan long after Bangladeshi women were enjoying subtle autonomy. Thus fertility in Pakistan failed to reach replacement level until 2030. Population growth began to slow earlier, but only because shortfalls in food production driven largely by water shortages raised death rates.

In Indonesia, some years of disarray and even armed

revolution followed the economic collapse of the late 1990s. From these troubled times emerged an extensive network of experienced local leaders, including women and men committed to women's rights who not only abhorred nepotism, corruption, and monopoly, but had the skills needed to move the country toward authentic democracy. Indonesia became a model for local democracy movements throughout Asia. The country's family planning program, famous for its vigor—indeed, even aggressiveness—suffered during the chaotic years but emerged more voluntary and firmly rooted in health care than it had been. Fertility reached replacement level in 2010 and continued to fall for some time.

Elsewhere in the world, different regions followed different paths. After years of resisting the drive to replacement-level fertility (despite relatively good health care and education), a continentwide feminist movement in Latin America began to operate businesses, significant aspects of government, and development programs without regard for the macho-dominated mainstream. Women provided women with microcredit, health care, and schooling, and a quiet revolution began. A long-held preference for male children was simply overwhelmed by the growing mastery women had over their lives. Fertility fell to—and below—replacement levels. The entire continent achieved population stability by 2025. Some countries continued to grow slowly; impoverished Bolivia and the small countries of Central America had positive growth rates in 2050 as the legacy of war, underdeveloped economies, health care, and education thwarted feminist movements. The economic and population giants of Latin America—Mexico, Brazil, Argentina—overcame this growth with very low fertility as early as 2025 and negative growth rates as early as 2035, driven by strong women's empowerment movements and adequate health care and education.

As Latin America and Asia came to sustainable development, as their economies grew stronger and more environmentally sound, as authentic local alternatives to Western mass culture flourished, and as local and distinctive women's movements changed cultures, the world's development assistance budget mushroomed. Around 2020, Latin American and Asian contributions to development assistance eclipsed those from the so-called developed countries of the last half of the twentieth century. In some shame, and out of concern that they would become irrelevant to world development, the developed countries reexamined their priorities and started to catch up.

The world focused much of its development assistance on Africa. A terrible flourishing of the AIDS epidemic, first in a few states of southern and western Africa, but eventually spreading nearly everywhere south of the Sahara, killed a quarter of the adult population and reduced overall life expectancy by as much as twenty-five years. A shocking percentage of all children in these countries were orphaned between 2010 and 2015, many of them condemned to a death sentence themselves, as they had been born infected with the AIDS virus. The horror of the epidemic and the social devastation that it wrought riveted the world's attention on emergency re-lief—nursing of the terminally ill, burial of the dead, care of orphaned children. Once galvanized by this shocking tragedy, governments and nongovernmental organiza-tions both within and outside Africa dug in and refused to leave these ravaged countries until basic health, sanita-tion, education, and economic measures were soundly in place. Where once nations went to war to protect the right of sovereign governments to make their own decisions and be free of interference from others, now the irrele-vance of political borders to viruses and disease shrank the list of "strictly internal" issues.

The hard work turned Africa around. Once the hor-rifying death rates associated with the AIDS epidemic normalized, non-AIDS mortality among infants and chil-dren fell, and overall life expectancy began to increase for the first time since the turn of the century. An unexpected benefit of the tragedy—as after the great plague of the fourteenth century in Europe—was a rise in land produc-tivity and an increase in the amount of capital available per person. Food production and nutrition status began to rise as healthy adults previously drained by care of the sick and dying returned to farming. Health care systems began to recover, actually revitalized by the skills and ex-perience gained in the course of the epidemic. During the crisis, old rules that limited women's roles became irrele-vant: every single able-bodied person, man or woman, had to work at everything that needed doing. Women emerged from the epidemic with skills, experience, and authority that no one could ignore, and they built health care, education, and economic systems around their own needs and priorities. The AIDS epidemic had devastated Africa's educated as well as its poor, and for many years Latin Americans, Asians, North Americans, and Europeans staffed Africa's hospitals, schools, universities, banks, and businesses. Aggressive training programs eventually brought Africans back to these workplaces in large numbers, even exceeding pre-epidemic levels.

Not surprisingly, when the epidemic began to recede, Africans responded by having large families. The feeling of needing to restore lost generations was strong indeed. But these children were born healthy and wanted. Near-universal condom use to prevent AIDS vastly reduced unwanted pregnancies and abortions. Even though women had four and five pregnancies for a generation, they used family planning to space them. The infant and maternal mortality associated with closely spaced pregnancies fell. As Africans struggled to their feet and economic conditions began to improve, fertility also began to fall. Now in 2050, Africa is the major source of positive population growth in the world, though populations are smaller than they were expected to be before the epidemic. But fertility is on its way from four children to three per family on average, and it is expected to reach two by 2075.

At the other end of the scale, Europe, with the strong economies, social programs, and women's status charac-

teristic of developed Western countries, had experienced
negative rates of natural increase—the difference between
births and deaths—before the turn of the twenty-first
century. With similar, though not identical, conditions,
North America's natural increase slowed soon after 2000.
For some years, migration from developing regions meant
that Europe experienced a slower decline than it would
have and North American growth rates hovered above
zero. At selected times and in selected places, large migration flows triggered hostility and resentment among
established residents. But not long into the twenty-first
century it became clear that migration from the south en-
livened and enriched the cultures of these two traditionally "Western" regions. A *café au lait* culture, as the
pundits called it, began to unfold—tan in skin color and
strong on urban sophistication and energy. By 2030, with
the exception of climate-change-induced emergency migration, improvements in people's economic and social
lives and population stability in Latin America and North
Africa reduced pressures to migrate, and growth reached
zero or negative levels in the two traditional migrant-
receiving regions of North America and Europe.

The migration triggered by sea-level rise, changing
rainfall patterns, and higher temperatures induced by climate change, created physical, social, and economic disruptions on a large scale. The extreme cases of a few Pacific islands, southern Bangladesh, and the Maldives,
all experiencing continuous flooding, sent millions of
refugees into the international community, straining the

atmosphere of cooperation that had grown over the previous decades. Europe and North America were not the
only destinations for these refugees, however, and the
international community shared the burden in the end.
Most people preferred to settle elsewhere in their own
countries, when that was an option, or in their country's
region. People of the Maldives migrated to India and Sri
Lanka; Bangledeshis settled elsewhere in Bangladesh, in
India, and in Pakistan; and Pacific Islanders migrated to
New Zealand or Asia.

Russia contributed strongly to Europe's negative
growth rates, both because fertility fell very low and because mortality rates continued the rise begun before the
turn of the twenty-first century. Economic and political
disarray—indeed, near-collapse—meant poor health care
and conditions hardly conducive to bringing children
into the world. Russia and its surrounding states, along
with Africa, became important targets of international development assistance after 2010. In an ironic reversal of
many long-standing traditions, Russia began to recruit
migrants from the developing world, to mitigate its feared
population decline. To be "Russian" became less important than having people to run the country.

Though vastly different stories had unfolded in the
countries of the world over the past half-century, ranging
from the tragic to the joyous, the international population
conference of 2044 declared that the problems of population growth that had dominated the attention of the world
for almost a hundred years were largely over. The con-

ference turned its attention instead to issues of aging, migration, and health; to further improving the status of women and children; and to truly fair trade and demilitarization of the global economy.

Thirty years earlier, in 2014, the United Nations had sponsored a joint international negotiation on population and climate change. The notion of sustainable development, as articulated in 1992 at the U.N. Conference on Environment and Development (UNCED), informed this negotiation. Representatives of every nation in the world, except the last remnants of OPEC (the Organization of Petroleum-Exporting Countries) and the Vatican, agreed that a way of life on earth that does not rob future generations of their prosperity must include stability of both population and the composition of the atmosphere.

Countries that successfully carried out the Cairo agenda of 1994 and countries that successfully responded to the global environmental crisis of 2010 told their stories to one another and to the world at the 2014 meeting. The consultations revealed two ingredients crucial for success in the new world: women's empowerment and full participation, both public and private, in their world; and efficiency in the use of energy and materials, driven by "getting the prices right" through tax policy. Those two elements made up the revolution that brought about the successes of 2050.

Will this or any other imaginative and optimistic scenario unfold? No one can know. Certainly we do not, though we had great fun imagining the satisfying parts. We fervently hope that something comparable, or even better, will indeed happen. We know that without envisioning an alternative to our current apparent destination, we will succeed in arriving where we are now pointed. We also know that a lot of work and a lot of luck *could* bring about such changes by 2050. Why we think that work is called for, and exactly what that work is, form the contents of this book.

We begin with three chapters on population issues. Chapter 2 examines the new world of population created by the ICPD in 1994. It describes the approach to population issues that prevailed from the time population became a widespread public concern in the 1960s and the shift in approach that took place as women's health organizations and other feminist groups weighed in on population at the Cairo conference in 1994.

Chapter 3 details the Cairo action agenda by telling the story of programs in Nigeria funded by an international nongovernmental organization (NGO), the Centre for Development and Population Activities. CEDPA-Nigeria's programs mobilize grassroots organizations of women who work in their neighborhoods and communities on family planning, other reproductive health, girls' education, income generation, and democratic participation of women in electoral politics.

The final chapter on population (Chapter 4) lays out the work ahead in a very specific context: how activists can best approach the population issue in the United

States. We argue for a rather new approach, one that reso-
nates with Cairo rather than with the older tradition
in which the roots of most American population activism lie.

Three chapters on climate change follow, Chapters 5–
7. The first of these outlines what we know now about the
science of climate change. We recapitulate the development of the science in the past hundred years. We explain
what the science means and why we have confidence in
the large computer models that underlie so much of our
understanding of global climate change. We summarize
major global reviews of climate-change research and suggest the implications for policy. We conclude by discussing likely impacts of the projected climate changes.

Chapter 6 focuses on the international negotiations on
climate change under way since UNCED in 1992. We describe the history and content of the negotiations, including the Rio and Berlin meetings and the Kyoto Protocol.
We discuss the difficult equity issues involved, continued
resistance to the negotiations, the economic models on
which much of this resistance is based, and some of the
reasons why we consider that resistance misplaced.

Chapter 7 focuses on the policy agenda that we feel
is most powerful for stemming an undesirable climate
change: a revenue-neutral tax shift. We cover the scale of
emission reductions required to stabilize the climate, the
importance of energy and materials efficiency, the power
of prices in achieving environmental policy goals, the
logic and efficiency of a revenue-neutral tax shift, and the

obstacles presented by existing subsidies and economic accounting. We end this chapter by suggesting some political strategies that we believe increase our chances of implementing the logically attractive but politically difficult task of "getting the prices right."

Chapter 8 considers population and climate change together. We look briefly at how continued population growth accelerates climate change and how climate change amplifies the troubles produced by rapid population growth. Most of the chapter describes the two revolutions required to bring about population and climate stability: a *social* revolution that improves equity, particularly women's status, and a *technical* revolution that yields vastly greater energy and materials efficiency than we have today. It is our belief that these two revolutions are essential if we are to strike the new balance between human beings and the environment required to sustain us on Earth.

Our final chapter, the Afterword, is counsel for the discouraged. It briefly examines the personal and psychological dimensions of activism on issues as enormous as population and climate change; it argues for continuing to try for success, even in the face of strong negative odds; and it urges readers to find joy, even where there is little hope.

2

The New World of
Population Policy

Advancing gender equality and equity and the empowerment of women, and the elimination of all kinds of violence against women, and ensuring women's ability to control their own fertility, are cornerstones of population and development-related programmes.

—ICPD Programme of Action, Principle 4

In the spring of my sophomore year in high school (in early 1969), two events conspired to stir in me a strong commitment to population issues. First, seven or eight girls—"good" girls, including three from the varsity cheerleading squad—suddenly disappeared from school. I was startled. They must have had plans for college and careers, and their dropping out of school made no sense. Then I heard the whispers: They were pregnant. All of them, pregnant at fifteen or sixteen and out of school because of it.

Then, during spring break that year, I went with my best friend, Betsey, to visit her older sister in Boston. It was a big deal for a girl from a small town in Maine. Something her sister Anne said during dinner one night made a stronger impression on me than the scale of the ice cream sundaes at Swenson's, the Harvard Coop, or the traffic on Storrow Drive. She said that she planned to have only two children—not remarkable until she said why. She envisioned a third child, she said, "taking food out of the mouths of the other two."

I did not know it at the time, but these experiences contain the two threads that weave the basic fabric of the global "population-issues" tapestry. Anne's remark is about the relationship between human numbers and resources. The case of the cheerleaders is about the quest to control individual fertility.

The Population-Resources Thread

Over the centuries, different people in different places have worried about the relationship between human numbers and the natural world. Joel Cohen cites many of them: a Babylonian poem of 1600 B.C. telling of the infliction of plagues and pestilence by the gods to "rid the Earth of the excess of humans"; nine centuries later, a

Greek poem narrating the story that Zeus created the Trojan War "to relieve the all-nurturing earth of men . . . that the load of death might empty the world"; and in another nine centuries, a Roman philosopher writing that "we are burdensome to the world, the resources are scarcely adequate to us" and that "pestilence and hunger and war and flood must be considered as a remedy for nations, like a pruning back of the human race becoming excessive in numbers."

Environmental and resource-scarcity arguments dominate the population movement that mushroomed in the 1960s, an outgrowth of the environmental movement in general and one that was specifically triggered by the 1968 publication of Paul Ehrlich's book *The Population Bomb.* Modern rhetoric is rooted in the concerns expressed by Cohen's Roman philosopher and calls for bringing human numbers into balance with resources and the environment, lest nature do it for us unkindly. Ehrlich and his wife, Anne Ehrlich, biologist Garrett Hardin, and Lester Brown of the Worldwatch Institute continue to articulate environmental arguments for stabilizing population. Numerous others, from leaders and members of the public-interest group Zero Population Growth (ZPG) to those in the Audubon Society and the Sierra Club, find in population growth the root of environmental problems and natural-resource scarcity—from deforestation, air pollution, and soil erosion to traffic congestion and urban sprawl.

Another manifestation of concern with population

and resources—in this case, economic resources—is a view, expressed by Europeans since the 1600s, that the distress of the poor and unemployed is due in part to the size of their families. Too many children, it is argued, strain household economies, and too many workers relative to jobs guarantee wages too low to move them out of their misery. Centuries ago, analysts focused on the poor of Europe. Today we can see this strand of argument when we consider high fertility in the underdeveloped world.

Thomas Malthus is the best-known proponent of the view that the poor are kept poor by too many children, and indeed that too many people guarantee misery for nearly everyone. He was not in favor of birth control, in his view "artificial and unnatural modes of checking population." Instead, he recommended (rather quietly in an appendix to the fifth edition of his *Essay on the Principle of Population*) delayed marriage and celibacy before marriage, what he called moral restraint.

Seeing in population growth the causes of poverty, resource scarcity, and environmental harm may involve the lives of individuals—whether the women bearing many children, the children themselves, or the men tasked with supporting the families they create. Economic theory, the progress of society, or the state of the natural world usually take priority in the analysis. In contrast, another dimension of the population issue, which corresponds with the disappearing cheerleaders, begins with individuals and their desire—indeed, need—to master their fertility.

The Family Planning Thread

As a personal matter, people for millennia have worried about limiting their fertility. The Old Testament refers, though not approvingly, to coitus interruptus. People have used condoms at least since the sixteenth century, and some analysts trace them to Egyptian times. John Riddle has documented that medical texts from ancient and classical times specified herbal contraceptives and abortifacients and that women used them, effectively, for centuries.

Cultural and religious precepts that limit sexual activity to marriage, that condemn births outside marriage, that govern legal marriage age, and that promote lengthy breast feeding (which suppresses fertility) all suggest that concerns with limiting pregnancy and childbirth reach far back in time. The widespread, if not universal, presence of abortion and infanticide are further indicators of unwanted pregnancies and births.

By the early nineteenth century, a British political reformer—a tailor by trade, named Francis Place—added another dimension to the population–birth control constellation. He is thought to be the first person to have argued publicly, in writing, that birth control is an effective way to avoid families so large that working-class incomes are insufficient to support them, yielding poverty, child neglect, and child labor. And he told people how to accomplish it: by inserting a sponge, "as large as a green walnut, or a small apple," before intercourse and removing it immediately after. Whether this method was in fact used widely is not documented. Whether it would work well is thrown into doubt by what science today knows about reproduction. But Place started something new: public concern, outside the medical and helping professions, with family fertility from the point of view of the families themselves.

Francis Place distributed his pamphlet in 1822 and died largely forgotten in 1854. His effort to bring practical birth control information to the working classes was resumed in earnest after the turn of the twentieth century, an outgrowth of concerns with women's rights and health. Margaret Sanger in the United States, Marie Stopes in England, Lady Rama Rao in India, and others elsewhere led much-resisted public health movements to bring family planning to women, arguing that the health of both women and children depended on limiting childbearing.

The Population Movement

By the time the population movement of the 1960s was under way, family planning was much more widely accepted. The strong consensus in the movement was that birth control is the obvious solution to high fertility and thus to the population problem. The view was not unanimous, however. One group, primarily social scientists, argued that people choose their family size for reasons driven by social, economic, and cultural conditions (poverty, religion, and the role of women); the sheer availability of contraceptive technologies would not overcome those forces. To bring about a fertility decline, these scholars claimed, one must (generally through economic development) alter the conditions that shape fertility choices—not simply introduce a "technical fix" in the form of birth control.

Another group, usually activists, was equally skeptical that family planning could solve the population problem. These activists argued that if people are simply enabled to have the number of children they want, while they will likely have fewer children, they will nonetheless have too many to stabilize the population. Thus they recommended two types of measures "beyond family planning." One overlaps strongly with the scholars' recommendations: we should change the socioeconomic climate in which couples make childbearing decisions, by overall economic development, education for girls, employment opportunities for women, and government rhetoric on the value of small families. These kinds of measures are actually commonplace in the year 2002. Indeed, improving the status of women is the cornerstone of current thinking about population, as the remainder of this chapter will demonstrate. The second type of measure is entirely taboo today: "involuntary" or "coercive" measures such as requiring sterilization after two children, issuing licenses for childbearing, or even the disoriented recommendation to put a sterilant (not yet developed) in the water supply.

Despite the early wild talk in some quarters, family planning emerged as the mainstream solution to the population problem. Official U.S. action on the population issue, both at home and abroad, took the form of funding family planning services. The U.S. Agency for International Development (USAID) undertook a population program in 1965 and focused on funding contraceptive research and overseas family planning services. Five years later, Congress created an Office of Population Affairs in the Department of Health, Education, and Welfare (now Health and Human Services) to carry out a new program to fund family planning services for poor women. Activist population groups such as ZPG focused on repeal of antiabortion and anticontraceptive laws, in addition to educating the public about population. International efforts to curb global population growth and the mainstream American population movement are in fact both correctly identified with family planning.

The world rose to the call for universal access to family planning and began in the 1960s to fund family planning programs. Since then, total expenditures around the world have multiplied several times. The United States led the effort by developed countries to finance programs in poor countries. In most years since 1965, U.S. government dollars have provided half or more of all international assistance for family planning. Inclusion of private foundations such as the Ford Foundation, the Rockefeller Foundation, and the Population Council pushes the figure higher and intensifies the picture of U.S. dominance of international family planning.

In keeping with that focus, the United States, through USAID, tackled family planning assistance with a particular outlook and approach. Getting family planning services to as many people as possible, or "mass distribution of contraceptives," claimed the highest priority. The leaders of USAID at the time made the explicit assumption that a technical fix, birth control technology, could solve population problems and that it was not necessary to address the social, economic, and cultural conditions that give rise to fertility.

Strong supporters of family planning seldom believed that the larger conditions were irrelevant to fertility. But they believed that birth control alone could accomplish a great deal, and more cheaply and quickly than programs to increase incomes, weaken the effects of religious doctrine, or improve education. This argument gained credibility from figures on the extent to which people wanted to control their fertility but could not, because they lacked access to contraceptives, a phenomenon called unmet demand for family planning. Today we would describe the policy choice to provide family planning to people who already wanted it as harvesting low-hanging fruit.

The pragmatic, focused U.S. approach also made it possible to develop specific numerical goals by which to measure the success of programs: the number of "acceptors" of contraceptives; "contraceptive prevalence," or the percentage of married women of reproductive age using a modern method of birth control; and "contraceptive years of protection," or the number of years that people were protected from conceiving.

The world's long history of efforts to limit fertility,

taken with the experience of women in most cultures with the anxieties of unwanted pregnancy, suggested that family planning programs would meet with success. And, indeed, a revolution has unfolded since the 1960s, in both contraceptive use and family size—something analysts often call the reproductive revolution. In the developing world outside China today, nearly 40 percent of women of reproductive age use modern methods of family planning, up from fewer than 10 percent in the 1960s. If China is included, the figure is 51 percent. In the developing world as a whole, family size is half what it was in the mid-sixties: 3.2 children per woman rather than more than 6.0.

Family Planning versus Development?

In the past forty years, have people increasingly turned to contraception because they already wanted to limit their families? Did the sheer presence of these services convince them to change their plans for a large family? Or did changing socioeconomic and cultural conditions give rise to changes in desired family size, which people implemented by using birth control? The answers vary, of course, for different countries and regions. Scholarly evaluations suggest that family planning programs are indeed associated with falling fertility, as are socioeconomic changes. The most powerful effect comes from the combination of socioeconomic changes *and* effective family planning services.

In 1991 W. Parker Mauldin and John Ross reviewed

the effects of family planning programs and socioeconomic changes on fertility in eighty-eight developing
countries. They found that between 1975 and 1990, fertility fell five times faster in countries with strong family
planning programs (such as South Korea, Thailand, Vietnam, and Bangladesh) than in countries with weak programs (such as Kuwait, Saudi Arabia, Cambodia, and
Chad). It also fell far faster in more developed countries
such as Mexico, Jamaica, Venezuela, and Chile than in
poorer ones such as Nepal, Senegal, Mali, and Niger. Fertility fell fastest when a country had both a strong family
planning program and improving socioeconomic conditions. On average, countries with both elements experienced a 3.5-child drop in average family size between
1960 and 1990. The opposite countries (with weak or
nonexistent family planning programs and less development) experienced no change in fertility.

Study findings about the synergistic effect of family
planning programs and socioeconomic changes have partially diluted the "family planning *versus* development"
arguments of the early days of the population movement.
Deeper examination of which socioeconomic changes
have the most powerful effects has advanced the debate
even more. It has guided population activists and scholars to asking the right question.

The Right Question

In the early days of concern with rapid population growth, writers frequently wondered, with evident

exasperation, how the people of Asia, Africa, and Latin America—and some in the developed countries—might ever be talked out of their apparent desires for large families. Two well-known advocates posed a question in 1970 that haunted many a population activist: "How can we convince a poor Pakistani villager or a middle-class American that the number of children his wife bears is of crucial importance not just to himself and his family but also to his society?"

If we ignore for the moment the old-fashioned emphasis on "*his* wife" and *his* family," putting the question this way makes solving the population problem indeed a discouraging business. One thinks first of the need to educate each and every person, so that everyone understands population growth and its consequences. But will people resist these ideas? Even if they absorb them, will understanding be enough to overcome the conditions that push people to have numerous children? Will people go against what their culture and economic interests tell them to do?

This is an analytical cul-de-sac. How much more powerful to pose the question this way: "What is it about life in developing countries that makes large families *good sense*?" If we can answer this question, we can move away from the exasperation that colored early analyses and begin to understand life in societies where families are large—and even feel some compassion. From there it is a logical step to the conditions that need changing so that *small* families make sense.

Of course, the weight of culture and religion encourages large families, directly through exhortations to marry early and have many children, and indirectly through admonitions to submit to the will of God. Yet many societies have broken through traditional religious and cultural teachings by choosing families that are small. Colombia is a Catholic country that has experienced a rapid fertility decline; Colombian women now average 3.0 children, despite annual incomes of just about $2,500. Bangladesh, an impoverished Islamic country, has experienced a rapid fertility drop that is astonishing, given conditions there; families now average 3.3 children. It is often pointed out that Italy for some years had the lowest fertility rate in the world. (Today Hong Kong, Bulgaria, and the Czech Republic have lower fertility, and several other countries match Italy's rate, at 1.2 children per family on average.) Even the local presence of the Vatican is not enough to prevent Italians from using birth control and even getting abortions.

The conventional wisdom tells us that wealthy countries have low fertility, while families are largest in the poorest countries. This is broadly true, with some exceptions. Fertility in China, Bangladesh, and parts of India are lower than one would expect from the economic conditions there. In contrast, fertility is higher in Saudi Arabia than one might anticipate from its high average per-capita income—though we know that Saudi Arabia's wealth is not evenly distributed, and Islam exerts a conservative force. Despite these exceptions, the demands of poverty, especially in a rural culture where a child's labor is a meaningful contribution to the household economy and where children provide a couple's only financial security in old age, do indeed cry out for many children. With poverty usually come illiteracy, poor nutrition and health, unsafe sanitation and water, and lack of schooling opportunities and other services.

Each of these by itself can drive high fertility. Illiterate couples (and women in particular) are less likely, even if they wish to limit childbearing, to know about family planning or its availability. Poor nutrition, inadequate sanitation, disease, and lack of health and other services to ameliorate these conditions all mean that more women face pregnancy with their physical resources compromised, more women die in childbirth, and more infants die before reaching age one. High infant mortality encourages high fertility; parents who have lost infants tend to have many children, even more than required to replace infants who die. Lack of schooling opportunities means among other things that children cost less and provide more. They require no school fees and are able to work at home, and they grow up without the education that can break the cycle of high fertility, poor health, and poverty.

Something else drives high fertility, too. If you were to ask a woman in a high-fertility country why she has many children, she might answer as follows: "I am nothing in my culture unless I bear children—in fact, I am nothing in my culture unless I bear sons. Sometimes the daughters keep coming, and I have to keep having babies until I've produced a son. Or two. And I was really nobody until I married, so I married young. As soon as I married, the babies started to come."

I have made up this answer, of course, because few people can move outside their culture to see themselves with such clarity. But the numbers support my fictional account. All over the world, where women live constrained lives with few options, and where their culture conveys prestige on them only through marriage and childbearing, especially of sons, fertility is high. Indeed, the exact kind of poverty that most strongly brings about high fertility may be the poverty that ranks women as second class.

Scholars and activists in the population movement, traditionally focused on encouraging fertility declines and stabilizing the world's population through family planning services alone, have for some years paid attention to these kinds of findings. They are less likely now to ask in exasperation, as so many of us did in the 1960s, why poor women have so many children. An examination of these women's lives provided the answers. The answers in turn weave a third significant thread into the tapestry of population issues, a thread that adds to the traditional warp and woof of family planning and resource concerns. A fourth thread finishes our embroidery and yields the final pattern of the population tapestry that we know as the Cairo agenda: that last thread is a feminist interpretation of women's reproductive health.

The Reproductive Health Revolution

The thread of reproductive health comes not from conventional population concerns, but from feminist critiques of population and family planning programs. Before we look at how reproductive health activists came to shape international population policy, we need to review just what women's reproductive health is.

Jodi Jacobson has written that the state of a woman's reproductive health depends on how she answers these questions: "Can she control when and with whom she will engage in sexual relations? Can she do so without fear of infection or unwanted fertility? Can she choose when and how to regulate her fertility, free from unpleasant or dangerous side effects of contraception? Can she go through pregnancy and childbirth safely? Can she obtain a safe abortion on request? Lastly, can she easily obtain information on the prevention and treatment of reproductive illnesses?"

It has become evident in recent years that few women the world over can answer all of these questions affirmatively and that, therefore, women's reproductive health is in abominable shape in much of the world. This understanding, and efforts to improve women's sexual autonomy; freedom from sexually transmitted diseases (STDs) including human immunodeficiency virus (HIV), acquired immunodeficiency syndrome (AIDS), and reproductive tract infections (RTIs); mastery over fertility; and

health during pregnancy and childbirth constitute the reproductive health revolution.

It seems a modest request to ask that a woman be able
to refuse unwanted sexual relations, but in fact many
women in the world cannot. In parts of Africa, refusing
sexual relations is simply not acceptable behavior by a
wife, even if her husband is known to be infected with the
HIV virus. A different sort of violence is female genital
cutting (FGC); in more than forty countries, mostly in
Africa, young girls are "circumcised"—all or part of the
labia and clitoris is excised, and in some cases the vagina
is almost entirely sewn up. Domestic violence, rape (mar-
ital and other), childhood sexual abuse, and trafficking
in women and girls, all more overtly violent than "accepted" cultural practices, add to the violation experienced by women and girls all over the world. In addition
to constituting internationally recognized human rights
abuses, and doubtless compromising mental and emotional health, each of these violations of a woman's control over her body compromises her physical health by
increasing the risk of infection, unwanted pregnancy, and
injury.

Diseases of the reproductive tract affect hundreds of
millions of women and constitute what many have called
a silent emergency. These conditions include STDs such
as AIDS and syphilis, and various other infections such
as chlamydia. The World Health Organization (WHO) estimates that a third of a billion new cases of curable STDs

emerged around the world in 1995, with most of the cases concentrated in the developing world. The National Research Council has written, "RTIs are a persistent global health problem: as syphilis preoccupied clinicians at the beginning of the twentieth century, RTIs are a major international public health problem as it ends."

The ability to delay, space, and stop pregnancy and childbearing is the third major element of women's reproductive health, all made possible by family planning. But family planning programs must be of high quality, or they risk doing little good and can do harm. High-quality family planning programs provide access to the full range of contraceptives, counseling, and safe abortion services. If only one or two birth control methods are available, a woman may in essence be forced to choose a method inappropriate to her needs, and suffer the consequences in side effects and ill health. Or she may fall back on no contraception at all and suffer the consequences in unwelcome pregnancy, abortion, or an unwanted birth. In programs with sensitive and complete counseling, a woman is more likely to come away with a birth control method that she understands well, and that she will continue to use. Such counseling also ensures that a woman has given voluntary and informed consent to medical treatment, whether in the form of reversible contraception or irreversible surgical sterilization. Also, in the best family planning programs, abortion is safe and readily available, as access to safe abortion can make the difference between life and death for a woman.

In many people's minds female reproductive health is defined by the medical and health issues surrounding pregnancy and childbirth, from anemia through toxemia and obstructed labor. Pregnancy and childbearing kill more than half a million women annually, the vast majority in the developing world, and two hundred thousand from the consequences of botched abortions. Five million women sicken annually from pregnancy-related causes. Seven million newborns die every year because their mothers are ill. The risks of pregnancy and childbirth prompted WHO, the World Bank, and others to undertake a joint effort in 1987. Known as the Safe Motherhood Initiative, it highlighted the risks associated with what is usually perceived, by its very commonness, as natural and unthreatening.

Reproductive Health and Population Policy

Reproductive health activists have clashed over the years with traditional family planners. The highest priority of the planners has been to deliver contraceptives to people, sometimes to the exclusion of other aspects of medical care that family planners consider outside their scope. While family planning is an essential aspect of reproductive health, feminist activists disapprove of delivering contraceptives alone, of providing only a limited range of contraceptives, and of doing so without screening for STDs and RTIs. Many, if not most, family planning programs around the world are not comprehensive: they deliver contraceptives. Thus, reproductive health activists see traditional family planning as yet another way to manipulate women against their will—to exhort them to have fewer children, simply by saying, "Take this pill" or "Use this device," without an understanding of a woman's broader health, or her life.

And activists point to a disturbing fact: during the decades that contraceptive use has increased, reproductive tract infections have, for reasons not fully understood, become more common all over the world. It shocks feminist observers that family planning services are reaching people, while screening for infections is not. Further, the discrepancy suggests that priorities are upside down. Most disturbing is the literal coercion that has occurred in some government family planning programs around the world. Eagerness to meet numerical targets for family planning "acceptors," contraceptive prevalence, and fertility rates has pushed programs to run roughshod over a woman's privacy and right to be free from medical interference without her knowing consent.

The antagonism between family planning and reproductive health activists led some women at the 1992 Earth Summit in Rio to condemn *all* government family planning programs as offensive to women. Preparations for the International Conference on Population and Development (ICPD) to be held in Cairo in 1994 had begun in 1991, with an initial Preparatory Committee or PrepCom meeting. The family planning community and women's reproductive health activists met in the early negotiations as enemies—with their animosity exacerbated by some of the talk at Rio.

Although they began as outsiders to the population and family planning community at the center of ICPD preparations, feminist reproductive health activists and the positions that they argued grew in strength throughout the three years of ICPD negotiations. Workshops, regional meetings, expert groups, and other forums created by the United Nations and nongovernment organizations (NGOs) in preparation for the Cairo conference produced statement after statement articulating the reproductive health agenda. Conversations and reports repeated the importance of "women-centered services"; the priority of individuals over demographic goals; and the need to consider STDs, RTIs, and maternal health.

The feminist agenda went beyond health. In addition to criticizing traditional family planning services, many feminists questioned the conventional wisdom that population growth causes poverty. They believed instead that poverty causes high fertility (and population growth) and that inequalities—between men and women, between classes and races, and between countries—lie at the root of poverty. They also argued that massive consumption of resources and production of wastes in rich countries is far more responsible for environmental harm than poverty and population growth in the Third World. Thus, in addition to reproductive health, feminists brought to the Cairo process a comprehensive agenda for radical social, economic, and political change. Central to this agenda was raising the status of women—indeed, redesigning development strategies around women's empowerment.

A London meeting in 1992 organized by the International Women's Health Coalition (IWHC), a leading international reproductive health NGO, was especially important in crystallizing the feminist approach and illustrating the power of the movement. In consultation with more than one hundred other women's groups, IWHC drafted a "Women's Declaration on Population Policies," which called for "a fundamental revision in the design, structure and implementation of population policies, to foster the empowerment and well-being of all women."

By the time of the second PrepCom, in May 1993, it was clear to the United Nations (U.N.) organizers that the new thinking in population, family planning, and reproductive health required negotiation of a fresh plan in Cairo, rather than revision of long-standing, more traditional agreements. The feminist reproductive health activists, influential as NGO observers organized into a women's caucus and as members of the official government delegations, made news at the second PrepCom by succeeding in placing reproductive health and the status of women squarely on the agenda. Indeed, these issues came to dominate the remainder of the negotiations, which included a third PrepCom and the Cairo meeting itself. They defined the Programme of Action that came out of Cairo, and redefined the world's approach to population.

Though feminist reproductive health activists and traditional family planners began as adversaries, in the course of the many conversations that culminated in the Cairo meeting, the two groups came to see their common ground. Family planners are usually medical people, sensitive to the need to deliver their services in an appropriate health care context. They are committed to informed consent and voluntarism. And a great many of them are feminists. The right of access to birth control has always played a strong role in feminist movements in the West, and women's autonomy lies at the heart of feminism. Also, the importance to fertility of women's status helped provide common ground between feminists and family planners—and even traditional population activists. Further, strong leadership by women within traditional "population establishment" organizations—Jodi Jacobson writing on reproductive health at the Worldwatch Institute and Judith Bruce of the Population Council writing about quality of care in family planning programs—helped move the traditional population movement toward greater appreciation of women's reproductive health.

Because family planning is one of the principal components of reproductive health, during the three years of preparation for Cairo—sparked in part by assaults from conservative forces like the Vatican on abortion, reproductive health, and sexuality—these two traditional enemies reached across their historical differences and built a political coalition more powerful than any previously seen at a U.N. population conference.

The Cairo Conference

The United Nations has since the 1950s called international population conferences in the fourth year of every decade. Early on, demographers and other scholars met to discuss esoteric issues such as census-taking techniques and mathematical modeling. Beginning in 1974, the meetings became forums for government officials to discuss and draw up population policy in the form of negotiated documents. In 1994, thousands of NGOs also participated and could lobby government delegations and influence the negotiated language.

Twenty thousand people from 180 countries gathered in Cairo in September 1994, thirty-five hundred on official government delegations and the rest from the press and NGOs. All four threads of the population issues tapestry as I have described it were present. Traditionally, issues of population, resources, the environment, and development drive international attention to population. At international population conferences, these concerns express themselves principally as support for family planning programs. In Cairo, some advocates of this view also called for inclusion of demographic targets and goals, to set the world's sights, in effect, on population stabilization. Family planners—including funders and program managers—with more than thirty years' experience of programs and international conferences were there in force, working to ensure that family planning received priority in the Cairo document. Most powerful in shaping the details of the ICPD document were the women's rights and reproductive health activists. They promoted the new understanding of the importance of the status of women and girls to population and development, of enlarging family planning to encompass reproductive health, and of reframing development around the empowerment of women.

The document negotiated in Cairo transformed the world's approach to the population problem by blending the various voices present. The Programme of Action essentially said that the world can restore to women the full measure of humanity that they deserve, and in so doing create the conditions in which fertility can fall and populations can stabilize. It also called for population and development programs to start with women's concerns, not to blame women for high fertility. On these points, the women's rights advocates prevailed.

The document also repudiated numerical targets, whether for fertility, birth control "acceptors," or population size; on this issue, some supporters of traditional population, resources, and environmental concerns lost. Still, the Cairo document did not reflect the concept that population growth is unimportant to development. (On this issue, some women's rights advocates lost.) Early in the document, the ICPD pointed out that the sooner the world's population stabilizes, the better. "Intensified efforts are needed in the next 5, 10, and 15 years, in a range of population and development activities," the Programme of Action stated, "bearing in mind the crucial contribution that early stabilization of the world population would make toward the achievement of sustainable development."

While denying that family planning alone can be a "technical fix" for population problems, the ICPD gave family planning far from a low priority. Indeed, its funding section called for family planning to receive the lion's share of allotted dollars. On this issue, clearly the vast majority of traditional population supporters and family planners won; supporters of the reproductive rights agenda would doubtless have preferred a different priority.

The Cairo document, like other international negotiations that fall short of international law (and even international law itself sometimes) was not everything that it might have been and often appeared to be merely rhetoric. But it was a bit different, for two reasons.

Unlike most international agreements of its kind, Cairo's Programme of Action commited countries to spending certain amounts on reproductive health, family planning, HIV/AIDS and STD prevention, and research and data collection by specific years. The figure for 2000 was to be $17 billion; for 2015, $22 billion. Rich donor countries were called on to contribute one third of the amount and developing countries two thirds—a fairer distribution than the quarter that wealthy countries contributed in 1994, leaving the remaining three quarters for poor countries to pay themselves.

Much hope surrounded the financial provision at the

conclusion of the Cairo meeting. Funding for the Cairo agenda, led by the United States, rose encouragingly for two years. Then U.S. funding fell by nearly 20 percent between 1995 and 1996, as anti–family planning legislators came to dominate the Congress. Funding for family planning services suffered the sharpest cut—in 1998, that category was only 70 percent of 1995 levels. Other donor countries too have lost interest in the issue, complaining of "compassion fatigue," or suffering economic reversals that undercut their foreign assistance budgets. While developing countries, taken together, contributed most of their share in 2000, wealthy donor countries did not.

Thus, a second distinction is that the Cairo enterprise is at its best as a symbolic and rhetorical device, to be used by activists as leverage against their governments, as evidence that we really know what is right and we all agreed to it—once. The document itself is less important than what lies behind it: the thousands of activist women, trained in lobbying and organizing, who banded together to achieve their agenda. Representing every interest present in Cairo, they are feminist and not feminist; they support traditional family planning, they believe reproductive health a vast improvement over family planning; they rate population the world's biggest problem, one of many, or not one at all. Most important, they believe in women. And these same women, who for three years worked tirelessly to build a consensus and craft language reflecting that consensus, will make the words of the Cairo document the most real. These same women will carry out the Cairo vision, working hard in their families, neighborhoods, and communities.

I think of the Nigerian woman with whom I shared a taxi in Cairo. She worked on AIDS prevention in the northern part of her country. "I've given up on men," she said, "we have to succeed without them." I have no idea how she is going to do it, but if anyone can, she can.

I think of an Indian woman with whom I sat on a bus at the end of a long and exhausting day. We were discussing the emotional and physical drain of constantly overcoming self-doubt. She said: "The women I work with, who cannot read, don't suffer from this! Once they learn they are not second-class citizens, they feel first-class for the rest of their lives."

I think of the Honduran judge with whom I visited Cairo's market. She dared to go on television to tell the story of her battering husband, so that Hondurans would know that educated, upper-class people share this nightmare.

And I think of the dozens of women who agreed with me that they were energized and inspired simply by seeing thousands of other women at Cairo dedicated to the same work and committed to carrying it out. Even after returning home to the obstacles and the resistance, these women said, they would not feel alone.

In changing the conventional wisdom about how to solve the problem of rapid population growth, Cairo has created a new world for population—the "new world" of this chapter's title. Times have changed in other ways, too. My two experiences in the spring of 1969 are out-

dated now: more adolescents have access to family planning, though many barriers remain. Pregnant girls stay in
school more often. And fewer people believe the drastic
vision described by my friend's sister—that of a third
child snatching food from his or her siblings.

Even if we *do* believe that population growth is likely
to have drastic consequences, Cairo provides us with an
agenda for action that is likely to succeed. It is an agenda
that paddles downstream, taking advantage of universal
commitments to healthy children and healthy mothers,
and of growing commitments to afford women the full humanity they deserve. People with differing views of population, society, development, and the world can work together from Cairo's constructive agenda and benefit from
its vision.

3

Putting Cairo to Work

Some leaders are born women.

—Anonymous

I once had an argument with a fellow population activist. In the midst of a discussion, over dinner in a restaurant, he professed not to know the precise agenda of action for encouraging fertility decline, and hence population stabilization. I felt sure he was being disingenuous in order to annoy me—we had a history—so I got irritated. It turned out, to my embarrassment, that a number of people committed to the population issue know more about the nature of the problem than about its solutions. This chapter is for them. And for my colleague, unjustly the object of my annoyance.

So what *is* the policy agenda for population stabilization? It goes far beyond merely (1) support of family planning or (2) education on population issues. Indeed, anything that increases the mastery that women and girls have over their lives counts as work to stabilize population, whether in a poor country in the Third World or a developed country such as the United States.

In the ideal world where populations *can* stabilize, women and adolescent girls have satisfactory reproductive health care, including high-quality family planning services, available either through private health care or through government or charitable programs; sexually transmitted infections are rare, and well treated when they occur; unwanted pregnancies and births are the exceptions; sexual and other family violence is an extraordinary event; births are safe; and women and men can practice birth control without disabling side effects. Infants and children are wanted when they are conceived and born, have adequate health care, and rarely die young.

Girls have every opportunity to attend school, from kindergarten through graduate school, studying subjects that range from child care and household economics through astrophysics. Women have every opportunity to do meaningful work at reasonable pay, earn sufficient livelihoods, and participate in public and political life, from the village through national governments.

The kind of poverty that robs people, especially women, of hope and of command over their lives is rare. Community-based development, economic reform, political change, new forms of business, and innovative and effective programs have banished the worst poverty from the planet.

To make progress toward *all* these conditions is our agenda. There are two ways of making this progress, both essential: one can work directly on it oneself, or one can support others as they work on it. In the first instance, one works for a nonprofit, a government agency, an international organization, or a foundation that creates programs, gets services to people, reforms governments and economies. Or one gets elected to Congress and works on reform and funding meaningful programs.

The alternative of urging others means supporting an activist organization that lobbies for funding of programs and reform of institutions, educates politicians and the public on the issues, and gets publicity. It can also mean electing the right candidates and writing letters of advocacy. Everything counts.

To illustrate the rich tapestry of projects and programs included in the action agenda for population stabilization, this chapter tells the story of the Centre for Development and Population Activities (CEDPA) and its work in the West African country of Nigeria. The most populous country in the African continent, Nigeria weighs in with about 123 million people (censuses here are not entirely accurate)—15 percent of the entire continent and one fifth of sub-Saharan Africa. Growth is rapid: 2.8 percent a year in 2000, a doubling time of twenty-four years.

CEDPA's experience in Nigeria illustrates a range of projects, from community-based distribution of contraceptives to the development of grassroots programs for women's economic empowerment through projects focused specifically on increasing women's political participation. Along the way, CEDPA touches on girls' education, literacy training for adolescents, immunization, and several aspects of maternal and child health. The story of CEDPA-Nigeria is about enabling women and girls to increase mastery over their lives.

A Tale of Three Leaders

In 1982, a forty-year old Nigerian woman, raised in a farming family and educated at the postsecondary level in the United States, founded the Country Women's Association of Nigeria (COWAN) in the southwestern state of Ondo. It was Bisi Ogunleye's vision that rural women joined together could pool their resources, get training, obtain loans, raise their productivity and earning capacity, and improve their standard of living and their families' lives. Indeed, it was Bisi's belief—well ahead of the popularization of microenterprise for women—that rural women hold the key to economic development for a country as a whole. She argued that the work of women is a critical piece of the entire economic fabric.

In a description of COWAN's early work, Bisi (now Chief Bisi, after her father bequeathed his hereditary title to her) argued that existing agricultural programs, intended to raise productivity and increase incomes, often failed because of their blindness to women's work. "No visitor or citizen of Ondo State," she wrote in 1983, "could deny the hard realities of rural women's participation in all aspects of food production. However, policy makers and development planners do not recognize this fact. [They ignore] the division of labor between husbands and wives. They think of women's participation in food production as just cooking in the home. [The programs] do not take into account the role of the rural woman but instead over-emphasize scientific farming and do not consider how rural women's resources fit into the scheme."

The technologies introduced in these programs, Bisi continued, "are mainly for men. Women will continue to do their own work in the old ways," falling behind in productivity and income. Also, "the beliefs and practices are that men are the ones capable of operating the machines."

COWAN undertook to change this. Bisi began by listening to a plan originated by thirty women in her state, of establishing a palm oil and cassava processing plant. She tried to get them a loan, but bankers refused because the women did not own the land they worked and had no collateral to offer. She gave them the equivalent of $45 herself. "They used the money to buy machines to process the plants and a used truck to haul their produce to the markets," Bisi writes of that time. "They did this for three months and then they came back with six times the amount of money."

It was just the beginning. Less than two years after its

founding, 135 members of COWAN cooperatives were raising yam, cassava, tomatoes, and vegetables. The association had also acquired a marketing depot, where members sold their products. Cooperative members saved money to generate individual and group credit and lent small amounts back to individual women so they could invest in simple food-processing technologies.

As Bisi was organizing the rural women of Ondo State into cooperatives under COWAN, activists in Washington, D.C., established an organization to bring managers of Third World family planning programs to Washington for training in management techniques and organizational skills. The Centre for Population Activities, or CEFPA, came into being in 1975 and through 1982 had trained more than fifteen hundred people from seventy-six countries—thirty-nine of them from Bisi's country of Nigeria.

Now our story shifts from Africa to Asia and from 1982 back to 1970. That year, the American Peggy Curlin accompanied her epidemiologist husband to Bangladesh, where he studied cholera. While there, she founded a community women's group known as Concerned Women. Among its first projects was an effort to vaccinate women in the slums of Dhaka against smallpox. The World Health Organization had succeeded in vaccinating men, but mortality from smallpox among pregnant women and children remained at 90 percent. The all-male WHO vaccination teams could not reach secluded Islamic women and their children.

"Everywhere we went to vaccinate against smallpox," Curlin reports today, "women drew us aside and asked, 'What is this no-baby pill? We want it!' " They were referring, of course, to the oral contraceptive. The nearest family planning clinic was twelve miles away from the slum where Concerned Women worked. If women would not enter the public rooms of their houses for smallpox vaccinations, they surely would not travel openly in the streets to obtain family planning. A program of community-based distribution of contraceptives, household to household, women to women, was born.

"There were five of us at first," Curlin says of those days. "We each had sixty thousand households to reach."

After several years in Bangladesh, Peggy returned to the United States. About that time, CEFPA's leaders in Washington realized that they needed a training program focused on women managers—on their special problems as women in their cultures, as well as the skills required to manage family planning programs successfully. They called on Peggy to develop the program. When CEFPA announced the first Women in Management program in May of 1978, 350 applicants from around the world responded.

In 1978 CEFPA also began to train women in their own countries. In just a few years, the corps of women trained by CEFPA grew into a network of women capable of recruiting other women in their countries for training, organizing, and building programs. They also served as consultants and participated in conferences nationally and internationally. By its own account, the organization's programs were producing "a vast resource pool spanning countries in Asia, Africa, Latin America, the Caribbean and the Middle East."

In the early 1980s, CEFPA expanded its scope beyond family planning to embrace a broader notion of development. It added nutrition, health, income generation, and institution building, all in the context of women's role in community development. Reflecting their mission's expansion, in 1981 CEFPA became the Centre for Development and Population Activities, CEDPA, and the organization felt that it had a model not just for improving family planning programs, but for community development more broadly.

"We began to see the management skills that were the focus of our training go to the next level," Curlin says today. "We saw our alumnae become catalysts for social change at the community level."

In 1982 CEDPA secured funding that allowed it to support $3,000 and $5,000 projects run by its alumnae. The organization saw these small projects as "in-country extensions of CEDPA" that worked "with local women's groups to develop and monitor community-based projects in family planning, health, nutrition, and income generation." CEDPA provided technical assistance in management, staff development, fundraising, program planning, and community organizing.

Today CEDPA describes its mission as "empowering women at all levels of society to be full partners in development." To accomplish this, CEDPA builds the capacities of individuals and nongovernmental organizations, mobilizes political and economic participation from the local to the international level, creates "gender-sensitive and inclusive reproductive health programs," and works to include youth in development. "All CEDPA activities," states the 1999 annual report, "are designed to advance gender equity."

In early 1983 a midcareer foreign service officer in the U.S. Agency for International Development (USAID), Elizabeth Keys MacManus, reported to her new overseas assignment in Lagos, Nigeria. Since joining USAID in 1961, MacManus had served in Indonesia, Vietnam, and Egypt, as well as in the Office of Population in USAID's Washington headquarters. In 1975 she was the highest-ranked woman in the agency. Long committed to family planning and population issues, MacManus looked about her in Nigeria.

Approximately 1 percent of married women of reproductive age used contraceptives in Nigeria at that time. Families averaged six or seven children in the country as a whole, with many families much larger. Maternal mortality was high, even by the standards of developing countries. So was infant mortality. "Contraceptive" meant "condom," which meant "prostitution." The notion of limiting childbearing was almost taboo. MacManus was not discouraged.

Approaching the medical profession first, she arranged for the training of doctors and nurses in family planning methods and services. Well aware of the health consequences of early, late, and closely spaced childbearing on women and their children, Nigerian medical professionals eagerly sought to introduce family planning to their patients—usually in the context of spacing children, rather than limiting their number. And the Nigerian army, which provided housing to the families of its soldiers in what have always been difficult economic times in Nigeria, signaled interest in making family planning available in its health care facilities.

Early in her tenure MacManus received a letter from Bisi Ogunleye, who told MacManus of her work and asked for her help. Always interested in development in general and women in particular, MacManus set out to visit Bisi. Driving for hours through rain forest, she reports, she finally emerged onto an open plain. After seeing virtually no human beings for miles and miles, there, gathered for market, were about ten thousand people. At the center was Bisi, surrounded by the women of COWAN's cooperatives, selling their wares.

MacManus urged Bisi to apply to CEDPA's training program and recommended to CEDPA that it accept her. Bisi did, CEDPA did, and a long and rich history began.

Chief Bisi and the Country Women's Association

Bisi attended the eleventh Women in Management training program at CEDPA in Washington in 1983. The five-week course relied on lectures, small-group discussions, case studies, simulation games, role-playing exercises, and field trips to cover population, health, and development as they relate to women; self-understanding for the professional woman; personnel management; and technical skills for building programs. Designed to promote a high degree of participation by trainees, the workshop also required each participant to develop a proposal for a project in her community.

Bisi's project was a $230,000 plan to equip COWAN members with tractors, harrows, shellers, ridgers, and other small-scale agricultural equipment; fryers, ovens, smokers, and grinding mills for food processing; two cold houses for food storage; and three trucks for transporting goods. She also included leadership and technical training for COWAN members and organizers, and a program to standardize market pricing, packaging, measuring, and weighing systems. The goals? "To increase the productivity and earning capacity of rural women; to provide training to improve women's basic skills and efficiency; and to relieve rural women farmers from spending so much time and energy in trying to sell their meager food stuffs with the present marketing system."

Bisi succeeded in bringing this project, and many more, to fruition—aided, in part, by a seed money grant of $5,000 from CEDPA soon after her training. Today COWAN has thirteen hundred community cooperatives in twelve Nigerian states. The members farm, process foods, make crafts, weave, and trade. COWAN is known globally for its grassroots projects designed and carried out by women, and Chief Bisi is known internationally for her work. She is the founding vice president of the Women's Environment and Development Organization—tapped for that role by the late U.S. congresswoman Bella Abzug—and in 1996 Bisi was honored with the Africa Prize for Leadership for the Sustainable End of Hunger.

According to Peggy Curlin, Bisi was not at first enthusiastic about family planning. Childless herself, from a culture in which a husband can divorce a childless wife with little ceremony, preventing pregnancy was not uppermost in Bisi's mind. A true grassroots organizer, however, she returned to Nigeria and consulted with the members of her cooperatives about family planning. Did they know about it? Were they interested?

They were indeed. Since 1988 several hundred COWAN members have received training in community-based distribution (CBD) of nonclinical contraceptives (usually condoms, foaming tablets, and oral contraceptive pills) and family planning counseling for women and men. In 1995 the project's scope widened to include education on minor health ailments; sexually transmitted infections, HIV, and AIDS; breastfeeding; nutrition; and immunization and oral rehydration therapy for children. COWAN members reach tens of thousands of rural Nigerians, in thirty of thirty-six Nigerian states, who would not otherwise have access to these services. They provide nonclinical contraceptives; discuss the health of women and children; and in general raise awareness of reproductive health, family planning, and women's participation in health care decisionmaking in the family and in the community.

COWAN members deliberately seek the backing of traditional rulers in the villages where they work, considering this support essential to program success. In fact, after twelve years of community-based family planning and health activities, Chief Bisi reports that "the traditional leaders have all become advocates for the program and encourage their subjects to participate."

Oba Ibrahim Akindoju (in southwestern Nigerian culture an *oba* is a traditional king) says of COWAN's work: "The reason why I support them is that I see a benefit in what they are doing. The most important is family planning and since family planning has been brought in, we are very happy."

Other elements of program success identified by Chief Bisi are the complete integration of activites—health with family planning, women's empowerment with health, and income generation with women's empowerment, for example; documentation of management, personnel, and organizational policies; simplified, culturally sensitive educational materials; and the need to have all methods of family planning available, either directly through the CBD agents or by referrals, "to ensure quality of care."

COWAN is a success story for its members, for Nigeria, and for CEDPA. It occupies a large place in CEDPA's work in Nigeria, representing, for example, nearly 95 percent of continuing family planning clients reached through CEDPA-supported programs in Nigeria in 2000. CEDPA also supports several projects run by grassroots women's organizations throughout Nigeria that provide integrated health services, including nonclinical family planning.

The National Council of Women's Societies

Among the oldest projects is CEDPA's partnership with the branch of the National Council of Women's Societies (NCWS) in Plateau State, in central Nigeria. Begun in 1986, NCWS is a national organization of women's groups. The Plateau State branch consists of seventy grassroots women's organizations working in trading, farming, food processing and selling, tailoring, textile working, and the professions. NCWS–Plateau State describes itself as "an umbrella institution coordinating the activities of these organizations."

The first NCWS project in the state trained a network of women who operated stalls in the Ultra Modern Market in Jos, the capital city, that offered nonclinical contraceptives and referrals to local family planning clinics. The volunteers also received training in child health (oral rehydration therapy and immunization), STD/AIDS prevention, and enhancing women's participation in health care—an expansion of the program that responded, in the words of an NCWS proposal, "to the yearnings of the target population."

Within a few years, several hundred trained volunteer vendors, including men, reached 130,000 people in ten markets throughout Jos. The market association at the Ultra Modern Market dedicated a stall to health services, and the Plateau State Ministry of Health volunteered personnel to staff it, creating a market-based clinic offering immunization, oral rehydration therapy, family planning, and basic first aid.

CEDPA, one of a handful of U.S.-based funders of this project, invested up to about $50,000 a year in this enterprise. Now U.S. funding has been phased out, and NCWS is operating successfully in Plateau State without it. In addition to the market-based services, projects include training of its personnel in workshops based on the Women in Management program; promotional activities that include "one-on-one motivational talks" on health, group presentations, and the development of educational materials; and a program in which men educate men about family planning.

COWAN works in southwestern Nigeria; NCWS–Plateau State, in the central part of the country. In both areas women traditionally play an active role in markets, and large portions of the population practice Christianity. In the far north of Nigeria, by contrast, deeply conservative Islam (which has a tradition of seclusion of women, and near-absence of the notion of ever wanting to limit the number of children one bears) generates a vastly different context for women's reproductive health, family planning, and women's participation in the family and society.

Work in Northern Nigeria

The starting point in the north is health. One CEDPA partner is the Grassroots Health Organization of Nigeria (GHON), based in Kano, the capital city of the northern state of the same name. Founded in 1993, GHON worked first in several Kano communities with women suffering from visico vaginal fistula, a disabling and stigmatizing condition that women often suffer in shamed silence. Deeply aware of the cultural context of these communities, GHON focused on "a cautious and person-to-person grassroots approach." It introduced family planning as a child-spacing strategy, to improve the health of women and their newborns, and worked through traditional channels.

Women of childbearing age are secluded in traditional Islamic homes in much of the north of Nigeria, forbidden to go out in public during the day, even to market. Elderly women are permitted this freedom, however, and the custom has arisen that some elderly women serve as the "eyes" of isolated women by going into the market on their behalf. These women, called *Dillalai* (roughly translated as "itinerant traders"), assist secluded women with errands, collect money for a local savings scheme, arrange credit sales, and bring clothes, kitchen utensils,

foodstuffs, and other sundries—including herbs and med-
icines—into the homes of these women. The Dillalai are
respected and can move freely in and out of the homes of
secluded women.

Another esteemed group in northern Nigeria that has
ready access to the homes of confined women is the
Wanzamai. These are local barbers—men—who not only
cut hair and shave faces, but act as local surgeons, performing male circumcision, removing tonsils, and con-
ducting a traditional procedure that is believed to remove
toxins from the body.

It is forbidden for a secluded woman in northern Nigeria to go to a hospital to deliver a child. Births customarily take place at home, with the assistance of another
group of elderly women, the Ungunzumoni, or traditional birth attendants. These women, usually widowed
family members or friends, are respected in the community; in addition to delivering newborns, they are also
herbalists who treat new mothers and their infants.

GHON recognized that all three of these traditional
groups had the capacity, with training, to bring reproductive health care to secluded women. With CEDPA
support, it developed a training program, tailored to
each group, for one hundred Dillalai, Wanzamai, and Ungunzumoni. Covered were child spacing; maternal and
child health, including immunization; and STD and HIV/
AIDS prevention. GHON members hope to reach sixty-
five thousand women in five Kano neighborhoods.

One Wanzamai, Muhammadu Usman, says: "Before

our training, when government wants to carry out immunization on children, sometimes the women would refuse to bring their children out. But now, they hear the
message from members of the community. There was a recent immunization conducted here, [and] a lot of women
and their children came out."

GHON trainees cooperate directly with local chiefs
and rulers. Kaltume Danabdu, a traditional birth atten-
dant, says of her work, "If I need to refer a case, I go to
meet the village head and together with others, he will
assist in getting the person to a place for treatment." A
young village leader in Kano is quoted as saying: "My
people are very happy. The traditional birth attendants
come here to inform me about what is happening to my
people. Before, we did not have that type of information
about births."

CEDPA supports similar programs in partnership
with grassroots women's organizations, at varying levels
of development and funding, throughout all Nigeria's
geographic regions. GHON works in Kano State with
CEDPA on a project aimed at youth; another group in the
north works with patent-medicine vendors to refer clients for family planning; programs in southeastern Nigeria organize women's cooperatives, work on adolescent
reproductive health, and care for AIDS orphans.

These projects are exciting—women helping women
to earn more money, harnessing tradition to bring health
care and family planning to confined women, reaching
rural areas, focusing on youth, caring for AIDS orphans.

Furthermore, they take place in the kind of setting that causes most people concerned with population growth to throw up their hands in futile frustration—a high-fertility, diverse, underserved, impoverished country where women have very low status and suffer all the disadvantages of discrimination and poverty. It is energizing indeed to learn of so much activity in Nigeria. More than twelve times the number of women use family planning in Nigeria today as did when Bisi founded COWAN, though fertility as a whole is only slightly lower; fewer infants die before their first birthdays, and fewer women die of pregnancy-related causes. Much, much more work remains. But the progress has begun.

The Democracy and Governance Initiative

Perhaps the most thrilling aspect of CEDPA's programs in Nigeria is its work in the realm of civil society. In 1996 it became clear to CEDPA, both in the Washington office and in Nigeria, that it was time to mobilize the astonishing energy and increasing power of women's grassroots organizations to expand women's participation in the Nigerian political process—to build nothing short of democracy in a country long ruled by military dictatorship. "The moment is right," CEDPA wrote in a $1 million proposal to the Agency for International Development's new democracy and governance program, "to support Nigerian women's empowerment through political participation."

The project, carried out in partnership with a Johns

Hopkins University program in communication and in-
formal education, planned to strengthen the political
skills of women's organizations and women leaders by
teaching advocacy, communications, and conflict resolution. It would improve the transparency and accountability of women's NGOs. It would build broad local,
national, and international coalitions to strengthen wom-
en's democratic participation. It would support community programs that empowered local women to participate in politics. And it would tell others of the lessons
learned by Nigerian women's groups as they increasingly
took part in democratic government.

Women's participation in politics is important both
for democracy and for women. Excluding half a country's
people from *any* effort is unwise; excluding women from
building democracies in Africa—and elsewhere—contra-
dicts the very notion of democracy. And women's lack of
political participation ensures the continuation of the
same barriers that prevent their advancement. Governments dominated by men, whether African or European,
have for centuries in Africa failed to overcome traditional
legal and political structures that deny women land
ownership and access to credit, or to replace traditional
cultural ideas about women's limited roles in society
and the family. Perhaps with women on the job, change
can occur.

In 1996 Nigeria had seen only ten years of civilian rule
in its forty years as an independent country. The military
regime governing that year had taken power in 1992, after

annulling a national election. Following three years in office, dictator General Sani Abacha announced a three-year transition to a democratically elected government, which in fact has occurred. But in 1996 the world was still reeling from the Nigerian government's execution of environmental and human rights leaders from the southeast of the country (Ken Saro-Wiwa being the best known). In fact, the United States, along with several other countries, withdrew its ambassador to Nigeria in protest and prohibited the transfer of U.S. funds to any level of the Nigerian government.

Hopes were not high in 1996 that General Abacha would allow a national election or respect its outcome. "The present military government detests every dissenting view and opinion," states CEDPA's proposal to USAID. "Overt calls for political change present a very real risk to all involved." Nonetheless, CEDPA forged ahead with its plan to build women's empowerment networks, broaden its advocacy efforts, and teach women at the grassroots level about their rights—all outside the government and partisan politics. The result has been nothing short of spectacular.

In the first two years of CEDPA's democracy and governance initiative, fourteen Nigerian women's organizations, some of them national in scope, representing hundreds of thousands of members, were trained in advocacy, coalition building, lobbying, civic and voter education, and the human rights of women. These women then organized local rallies, events, and educational sessions—in markets, on radio and television, and in villages, using drama, print materials, posters, T-shirts, and just plain conversation. They talked about wife beating, the rights of widows, female genital cutting, inheritance, voter registration, how to withstand pressure to *sell* one's vote as a woman (a common practice, apparently, averaging about four dollars per vote); how to register with the political party of one's own choice, rather than of one's husband; political corruption; and local disputes. They visited local leaders and dignitaries. They networked and mobilized. They made up songs and taught them to local women, to bring home the message of political participation and human rights. Many groups endorsed the message with modest loans to enable poor women to build small businesses—and to create the conditions in which women could exercise the political rights about which they had learned.

The 100 Women Groups

A pillar of CEDPA's democracy and governance initiative in Nigeria is the 100 Women Groups. This brainchild of Dr. Entyantu Ifenne, resident adviser to the CEDPA-Nigeria field office, joins women into groups of roughly a hundred to carry out their political training and mobilization. It began with one hundred national women leaders who met in 1996. Today more than a million Nigerian women are part of 100 Women Groups all over Nigeria.

The 100 Women Groups, and other CEDPA participants, have been in touch with two and three times the
number of women they expected to reach with their messages and training, "stretching their budgets to train more
women than originally planned due to an overwhelming
response," according to a CEDPA report on the projects.

In the midst of all this activity, in May 1999 Nigeria
actually called national, state, and local democratic
elections. CEDPA's Nigerian partners—the women of
COWAN, NCWS, and others—registered over 2.5 million
voters and supported 125 female candidates for elective
office. More than a third of these women were elected.

Since 1999, the 100 Women Groups and their CEDPA
partners have participated in the difficult transition to
democracy in Nigeria, a process far from completion. In
addition to continuing their mobilization and education
efforts at the grass roots, they have participated in a
Women's summit at the national level to draft a national
policy on women and to advocate for inclusion of affirmative action in the Nigerian constitution.

In the most recent phase of the democracy and governance initiative, Nigerian women's groups have joined
their work to empower women politically with health
messages. Some 100 Women Groups have held rallies to
promote immunization of children, HIV/AIDS prevention, breast feeding, and child spacing. The proposal for
work after the year 2000 scales up the grassroots activity,
focusing on linking the local networks with national and

regional women's professional organizations. The plan is to develop legislation on women's rights, lobby elected officials, and get the legislation passed.

CEDPA has gathered stories of women's experience with the democracy initiative, stories told in their own words. Bilkisu Muhammed, of the Knitters Association, a member organization of the United Women's Association (UWA) in Kano, says of CEDPA's democracy training: "Many of us did not even know where to put our thumb prints when voting. So a lot of votes were lost this way. In the last election, UWA taught women how to correctly apply thumb prints on the right spot. So we now know how to vote properly."

Danejo Ibrahim, also of UWA, comments: "Now no one can buy my vote with money. We have been told this several times. Now we are telling others."

"Women are so bold now," says Mrs. V. A. Bedu, of Community Women and Development in the southwestern state of Osun. "Before, we used to be shy. Even illiterate women, in their 100 Women Groups, are determined to do something at the elections. What we are telling the women now is that even if the men give you [the Nigerian equivalent of four dollars], do not take it."

Chief Bisi says of the 100 Women Groups in her state: "We told our members 'Go to your own backyard and take one poor woman and give her [the equivalent of $6.50].' We have given out over [$25,000]. A woman who is now able to get that [$6.50] will start to trade; by the end of each year, each woman will have more than [$6.50]. This helps to take care of the poorest of the poor so that they will not, because of poverty, sell their votes to the men. We are hoping that through this base we will be able to get people to vote rightly in this country."

Men are included in CEDPA's democracy initiative. "We also invite the men [to training]," remarks Rosemary Ofem of the Northern Cross River State Women's Association. After the training, "they now have the zeal that their wives should be part of us. They feel the women are really doing something."

And 100 Women Groups work with local governments. Chief Bisi tells the story of one group that, in order to improve a road, obtained a load of sand. The women went to the local government and asked for cooperation. " 'We do not have so much money, but we have got sand,' " Bisi reports the women said. "The local government chairman got a contractor to spread the sand properly. Everything was finished in three days. This is part of what the 100 Women Group has achieved." Bisi continues, "To know your civic responsibility is to be the eyes and ears of government."

"I won't mind a woman president because I have seen men handle the affairs of the country, but I have not seen any positive change," says Mariam Sule, of the Grain Seller's Association, a member of the United Women's Association. "Maybe this time around, a woman can do it better."

"There is nothing that a man can do," says V. A. Bedu, "that a woman cannot do."

CEDPA has been at work in Nigeria for about twenty-five years. At the beginning, its work was limited to bringing a few Nigerians a year to Washington for management training. Then CEDPA began to support small projects run by Nigerian community-based organizations such as COWAN, at a few thousand dollars a project. In time, a several-hundred-thousand-dollar USAID grant over several years allowed CEDPA to build a network of family planning and health projects in Nigeria, all run by grass-roots women's organizations. Annual budgets for these groups reached $15,000 and $25,000 in the early 1990s. CEDPA's programs and trainee network became large enough so that in 1993 the organization opened a Nigerian office, staffed entirely by Nigerians, to coordinate its many activities there. Today CEDPA works with twenty-nine community-based organizations in twenty Nigerian states, and CEDPA invests roughly $2.5 million in Nigerian programs annually. For what it buys, it is a small amount of money.

Scarcely a single feature of Cairo's Programme for Action is not present in CEDPA-Nigeria's programs. They embody a great deal—indeed, nearly all—of both the reproductive health agenda and the agenda for broadly conceived women's empowerment. This should perhaps not surprise, as CEDPA alumnae from all over the world constituted the largest single presence at the nongovernmental forum in Cairo, CEDPA alumnae served on many official government delegations, and Peggy Curlin was a member of the U.S. delegation. Rather than saying that CEDPA's programs follow the Cairo Programme of Action, it is perhaps more accurate to say that CEDPA's experience led it.

Nigeria is only one of CEDPA's programs. The organization supports scores of grassroots nongovernmental organizations in fifteen countries of Latin America, Africa, Asia, eastern Europe, and the newly independent states of the former Soviet Union. Though every country has a different story, COWAN has counterparts in Nepal, Bisi has counterparts in Guatemala, and every Nigerian quoted in this chapter has counterparts in the other countries where CEDPA works.

CEDPA is not alone in working to carry out the Cairo agenda. Large and small international NGOs such as the International Planned Parenthood Federation, the Pathfinder Fund, and CARE; universities in the United States and abroad; entities such as the U.N. Population Fund and various European government foreign assistance ministries; donors such as the Packard and Hewlett foundations and the Population Council; and some for-profit organizations such as the Female Health Company, manufacturer of the female condom in the United States, all labor to bring the Cairo agenda to fruition.

The Cairo agenda is revolutionary, and the work required to make it a reality is staggering. Almost certainly, no national government, no foundation, no business is doing enough—and the sum of all of our actions is not enough—yet. But the story of CEDPA-Nigeria teaches two very important lessons. First, we know what to do: build from the grass roots up, asking women what would improve their lives, and enable them to create it. And second, we know that much is going on, even in places as discouraging (on paper) as conservative, impoverished Nigeria, where women are as disadvantaged as anywhere else on Earth.

Peggy Curlin says that for every problem in a village, a solution exists—in that village. Let us hope so. CEDPA-Nigeria's story suggests that Curlin is right.

4

U.S. Population Activism in the New Century

In a book that is essentially about global population policy, the efforts of activists based in the United States nevertheless deserve attention. There are probably more self-described American population activists than those of any other nationality, with a movement more than three decades old and several large national organizations focused on population matters. We U.S. activists work to affect the fertility and growth rates of an important country: the United States has the third-largest population in the world and is the most rapidly growing industrialized country of any size. We lobby to affect an enormous resource, in the form of American foreign aid, vastly more capable of furthering our agenda than it has done in the past.

How well U.S. population activists do their job may determine a great deal about population issues, both domestic and international. How much is spent on international assistance related to population, including women's empowerment; whether women's empowerment and reproductive health settle into the central position they should occupy in thinking about population, both domestic and international; whether and how soon the U.S. population stabilizes; whether every child born in the wealthiest country in the world is wanted; whether we provide a creditable example to the rest of the world as we handle domestic population and resource issues—all these are critical matters for the United States. How American activists approach their work on population issues may in turn determine whether we succeed or fail.

We are guided in this task by our legacy of early writings by the "masters" in the field. The groundbreaking publications of the 1960s and 1970s first led the cry for population stabilization, globally and in the United States. They include Paul Ehrlich's powerful *Population Bomb*, which ignited the U.S. movement in 1968, the year that he and others founded the organization Zero Population Growth (ZPG); the many books and articles of Lester Brown, which cover population, food, and sustainability; and Garret Hardin's elegant 1968 essay, "The Tragedy of the Commons," which still frames essential dilemmas of population, resources, and public policy.

In the early years, these analysts and others in the movement shared an outlook and approach that has dominated the U.S. population movement for most of its history. When they first set to work, the world they faced was different from today's. Fertility and population growth were high everywhere. Even in wealthy countries like the United States, families had more than two children. In 1960, women in the United States had slightly higher fertility on average (3.4 children) than women in the developing world (including China) have today (3.2)! Society welcomed population growth. Laws still banned contraceptives in many places and abortion in most. The notions of scarcity and of "limits to growth" were alien to all but a few. The public had only just begun to recognize environmental problems and saw them largely as local problems, soluble simply by "cleaning up after ourselves."

In attempting to get population on the public agenda against these odds, the early analysts shaped their arguments in a particular way: they described population as the most important global environmental issue—indeed, crisis—faced by the world. The growing human population was likened to a ticking time bomb set to explode. Human populations on the earth were compared to bacteria in a petri dish, where excessive growth in numbers would outstrip food supply, causing starvation and population collapse. Most of the world's ills, from environmental destruction to poverty, hunger, and war, were traced to population growth. At the same time, analysts downplayed other causes, such as inequitable social and economic systems, disparities in resource consumption levels, and differences in technologies. They argued that if *we* don't solve the population problem, nature will do it for us—by killing us.

Much about these principles is true and useful, and we would be unwise to ignore the early insights of the masters. Rapid population growth *is* a crisis. In my view, the "bomb" has already exploded, though perhaps not exactly as the image suggests. Certainly the population problem is no smaller today than it was when the early writers published their work. Indeed, the world's population has nearly doubled since 1960, and environmental problems have mushroomed. Yet aspects of the early approach would serve the population movement better today if refined and supplemented. (And indeed, the masters' writings themselves have evolved. For example, in recent writings, both Ehrlich and Brown refer to the importance to population of gender equity and education for women and girls.)

In this chapter I outline some principles that I believe should be added to our traditions, to guide the population movement in the new century. These principles join social science to the biology that has traditionally dominated population issues and add political understanding to the focused commitment of the first generation. Refining our activism in this way increases our chances of broadening the movement beyond its current membership and raises our chances of success. It also matches our activism more closely to the inclusive, constructive, and complex vision of Cairo.

Principle 1:
Population Growth Is Not the Only Problem

It is true that if the world does not solve the population problem, it will have a much harder time accomplishing virtually every other desired goal: cleaning up and preserving the natural world, working toward peace, eradicating poverty, making the world more equitable. Indeed, continued population growth can totally prevent us from solving some problems. Many say justifiably that population is the world's biggest, most fundamental problem.

Still, solving the population problem is not enough. Were we to do only that, in some magic, isolated way—without improving our use of resources and preventing waste, without governing ourselves more wisely, and without changing unjust social and political systems—we would have a dirty, warring, unjust world with a stable population. The population problem is one of several equally critical, equally fundamental problems, no less important because other issues are equally so.

When we say that population growth is the only, or the biggest, problem, we sound to those we wish to convince—those not already on our side—as if we are insensitive to much that they care about, and that we care about too. We seem to believe that poverty is not a serious problem, when it lies at the heart of many environmental and social difficulties, including high fertility—and we *do* care about poverty. We seem not to believe that technologies can change the impact of human beings on the world, when they clearly do—and we believe it too. We appear to deny that small numbers of people consuming vast amounts of resources and producing huge quantities of waste is a major dimension of environmental degradation, when it is—and we agree. And we seem to believe that war and weapons do not, in addition to hurting people, harm the environment and hold back development, when they do—and we know it.

In other words, population activists who today insist on the sole primacy of the population issue have a serious public relations problem. Only it is not trivial or superficial, as the term "PR" suggests. A critical part of the bitter conflict in the United States over immigration policy in recent years is the perception by communities of color that the exclusive emphasis on numbers by the population movement means that we want to protect our wealth. Though a shock to liberals in the population movement, it is, in fact, part of the debate.

The first principle is that population is not the only problem. Other factors are equally important.

Principle 2: The Population Issue Is Complex

With their almost exclusive reliance on biological ways of thinking about how human beings interact with their world, the early writings were deterministic and oversimplified. The analyses suggested that human numbers *necessarily* and *always* produce adverse effects and that human life is summarized by its biological character. Human life *is* biological, but it is also social, political, technological, religious, and a lot else. Those dimensions affect a human being's impact on the world; they can make it better or worse.

Human beings affect the environment not simply because of their numbers. It is more accurate to think of many factors, all swimming together in a soup, like flavors. Sometimes one flavor masks another. Sometimes one flavor brings out another. Sometimes two flavors mix to create a lovely taste; sometimes they mix to taste like mud. The flavors in our soup are numbers of people, resource consumption patterns, technology, and social and political arrangements. Thoughts of this much complexity have less punch than the petri dish illustration of early writers. But the longer sentences are more appropriate for today.

Consumption patterns and technologies can worsen or mitigate environmental impact. A town of ten thousand people who drive sport utility vehicles to work harms the environment more than a town of ten thousand people who walk to their offices. A town of people each driving 350 miles a week harms the environment more than a town of individuals who drive that far in a month.

Social and political arrangements can also improve or worsen the effect of numbers of people, consumption patterns, and technology. Imagine a population of 50 million people that produces 50 tons of nuclear waste. If that population has an isolated totalitarian government and active terrorists, and is otherwise not very effective, the environmental and human impact of that 50 tons of nuclear waste is likely to be worse than if the same number of people had a true democracy, a responsive government, and active peace and environmental movements. Similarly, the consequences of crowding are worse in a society of aggressive people committed above all to maximizing their own welfare than in a society of civil residents who have worked out ways of discussing complex problems and dealing with them.

Thus, no single answer exists to the question so often posed by population activists: How many people constitute the right size population, or what is the Earth's optimum population? There are many answers, all dependent on details of the surrounding conditions. A smaller number may be too many if governments are oppressive, wealth is unevenly distributed, individuals are surly, and some people consume a lot more than if the opposite conditions prevail. And "too many" depends in part on what the people involved consider too many, not just on whether the resources are sufficient.

Lester Thurow summarized these complexities eloquently when he wrote: "If the world's population had the productivity of the Swiss, the consumption habits of the Chinese, the egalitarian instincts of the Swedes, and the social discipline of the Japanese, then the planet could support many times its current population without privation for anyone. On the other hand, if the world's population had the productivity of Chad, the consumption habits of the United States, the inegalitarian instincts of India, and the social discipline of Argentina, then the planet could not support anywhere near its current numbers."

Another aspect of population's complexity is relevant. The notion that the human population on Earth will grow beyond its resources—"overshoot" them—and experience dieback—or "collapse"—is a dominant piece of the population canon, still employed by activists today. It is indeed what happens in many predator-prey relationships in the wild, and when the bacteria in a petri dish grow beyond their food supply.

Speaking of human populations in this way is rather more a conclusion about how the world seems than a data-based prediction. Those committed to the idea that "overshoot and collapse" describes what is most likely to happen to human populations should elaborate and strengthen their arguments. They could incorporate data on the health of ecosystems, the identification of thresholds of stability and instability, the development and spread of diseases, and the geographic scale and size of the populations involved. It is not enough to simply repeat the metaphor of "overshoot and collapse" as if it were a prediction; population activists who speak in this fashion are not believed, except by already committed activists.

Other metaphors, not rooted in biology alone, also illuminate the population problem in all its severity. For example, the tragedy of excess population growth may *not* be that it kills us, but that it does not—that as we adapt to slowly developing, ever grimmer conditions, we lose our memory of clean air, freedom of movement, privacy, and dignity. C. S. Lewis said, "The safest road to hell is the gradual one—the gentle slope, soft underfoot, without sudden turnings, without milestones, without signposts." He doubtless had something in mind other than environmental deterioration, but the point applies.

The second principle is that the population issue is complex and is not readily reduced to simple ideas.

Principle 3:
Adopt a Constructive, Rather than a Punitive, Attitude

The Cairo agenda argues that we should avoid any sort of condemnation as we address issues related to high fertility and rapid population growth. It urges us to look instead at the conditions that give rise to high fertility and change those, thereby providing women and men the opportunity to solve the population problem themselves, on their own terms. The lesson that we can move ahead more effectively by being constructive than by being punitive can be applied to other dimensions of the population problem and to places other than the Third World.

We can try hard to create the conditions that enable people to find a sufficient livelihood at home, so that they

are not pushed by enormous disparities in wages to migrate in large numbers to wealthy countries. This task is
admittedly *huge*—the ultimate job of global development,
in many ways—and not one that can yield a reduction in
U.S. immigration levels, for example, anytime soon. It is
also a more constructive approach to curbing unwanted
immigration into wealthy countries, almost certainly
more effective in the long term, and more likely to earn
more coalition partners, than erecting militarized borders
and fashioning punitive laws. Immigration laws with
ceilings and quotas will always have a place; they are a
fact of life among sovereign nations. But let us not imagine that they are the only or the most effective approach,
especially for the long term.

A related issue for population activists involves our
sense of urgency—and, often, of despair—about population growth and the future of the planet. We should not
turn this anxiety into hostility toward those we consider
keep us from population stabilization: people in our
country with above-average fertility or young single
mothers on welfare. We are more effective when we get
our numbers right, attribute causes correctly, and avoid
fashioning punitive remedies.

Fertility in the United States has averaged around two
children per woman for some years. Yet if every child
born in this country were wanted, fertility would be
lower. How much lower is not clear, but the difference
would be nontrivial. American women, from teenagers to
women in their forties, experience much more unwanted

fertility than one would expect in a country as wealthy as ours. The causes are complex, but poverty, powerlessness, and sexual violence—including sexual abuse of children—are among the most important. Studies find that between half and two thirds of girls who become pregnant as teenagers have been sexually abused at some time in their lives. For causes like these, blame is cruel, and withholding welfare is barbarous punishment. Making services available, raising the minimum wage, reducing domestic violence, protecting children from rape: these are appropriate responses.

The third principle is that creating conditions for change is better than blaming the persons involved.

Principle 4: Laws Have Limits

The U.S. population movement needs to be more sophisticated in its understanding of how public policy works and of the limits of public policy in realms as personal and complex as those connected with population growth.

Laws definitely have a place in the effort to bring about population stabilization. Our federal law that supplies family planning services for poor women is essential, though insufficiently funded. We assist family planning, women's empowerment, child health, and related programs overseas through legislation. Immigration laws, welfare laws, and funding for sex education are all legitimate devices for influencing population. States also address family planning funding and welfare. Localities can affect population issues through ordinances on land use and growth control. Though not by means of ordinances or laws, school districts have a strong hand in sex education and family planning services for adolescents. There is room for more legislation at all levels in the United States in the areas of domestic violence, child abuse, and poverty—all issues that affect fertility, and therefore population.

Population activists in the United States usually support legislation of this kind. But we also tend to have an overdeveloped sense of how much a technical solution can accomplish. Simply declaring in a law that population stabilization is a worthy goal for the country may feel satisfying to those who are desperate to stem population growth, who have watched the public landscape change radically in the United States through civil rights legislation and other laws. Still, we must have a realistic sense of what such a declaration can accomplish.

At the urging of the organization ZPG, in 1999 Congressmen Tom Sawyer of Ohio and Connie Morella of Maryland introduced a population policy bill. No action was taken on it before the end of the session, and new bills are customarily introduced with each new session. The old bill contains some stirring language characteristic of all the bills:

- Rapid population growth causes serious problems both in the United States and abroad.
- The people of the United States envision a world with a healthy environment, clean air and water,

uncluttered land, ample open space, natural beauty, wilderness, and abundant wildlife, in which the dignity of human life is enhanced.

- Delaying efforts to slow population growth will increase the difficulty and cost of achieving that goal.
- The United States should develop, promote, and implement, at the earliest possible time and by voluntary means consistent with human rights and individual conscience, the policies necessary to slow the population growth of the United States, and thereby promote the future well-being of the people of this nation and of the world.

It sounds wonderful! However, let us not imagine that the bill has a real chance of affecting U.S. population growth. It is entirely limited to a rhetorical declaration. Anything with real content—such as expanded reproductive health, opposition to domestic violence, antipoverty programs, or changes to immigration laws—would face even more political obstacles than the simple declaration. It is true that even rhetorical support at the highest levels of government can create awareness of population issues and might affect fertility rates slightly. But a campaign of presidential-level leadership—or by the First Lady—would be likely to do more than a one-time legislative declaration. To be effective, such declarations have to be the result of widespread public support, not the reverse.

ZPG is realistic about its work on population policy bills. It aims to create opportunities to educate individual legislators, and to use bills as an organizational tool for the members. ZPG knows well that simple declarations cannot overcome the economic forces that promote growth, the social and cultural forces that affect fertility, or the wage disparities that fuel immigration. It knows that in this field one must attack causes, not simply rely on declarations.

In addition to realism about the likely effects of population policy legislation, we must never forget where we are: this is the United States at the beginning of the twenty-first century. We have struggled for years not to lose domestic funding for family planning for poor women. In the 1990s Congress decided to close down the government rather than fund family planning services for poor women overseas. Abortion providers are murdered, and the availability of abortion services erodes yearly. Focusing on population policy legislation for other than education purposes risks making the population movement look irrelevant and ineffective.

The fourth principle is that laws have limits, and we should work for those that are effective.

Principle 5: Work Wisely on Immigration

To have a stable population in the United States, it is indeed necessary to bring annual immigration levels down from the million or so that they are today. This is a demographic fact. Today immigration constitutes close to 40 percent of the annual population increase in the United States. As time passes and the baby-boom generation ages out of the childbearing years, immigration will make up an even higher percentage of expected annual growth unless it abates significantly—although that may be a high percentage of a relatively small absolute increment.

Immigration policy has been an inflammatory issue in the population and environment debate in the United States, with a great deal of name-calling and extremely hard feelings. On one side are people who insist that immigration is the main cause of population growth in the United States, that population growth is destroying the country's environment, and that we must curb immigration if we are to save the environment. Arguing for this position, some people feel that they must find every reason why immigration—and, often, immigrants—can be considered undesirable. In the middle are people, some of them environmentalists, who say that population growth, while important, is a global phenomenon and that it does not really matter where it takes place. Whether people born in Mexico, for example, live in Mexico or in the United States, the argument goes, has no effect on global population numbers and need not enter the debate.

On the other side are those who say that wasteful resource use and social inequalities, not population growth—and certainly not impoverished immigrants—lie at the root of environmental problems. They add that people who wish to curb immigration are principally interested in protecting their own wealth and in preventing the ranks of people of color from growing in the United States.

These are not grounds for forward movement, and indeed make for anguish and conflict. Yet we can advance the immigration debate with grace, though slowly, if we bring a certain wisdom to the issue, correct our past mistakes, and work with those who have disagreed with us on substantive issues that we have in common.

Those who have argued for restricting immigration on the grounds that it is the chief cause of U.S. population growth and, by implication, of U.S. environmental degradation, should speak of fertility as often as of immigration, and of resource use as often as of population growth. Otherwise a cascade of false impressions is set in motion. We appear to single out immigration as the main cause of population increase, when natural increase currently contributes more growth. We look as if we wish to protect U.S. fertility levels, when many people of all ages and incomes in the United States want fewer children than they currently have. We appear to focus exclusively on population growth, when wasteful resource use contributes enormously to environmental degradation.

Those in the movement who argue that migration between countries is irrelevant to total global population numbers and hence has no significance for the population debate are leaving out half the issues. If population growth counts, it counts both globally *and* where it happens. In addition to having global effects such as increased carbon dioxide emission, population growth occurs in particular places, affecting particular resources. To argue that population is *only* global omits these local impacts. They matter—and so, then, does migration between countries.

If the environmental movement, the population movement, and the movement for social justice were to join to reduce wasteful resource use and economic inequality, all three movements would progress. Modifying immigrants' rights so that tighter immigration levels do not translate into more discrimination against people of color is critical. Access to reproductive health care, women's empowerment, and community development in all communities, including those made up of immigrants, is also crucial. Even as such work strikes a major blow for improving people's lives and achieving a stable population, it fosters cooperation. In addition, it would build bridges on which the movements may eventually be able to walk, together, to a fair and enduring immigration policy.

Readers uneasy with the immigration issue may feel relieved at this recommendation; readers devoted to curbing immigration are doubtless unhappy. The approach I advocate has been born not of my discomfort with immigration issues but of hard experience over fifteen years of population activism at the national scale and the cold calculation that it is simply impossible, in the current political climate, to be heard accurately if one advocates limiting immigration into the United States. Indeed, one is heard as a demon by all but those who already agree with immigration reduction. This is a political reality, making it impossible to move forward meaningfully on legislative reduction of U.S. immigration levels.

Given this hard, cold fact, I argue for a long-term approach that seeks first to change the climate in which immigration policy is debated and only later—in a future I hope is closer to five years away than ten or fifteen—to reduce annual immigration levels. No debate can occur unless the two sides—those who wish to stabilize the U.S. population sooner rather than later, and those who defend the rights of communities of color, especially Hispanic communities—know each other. If that happens—and acting together on shared issues can accomplish it, I believe—then and only then can we move forward on immigration policy.

The fifth principle is to bring wisdom and patience to the immigration issue.

Principle 6: There Are Many Roads to Mecca

We will be more effective as a movement if we give up the idea that if everyone knew what we know, they would feel as we do about population. It is tempting to believe that if everyone simply understood the nature of exponential growth, the extent of unwanted pregnancies, the laws of ecosystems, or whatever collection of facts and principles settled things for each of us, they would join us and work for the cause. But there are many, many different ways of thinking about the world, to which we must be open. One individual perhaps might find the religious notion of stewardship most moving. Someone else might be convinced most readily by the concept that corporations benefit from population growth while "the little people" do not.

It is vital to remember the many ways of *resisting* beliefs, all operating through political interests, values, and culture. A successful political movement of any kind never underestimates their importance, whether it is an African woman's belief that without children she is nothing, or an American's belief that he is entitled to all the material goods he can buy. Sometimes rational argument is not the most appropriate response. Sometimes political action is.

It is also important to remember that some people are never going to agree with us. Some will forever see an upward-moving population growth curve as increasing profits, as progress, and as the way the world is supposed to be.

A few years ago I participated in an effort in Boulder, Colorado, to develop "principles of sustainability" as part of a "healthy communities initiative." We had, like many communities, held large meetings with an array of "stakeholders," all of whom "envisioned" the kind of Boulder they wanted to see in the future. At the end, the sense emerged that the group thoroughly understood "healthy," but not "sustainable." So a small group began outlining the basic principles that a community, a business, a public group, or an individual would have to follow to generate "sustainable" activities. We covered the environment, the economy, and social equity and diversity. In the course of our discussion late one summer afternoon, someone proposed that sustainability requires that everyone understand and believe in certain basic ideas: regard for the environment and all creatures, intergenerational equity, and respect for other cultures, for example. Something felt wrong about that, sensible as it sounded at first. Eventually I realized what was wrong. We have to create a sustainable society even though people do *not* believe in it. We have to win without them on our side.

If we remember this, perhaps we can avoid framing our strategies for success like this: we could win "if only everyone understood ecology . . . or believed in the value of other species . . . or gave up the paradigm of domination . . . or gave up greed." Even though these statements are true, they are largely irrelevant in the short term. We need to succeed without perfection.

The seventh principle is that there are many roads to Mecca.

Population stabilization, whether in the United States or in the world as a whole, is too important to fail for bias, overzealousness, incomplete understanding, or ignorance of its vulnerabilities as a political movement. The enormous challenge of bringing human populations into sustainable harmony with the earth requires the most informed and powerful strategies and the broadest, most effective political coalitions. A population movement that follows the principles outlined in this chapter has a greater chance of success than one based solely on the early works of the masters in the field. The movement in the new century would be constructive; it would open itself to a larger membership and to broader political coalitions; and it would present a vision of population issues and their place in the economic, political, and environmental world whose complexity matched reality. We stand on the shoulders of the masters in the population field, and we see farther than they did two and three decades ago. Real success with regard to population in the world today requires this longer, larger vision.

5

A Warming World

In 1988 I attended an international conference in Toronto arranged by the Canadian government, a conference designed to discuss the problem of human-induced climate change. During one plenary session, a participant stood up and introduced himself as the ambassador to the United Nations from the Republic of Maldives. Then he sat down. There was puzzlement among the delegates in the silence that followed, and one could sense wheels beginning to turn in many heads: "Where on Earth is Maldives? Oh yes, it's that group of islands in the Indian Ocean. That large group of small, low islands. Low islands! Oh my goodness! With sea-level rise, he could lose his whole country!"

This momentary drama may have moved the delegates to adopt a goal—countries to reduce their emission of greenhouse gases by 20 percent below their 1988 amounts by 2005—but it also epitomized certain features of the climate issue. Most directly, it signaled that fairness would be a factor in international discussions about how to deal with the threat of climate change, and that debates about the details of climate science were now joined by other equally important topics. It also reminded us that the most global result of a climate warming would be a rise in sea level, affecting the billions of people who live in low-lying coastal areas.

Global Warming

Earth's average climate has warmed strikingly since 1860. Climate experts have deduced the warming from records of temperature measured at meteorological stations around the world and by observations made from ships at sea. Assembling these scattered records has been a grueling task. Global temperature trends emerge only after the raw data are corrected for missing days, for times when a particular thermometer was replaced with a new one, and after studies have determined the difference between temperatures measured in cities and those in rural areas. The experts must then average the corrected numbers to derive a global temperature trend. Different scientists have quoted slightly different numbers for the global average temperature during this 140-year period, but all of the studies show a rapid warming trend beginning about 1910, leveling off about 1940 for the next three decades, then climbing steeply to the end of the century. A simple graph shows this warming clearly. Figure 5.1 demonstrates the variation of global average temperature from a fixed baseline for each year.

Attempts in the 1950s to arrive at a history of global average temperature used data assembled painstakingly from many places around the world, with time lags of up to a decade in data gathering and analysis. In recent years, more rapid communication and a better system of meteorological data exchange make assembling the history much easier. Climate study groups collect data rapidly and process the temperature information more quickly—usually a few weeks after the end of each month.

This rapid data dissemination serves the heightened interest today in whether the global temperature has continued its rapid rise. A record warm year, or even a record month, can find a place in the morning newspaper, and the 1990s rewarded us with frequent records. In one ranking, 1998 was the warmest year recorded by the global network of thermometers, 1997 was second, followed by 1995, 1990, and 1999. The 1990s stand as the warmest decade on record.

The high temperatures observed at weather stations near the end of the twentieth century are supported by a

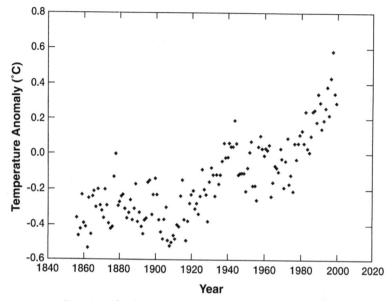

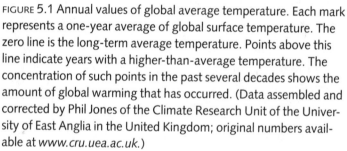

FIGURE 5.1 Annual values of global average temperature. Each mark represents a one-year average of global surface temperature. The zero line is the long-term average temperature. Points above this line indicate years with a higher-than-average temperature. The concentration of such points in the past several decades shows the amount of global warming that has occurred. (Data assembled and corrected by Phil Jones of the Climate Research Unit of the University of East Anglia in the United Kingdom; original numbers available at *www.cru.uea.ac.uk.*)

number of other observations. Bore holes (dry oil wells and other drilled holes) provide access to soil and rock temperatures at various depths. High or low temperatures at the surface are slowly conducted downward away from the surface, so temperatures measured deeper indicate earlier surface conditions. These measurements show warming over the past hundred years. Mountain glaciers in many locations around the world are melting and retreating up their valleys, again indicating warming, as does the loss of a considerable portion of the famous snows of Kilimanjaro. Observations of sea ice in the region around the North Pole show that the ice has thinned rather dramatically in recent years, and the area of sea ice that endures through one or more summers has decreased over the same period. Sea level has risen in the past century, a change that is consistent with the expansion of sea water as it has warmed and as the oceans have received the runoff from melting glaciers. These observations add significant confirmation that Earth's surface has indeed warmed in the past 140 years.

Temperature changes over much longer periods also validate the temperature record. Scientists have developed a number of techniques for using "proxy" data—factors that depend on temperature and can be used to derive temperatures over time. For example, analysts in Great Britain have summarized historical records—the dates that rivers froze and thawed, the dates of the wine-grape harvests, accounts of crop failures due to late cold spells—to reveal European climate conditions several centuries back. Exotic features of polar ice related to the temperature at which the snow contributing to the ice formed also reveal temperatures, with the ice's layering providing estimates of the dates on which the snow fell. The width and density of dated tree rings provide information about growing-season temperatures. Pollen grains found buried in peat bogs and mud at the bottom of

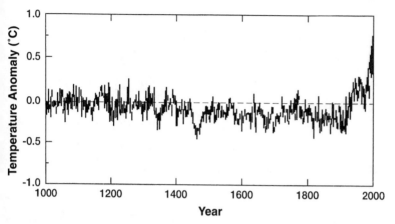

FIGURE 5.2 Northern Hemisphere surface temperatures during the last millennium, deduced from proxy data. The dashed line shows average temperature 1902–1980. The vertical lines represent the proxy data until approximately 1900; later data points represent the thermometer measurements used in Figure 5.1. (Redrawn from M. E. Mann, R. S. Bradley, and M. K. Hughes, "Northern Hemisphere Temperatures during the Past Millennium," *Geophysics Research Letters* 26:759–762 [1999].)

lakes indicate what vegetation grew nearby, and hence what climate regime existed there.

Such analyses indicate that 1998 was the warmest year not only of the twentieth century but also of the entire millennium. Figure 5.2 shows the average surface temperature of the Northern Hemisphere as reconstructed from the proxy evidence available. The first half is slightly warmer than the millennium average. A slight cooling is discernible during the second half, a change that may represent the Little Ice Age, during which much of Europe had noticeably cooler temperatures than the usual. But the large, rapid warming at the end of the graph is unprecedented in the thousand-year record.

The majority of climate scientists today believe that this millennium-end warming, of which the 140-year temperature rise is a part, is partially if not entirely caused by changes in the composition of the atmosphere produced by human activities. Careful measurements document these changes, particularly the increase of heat-trapping gases. Such increases, accompanied by the rise in the global average surface temperature, strongly suggest that human activities are warming the climate.

Global average temperature is just that: an average of many measurements made over large portions of Earth. On land these measurements are made with thermometers mounted in standard shelters that allow air to move freely around the instruments but shield them from sunlight. At sea, some ships measure the water temperature quite near the surface, which is close to the temperature of the air just above the surface. Although the global average is frequently referred to as surface temperature, purists describe it as "near surface." More important is the fact that global average temperature, in a certain sense, does not exist; it is a derived number that resides only in the minds of climate scientists and does not appear on any thermometer. That global average is useful to scientists as an index of trends that tell us if the energy being absorbed by Earth is in balance with the infrared radiation escaping to space. But the interaction between people, plants, and the atmosphere takes place on a local scale, and local temperatures may vary widely from the global average.

As an example, look again at Figure 5.1. During the 1980s every year, globally, was warmer than any year between 1860 and 1940, and no year in the 1980s was cooler than the coolest year in any preceding decade. Yet in those warm 1980s, five serious freezes hit the citrus-growing area of Florida. Orange trees there were so damaged that much of the frozen orange juice industry relocated either to more southern parts of the state or to Brazil.

The use of a single number—an index—to represent a large set of numbers or a series of events is fraught with difficulties. Some are philosophical. A famous and colorful economist, Kenneth Boulding, who popularized such terms as "spaceship earth" and "cowboy economy," wrote in 1970 about the problems that occur when we create an index. An index tends to become an ideal. "We are all Pythagoreans," Boulding said. "Once we get a number, we sit down and worship it."

His particular target was not global average temperature, but Gross National Product (GNP)—an index, he said, that indeed was "gross." He pointed out that GNP is useful in managing some overall features of an economy, but we have begun to regard it also as an indicator of human welfare, even though the data used to calculate it include the cost of items that detract from human welfare as well as those that benefit it. GNP is driven up by increases in imprisonment, hospitalization, and toxic waste remediation, as well as by better schools, fewer people living in poverty, and more universal access to preventive medical care.

I will return to the grossness of GNP when I discuss estimates of the cost of taking action to stem human-induced climate change. All the same, we do worship GNP. In some recent years, the business page of the morning newspaper frequently was able to report with pleasure that our GNP had grown at a faster rate than in the previous year, or faster than predicted. Yet such stories almost never included comment on, or even evince knowledge of, whether the growth came from increases in good things or bad. Thirty years after Boulding's warning, and more than seventy years after a similar warning by the economist who developed GNP, other measures have been devised in order to more closely represent human welfare—but none comes close in status to GNP.

Boulding was also ahead of his time on the climate-change problem. He speculated that the first natural resource we will run out of is not food or oil or copper, but places to put the waste products of our industrial society. We are seeing his expectation come true in the major increase of our index: global average temperature.

The Greenhouse Effect

When sunlight arrives at the top of the atmosphere, some is reflected back to space from the tops of clouds and small particles in the air, while some penetrates to the surface and is reflected by snow cover, sea ice, and other light-colored areas. The atmosphere and surface of Earth absorb the rest. With warming, this energy attempts to leave Earth in the form of infrared radiation or heat. But heat-trapping gases in the air absorb much of it, radiate some back to the surface, and thereby produce additional warming of Earth's surface. Water vapor plays a significant role in the natural trapping of heat, with carbon dioxide, methane, and nitrous oxide playing smaller roles. The recycling of energy produces an average temperature of Earth's surface higher by 33 degrees Celsius than it would be if none of the gases absorbed infrared radiation. This is a natural effect of our atmosphere—the "greenhouse effect"—and a benefit that allows life to exist as it does. Indeed, were it not for this natural warming effect, Earth would be mostly frozen and creatures such as human beings would not likely have evolved.

Since the natural, preindustrial concentrations of heat-trapping gases warm Earth substantially, it is logical to assume that adding more of such gases will heat the surface even more. Indeed, increasing the concentration of heat-trapping gases, thereby upsetting the balance of energy-in with energy-out, is the essence of the idea that human activities are pushing Earth to a warmer climate.

The History of Climate-Change Calculations
Determining how much warmer the climate will be, and what other changes will follow, requires a complex mathematical calculation based on deep understanding

of how the climate works. The history of progress in achieving this understanding reaches back at least to Jean-Baptiste Fourier, a French scientist and mathematician of wide interests: he traveled to Egypt with Napoleon and became an expert Egyptologist; later, back in France, he skillfully administered a *département* for twelve years. Fourier learned in the early 1800s that the atmosphere could absorb energy in the form of infrared light, and he postulated that this fact might keep Earth warmer than it would otherwise be.

He compared this phenomenon to placing a piece of glass over the top of a bucket in sunlight, thereby warming the contents of the bucket. Very likely this comparison gave us the term "greenhouse effect." It is a convenient name, widely used to describe both the process and the heat-absorbing substances (as in "greenhouse gases"). We now know that actual greenhouses (and glass-covered buckets) do not work primarily because of the greenhouse effect, but instead by preventing warm air from escaping and being replaced by colder air from outside. Nonetheless, the result is the same, and a warming climate is widely known as the greenhouse effect.

A few decades after Fourier's insight, the Swiss scientist Louis Agassiz, an expert on tropical fishes, rather accidentally took a large step in the progress of climate science. His work was not intended to be relevant to a human-induced climate change, and it is rarely mentioned in that connection. Nonetheless, he made a major contribution and deserves much credit.

While vacationing in the Swiss Alps in the 1840s, Agassiz examined boulders found far from other rocks of the same kind, and grooves in rocks in valleys and elsewhere. From these observations he developed a stunning hypothesis: not only had glaciers once reached farther down valleys, a fact already known, but ice had covered much of Europe. The slowly moving ice had displaced boulders and gouged rocks at many locations. The scratches and displaced boulders had, until then, been explained by some as the work of the biblical flood experienced by Noah. Thus, Agassiz faced not only the usual doubts about any new scientific hypothesis, but also religious objections. It took twenty years of arguments and examination of rocks and scratches in other countries for most of the geophysics community to concede that Agassiz was right and for others to join in the study. The objections of the "religious right" of his day faded as numerous calculations showed that a flood could not account for the observed evidence. Later studies showed that Agassiz's "ice age" was not unique, but was one of a sequence. His work thus revealed that large climate changes are possible but, more relevant to this discussion, it also introduced an interesting scientific question: What caused this repeated sequence of several thousand years of warm weather followed by a longer period of cold weather and a mile or more of ice covering large areas of midlatitude continents?

Agassiz did not follow up on this question but, after a time, others did. Nearly sixty years after Agassiz's ice age discovery, Svante Arrhenius, a Swedish chemist, thought that perhaps some process removed part of the carbon dioxide (an atmospheric gas that readily absorbs infrared radiation), allowing extra heat to escape and leading to cooler times and continent-wide glaciers. The calculations he devised to test this notion indicated that an appreciable cooling would indeed result if the air had only half the normal carbon dioxide concentration.

Without evidence, he was reluctant to speculate on any way that nature could remove half the carbon dioxide from the atmosphere. Sitting in his office, however, looking out at chimneys belching smoke from factories, he could suggest a way in which atmospheric carbon dioxide would *increase*. Burning coal releases carbon dioxide, and the coal-based industrial revolution was in full swing. By 1896 Arrhenius had reversed his calculations and found that if the amount of carbon dioxide in the atmosphere were doubled, Earth would warm by roughly the same amount as it would cool with the reduced carbon dioxide. Coal burning *was* increasing carbon dioxide concentrations in the air. He guessed that it would take centuries to double the concentration. As he lived in Sweden at a cold northern latitude, he was not averse to warmer winters and did not present his conclusions as worrisome. That idea came decades later.

The Greenhouse Gases

Arrhenius dealt only with carbon dioxide, the gas principally responsible for the current warming of the air.

But CO_2 is helped by a number of other gases that trap heat trying to escape to space. Some of these grow in concentration sufficient to add appreciably to the effect of carbon dioxide. At the same time, a few other substances arising from human activities either increase or decrease the effect of carbon dioxide and the calculated rate of warming.

In order of overall importance, the heat-trapping gases that tend to warm the climate are carbon dioxide, methane, chlorofluorocarbons (CFCs) and related chemicals, nitrous oxide, and ozone. Water vapor is a powerful heat-trapping gas, and more of it occurs in the air than the gases listed above. But it is nature, not human activities, that controls the amount of water vapor in the air. Too much of it causes rain or snow and brings the atmospheric concentration back down. Dry air encourages evaporation from the oceans and elsewhere and raises the water vapor concentration.

Use of fossil fuels contributes most of the heat-trapping gases controlled by people. In the years from 1987 to 1996, human fossil-fuel use annually emitted roughly 22 billion metric tons of CO_2 to the air. As a source of extra carbon dioxide in the air, fossil fuel is joined by changes in land use. A mature forest contains much carbon in the wood of the trees; should that forest be cut and burned to convert the land from trees to agricultural crops, the carbon would be converted to CO_2 and released with the smoke from the fire. Conversely, when trees are planted on grassland or former crop fields, they absorb carbon from the air and store it in the wood during the years the new forest is growing. In 1991 emission from such change in land use was estimated to be roughly 4 to 6 billion metric tons of CO_2.

The oceans annually absorb some of the atmosphere's extra carbon dioxide; enhanced plant growth, caused by the extra carbon dioxide, takes up more. As a result, the amount of carbon dioxide in the atmosphere increases by only about 12 billion metric tons each year, enough to make the current concentration of CO_2 higher than at any time in the past 420,000 years—and possibly the past 20 million years.

Methane emissions also arise from fossil-fuel use. Of the 360 million metric tons a year of methane emitted as a result of human activities during the 1980s, about 100 million metric tons came from fossil-fuel sources. Methane can leak from natural gas pipelines and wells, and some escapes from coal mines. Trapped within the coal deposit, methane has presented a threat of explosion and foul air in underground mines for as long as people have dug coal. Additional methane is released from biological sources. Like CO_2, the current methane concentration has not been exceeded in the past 420,000 years.

Halocarbons are synthetic compounds of carbon with chlorine, fluorine, or bromine atoms attached. The best-known are the chlorofluorocarbons, which came to public notice when scientists determined that they help destroy the protective layer of ozone in the stratosphere. None of the halocarbons have concentrations greater than one part per billion of air; indeed, CFC concentrations are measured in parts per trillion. But a molecule of some halocarbons is twenty thousand times as effective as a carbon dioxide molecule in trapping heat, and some will remain in the atmosphere for thousands of years. Thus they can contribute to warming even in small concentrations.

After the discovery that CFCs destroy stratospheric ozone, international agreements, beginning with the Montreal Protocol, scheduled the phase-out of almost all manufacturing and use of these chemicals. As a result, the concentrations of CFCs and some other halocarbons are beginning to stabilize or decrease.

Smaller contributions to greenhouse warming are made by nitrous oxide, which is emitted by biological activity in soils encouraged by nitrogen fertilizer use, and is produced in some industrial processes. Ozone both near the ground, where it is a pollutant harmful to human health, certain trees, and agricultural crops, and high in the atmosphere—but below the stratosphere, that is, in the upper troposphere—is a greenhouse gas. Ozone is created by a chemical interaction powered by sunlight, between methane or volatile organic carbons such as evaporated gasoline, the starter fluid used for backyard barbecues, and gases given off by trees, with oxides of nitrogen emitted by cars, power plants, and jet engines.

Both methane and CFCs have indirect effects that add

to or subtract from climate warming. Methane reacts to produce more water in the stratosphere, increasing total heat trapping; CFCs destroy some stratospheric ozone, allowing more heat to escape from Earth and thus slowing climate warming.

Two other substances, released by human activity, also tend to change the rate of climate warming. Coal and oil usually contain small amounts of sulfur which, when the fuel is burned, produce sulfur dioxide. This gas reacts in the air to yield small droplets of sulfuric acid and small particles of various salts such as ammonium sulfate. These particles remain in the air for a week or two before falling to the surface or being washed out by rain—as acid rain. While in the air, they reflect sunlight back to space, slowing the accumulation of heat near the surface. Coming from fossil fuels, atmospheric sulfur particles have increased over the past century even as carbon dioxide emissions have. Soot, released from a variety of fires, is black and readily absorbs sunlight, warming the particles and the air around them.

Modern Climate Modeling

The paper Arrhenius published in 1896 on the potential effects of extra greenhouse gas concentrations on the global temperature increase led over the next century to an enterprise that continues vigorously today. Dozens of groups around the world make ever more complex calculations, carried out with the help of some of the world's largest computers, to try to foresee how Earth will change as we continue to burn coal and otherwise modify the composition of the air.

Modern calculations start with a simulation of the global climate in mathematical terms. Facts such as Earth's diameter and its rate of rotation; the physical and geographic characteristics of the air, water, and land surfaces; and the intensity of sunlight are combined, using well-established principles of physics and chemistry, to calculate a possible Earth climate. If the "computer climate" so produced strongly resembles the one Earth actually enjoys, this calculation (or model) could be useful in investigating features of the real climate.

Arrhenius did not have an electronic computer; his calculations were limited to describing the transfer of radiation up and down through the air at one (perhaps typical) spot on Earth. Today not only is radiation transferred up and down in the models, but winds move heat and moisture, clouds reflect sunlight and influence outgoing radiation, and all these factors are calculated at several thousand different locations on the planet, at ten or more levels in the air above each location; even more levels are required to simulate the oceans.

Despite the vast complexity of a modern model of climate, simulations are only approximations of the incomprehensibly complex actual climate. The limitations of even the most powerful computers do not yet allow accurate description of crucial details of the surface, such as hills and valleys, trees and grassland, temporary coverings of snow, crops and fallow land, wet and dry soil, cities, and lakes. Moveover, climate models must simultaneously model the ocean as fully as the atmosphere is simulated, because the interaction of the atmosphere and oceans is strong indeed. Winds drive ocean currents, which affect the temperature of the surface. That temperature in turn strongly influences the temperature of the air just above it, as well as the evaporation of water vapor into the air.

Nevertheless, climate modeling is a valuable research tool. A scientist in the laboratory making measurements to confirm a hypothesis about how certain nuclear particles should behave in a changing magnetic field may find the hypothesis not confirmed. The scientist must then devise a new hypothesis and devise new measurements to test it. A climate model, by contrast, is a versatile hypothesis that can be modified in many ways without the need to start again.

Every set of observations of today's atmosphere, or deductions about past climates, suggests ways in which the model can be modified to mimic more closely the actual working of Earth's climate. And every test that shows the model is correctly simulating important processes in the climate, such as the generation of jet streams or the nature and amount of clouds over the warm ocean of the western equatorial Pacific, allows the modelers to claim more credibility for the model's usefulness as a research tool. There is no way to guarantee that model builders have included every significant process, so no amount of process-by-process testing will *prove* that the model is realistic in projecting future climates. Only evaluation of the model's output when asked to "predict" the amount of some past climate change for which we have sufficient observations can adequately raise our confidence. The crucial test of a model is how accurately it represents the well-established climate change observed from 1860 to 2000. The results of this sort of test are featured in several international reviews of climate science since 1990.

International Scientific Reviews

In the 1980s, models achieved a high degree of sophistication, but they rather consistently showed a warming during the twentieth century about twice as large as that which the data experts deduced from the available temperature records. In 1990 the Intergovernmental Panel on Climate Change (IPCC), an international scientific group established by agencies of the United Nations, examined the data showing a rapid temperature rise, the progress in construction of climate models (including their overestimation of the twentieth-century warming), and their use in estimating future change. The report issued by IPCC concluded that there was at least a possibility that human-caused emissions of gases that trap heat could warm the global climate to an extent that would be harmful. The adverse effects included damage to ecosystems influencing species diversity, loss of soil moisture during the growing season, damage to forests and agriculture, and a rise in sea level as warmer weather expanded sea water and melted glaciers.

IPCC conducted a second assessment of climate-change science in 1995. By that time the newly identified cooling influence of sulfates, along with ozone depletion in the atmosphere, had improved the realism of model calculations. Also, in 1991 a large eruption of the Pinatubo volcano in the Philippines allowed a direct test of the models. We know that sulfate particles shot into the atmosphere by major volcanic eruptions reach the stratosphere and remain in place for a year or two, rather than the week or two such particles stay in the lower atmosphere. The measured concentration of the stratospheric particles after Pinatubo could therefore be used to predict a cooling followed by a recovery a year or two later. One research group produced and published a prompt prediction of the magnitude of the global cooling that would occur and the schedule on which the temperature would return to its pre-eruption value. The reasonably close agreement of this forecast with what actually happened added one more step to the climb of model calculations toward respectability.

In 1995 IPCC best estimates of change, assuming a business-as-usual continuation of emissions, were a warming by the year 2100 in the range of 1 to 3.5 degrees Celsius, with a best guess of 2 degrees. Similarly, IPCC foresaw a 50-centimeter sea-level rise above the current level, reduction of the day-night temperature difference, greater warming of the land surface than the sea surface in winter, a maximum warming of high northern latitudes in winter, and an enhanced global mean hydrological cycle. In its overall summary, the 1995 IPCC report concluded that even though the committee recognized that uncertainties remained in key factors of the calculations, it felt that "the balance of evidence suggests that there is a discernible human influence on global warming."

This conclusion, which went further than any previous statement, balanced the committee's appreciation of the rapid scientific progress during the previous five years with its awareness of the work still needed on uncertain features of the model—specifically on the simulations of clouds and sea ice, and the role of water vapor.

With continuing improvements in climate modeling and observations, IPCC remains active and a Third Assessment Report (TAR) was released in 2001. In addition to the main greenhouse gases, the new review considered additional climate-forcing factors such as modest changes in the intensity of sunlight and the cooling effect of small particles produced by human activity. The panel found that these improvements not only reinforced the agreement of the models with the average rate of observed warming, but also that model calculations now were following some of the finer details—the short-term ups and downs—of the observed warming of the past 140 years. The committee felt required by the evidence to state that, in its judgment, human activity was the primary cause of the observed warmer climate.

As committee members reviewed the emissions to be

expected in the new century, they realized that countries that have not yet taken steps to decrease their sulfur emissions might do so, to reduce both acid rain and the demonstrated health damages caused by sulfur dioxide and sulfate particles. With fewer sulfates in the atmosphere and a reduced cooling effect, the warming projected by 2100 became larger. The revised figures ranged from a minimum of 1.5 degrees Celsius to a very disturbing maximum of 5.8 degrees, barring prompt and energetic efforts to decrease CO_2 emissions.

Continuing Controversies

Several kinds of scientific argument urging caution in interpreting such results have received thoughtful attention. The climate system is much more complex than even the most elaborate model, so the chance that the model is missing some important factor cannot be entirely dismissed. Further, a few experienced atmospheric scientists, with long careers collecting, using, and interpreting atmospheric measurements of various kinds, assert that the world does not work in the way model calculations say it does. Modeling enthusiasts sometimes point out a detail of typical climate models that could give trouble, and some challenge the emission scenarios used in projections of future climate change.

The answer to such criticisms cannot come from knowing that everything in the model is correct; the complexity is too great to expect such perfection. Only comparisons with what happened in the actual climate, particularly for periods during which the climate was changing, can ensure that model credibility has risen to a level useful for public policy considerations. The reviews in TAR summarize an impressive list of model tests, and observations of climate changes already indicate, despite the continuing controversy, that the science of climate change has now reached a level such that the probability of a serious climate change is high enough to require serious attention by all responsible leaders.

Climate change is not unusual in its creation of scientific controversy. In the past, many new explanations of complex phenomena have resulted in vigorous scientific disagreement. Agassiz's ice age is one example. Later, continental drift as an explanation for the shape of continents and for "misplaced" fossils—the bones of warm-weather creatures found in Alaska, for example—was argued for decades. With time, some opponents retired and more convincing evidence was brought up from the floor of the Pacific Ocean. Even so, not everyone was convinced. The controversy over continental drift lingered until mainstream scientists found it nonproductive to respond to the few remaining critics.

The all-time champion controversy that continues despite mounds of evidence is the explanation given by Charles Darwin and Alfred Wallace for the origin of species. Evolution did not project fearful future consequences; it did not threaten entrenched economic interests, but it did challenge strongly held beliefs about the uniqueness of the human species and, in the process, confronted the creation myth of virtually every culture and religion.

This feature is shared with greenhouse climate warming. There are strongly held beliefs that help shape our interpretation of the science. To those discouraged by the haste and crowding of modern life, climate change seems to epitomize all that is wrong with the relationships of humans to their surroundings. Earth seems so large that many cannot imagine that it can be appreciably modified by the daily activities of ordinary people. To those in the fossil-fuel business, in some ways a romantic enterprise (think of wildcat drillers and the risky search for new oil fields, an activity that gets much credit for bringing our industrialization to its current high level of achievement), it must be incredible to hear themselves branded as polluters who are ruining the climate. To those charmed by the excitement of urban life and unimpressed by the natural world, it seems likely that any climatic problem will bring forth new technological solutions that do not require changes in their present activities. Our own judgment is that, despite the ongoing controversy, *now* is the time to take effective action to reduce our annual changes to the composition of the atmosphere. And we need to plan our adaptation to the changes to which we have already committed ourselves by previous emissions.

Climate-Change Impacts

The simplest, most direct impact of a climate warming is, of course, a higher temperature in most locations, while a few locations remain the same or cool. Early on, this fact led those hoping not to worry about climate change to comment that since people vacation in warm places (and retirees move from North Dakota to Arizona), a warmer climate must be advantageous. Such statements overlook two factors. The first is that, although humans are quintessentially adaptable, other features of the biosphere are more tightly tied to a particular climate regime. The range in which most bird and tree species prosper is determined by climate, for example. The second factor is that heat waves are the largest meteorological cause of death in the United States, mostly of poor people trapped in low-quality urban housing. The retirees in Arizona require air conditioning in their automobiles and housing to make their new homes successful. Studies of climate-change impacts require that we consider much more than the ways prosperous people can remain comfortable.

An average warming is not the only physical change that comes with climate change. Sea level rises, and is already some 10 to 20 centimeters higher than it was a hundred years ago. It is projected to rise 5 millimeters per year during the twenty-first century, a rise that threatens the lands of those living in the Nile Delta, low-lying Bangladesh, and many island nations. It also portends higher storm surges and saltwater intrusion.

Since the air can hold more water vapor in a warmer world, global rainfall and snow amounts will increase and the rain will frequently arrive in heavier storms than formerly. This change, too, has already started and has been documented in several regions. Glaciers are retreating and will continue to do so. Cloud cover has increased; day-night temperature differences have become smaller; winters will get shorter; there will be more drying in continental regions, with an increased risk of drought; and peak winds and precipitation in tropical cyclones will probably increase.

Many of the projected changes will have their first impact on features of the biosphere. Forest damage, in particular, has received much attention. There is evidence of forest response to long periods of slowly increasing temperatures 16,000 years before the present (BP) to 9,000 BP, when North America and other regions were emerging from the most recent glaciation. Pollen grains deposited in the bottom of lakes and elsewhere that have been retrieved, attributed to a particular time, and identified as to species show that, as the climate warmed, forests migrated northward to remain in a climatic region most favorable to their reproduction and growth. In comparison to the projected rate of temperature change for the twenty-first century, however, the global warming at the end of the ice age was quite slow. It is doubtful that today's forests can migrate at a sufficiently rapid rate to avoid major damage, especially since there are now many human-made obstructions to forest migration such as highways, cities, and cultivated fields.

A more rapid forest response to warmer winters will occur where forests include species such as Douglas fir that require a certain period of cold weather if the trees are to resume growth in the spring. This feature of tree physiology protects against renewed growth too early in the year, but with warmer winters it could result in slower growth, or no growth, the following summer. Other natural systems vulnerable to climate change include coral reef ecosystems, mangroves, remnant native grasslands, and species facing extinction.

Agriculture is the sector of our society that most readily comes to mind as sensitive to climate. Early frosts damage orchards; a dry spell decreases production; a wet spring delays planting; high temperatures at certain stages of plant development reduce production. Most agricultural experts believe that the most harmful long-term climate change would be one that increased the variability of weather. Other alterations such as a change in the average temperature or average rainfall might require planting a different crop on a different seasonal schedule, and adaptation would therefore be relatively straightforward. Many agriculturists expect the rapidly advancing science of genetic modification to offer opportunities to create crops that can prosper in altered climates. They admit, however, that to meet the needs of growing populations they will need more than the ability to sustain current food production, and that there are at present no clear paths for large production increases. The expansion of farming onto unmanaged forests and grasslands has already created problems with loss of species diversity; improved technology to get more productivity from each hectare is not in sight.

Ameliorating these troubles to some extent is the fact that carbon dioxide is food for plants. Studies in actual greenhouses show that plants, if they have adequate water and soil fertility, grow better in an atmosphere with increased carbon dioxide concentration. It is not yet feasible to predict how much this effect will increase production when it is applied to plants growing outdoors, plagued by a warmer climate and assaulted by ozone on their leaves. Open-field studies are under way to answer this question.

Climate-change impact studies, involving as they do the reactions of people, are necessarily less precise than global climate-change models. In addition, local-scale climate models that could be used in impact studies do not yet produce credible results. There are few detailed indications, only general expectations, of how the climate change will play out in specific localities. Furthermore, the impact of any climate change in a region depends on the region's vulnerability—how poor its people are, how otherwise stressed its ecosystems are, and whether its society is organized to adapt readily to change. Finally, assessing climate-change impacts requires that we imagine these dynamic and qualitative features of a place some decades in the future.

We have gained some insight into possible climate-change impacts on human activities by looking at the impacts produced by past climate changes. The Little Ice Age, a cooler period in parts of the Northern Hemisphere in the sixteenth through nineteenth centuries, forced changes in agricultural practices and crop selection in Europe and contributed to the demise of small Norse settlements in Greenland. These impacts were produced by a regional climate change associated with a global change of less than half a degree Celsius, suggesting that a change of this magnitude is worth careful attention. One degree sounds trivial to most people, even though a change of this magnitude would likely be severe in some regions. From this perspective, the IPCC projection of a possible warming of more than five degrees by 2100 takes on frightening proportions.

Not all climate-change impacts will be regarded as detrimental. Longer growing seasons in middle- and high-latitude areas, when combined with the fertilization effect of carbon dioxide on some crops, should produce higher yields and more efficient use of irrigation water. Increases in rainfall in some arid areas are also possible. Some people in cold climates, like Arrhenius, will see a warming as beneficial, especially since both model calculations and recent observations indicate that most of the warming will occur in winter and at night. The number of deaths of people from winter cold periods should decrease.

Adverse health effects of a climate warming could include expansion of the range of the insects that carry malaria or dengue, which has already extended into the southern United States. Prosperous countries with modern public health establishments should be able to prevent an increase in such diseases. Poor countries are not so fortunately situated (and even prosperous countries experience additional deaths during heat waves).

Furthermore, burning fossil fuels can, through the production of atmospheric sulfates and ozone, cause direct lung damage to athletes and young people (that is, those who breathe deeply) and exacerbate asthma attacks among those afflicted. Studies attribute twenty thousand or more extra deaths a year in the United States to fossil-fuel air pollution. Mining and drilling for fossil fuels produce land degradation; transporting them produces oil spills. Reducing a surge in these problems would be a welcome bonus of the steps taken in the name of slowing climate change.

The results shown in Figure 5.3—and earlier similar, but cruder, calculations of thirty years ago—present the essence of concern about a human-induced climate change. Even before details are studied and explained, the idea that we humans are now powerful enough to change the global climate, entirely by accident, is frightening. What else are we changing? Will we know in time to prevent the changes that are harmful? How will we prevent the harmful changes, even if we recognize them in time? It finally dawns on us that we are approaching the condition of being in charge of keeping the whole, previously natural, global system running smoothly—a monstrous task that we have thought little about and one that our political systems are ill equipped to handle. A decade ago I wrote, "For a people who are not yet able to describe fully the workings of a tree or the chemistry of an

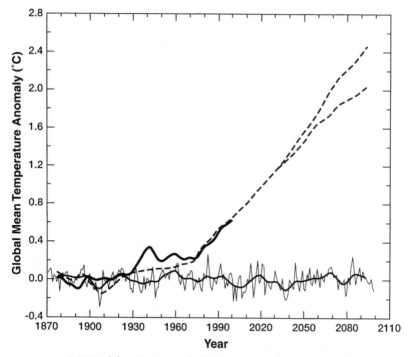

FIGURE 5.3 Model projections of global average temperature. The thin fluctuating line near 0° C shows the calculated annual average temperature in the control run of the model, a run in which no changes in greenhouse gas concentrations occur. The thicker dark line through the thin line is a running average of the control run temperatures. The heavy solid line with a peak near 1940 is a smoothed version of the measured surface temperature on Earth. The upper dashed line shows the calculated temperatures produced when the model is forced by the observed changes in greenhouse gas and sulfate concentrations from 1880 to 2000, and beyond 2000 by an increase in forcing that follows current emissions trends. The branch that bends lower results from the same forcing except that greenhouse gas emissions beyond 2000 are reduced to stabilize atmospheric concentrations after 2050 at 550 parts per million, approximately double the preindustrial concentrations. (Redrawn from Aiguo Dai, T. Wigley, B. Boville, J. Kiehl, and L. Buja, "Climates of the Twentieth and Twenty-First Centuries Simulated by the NCAR Climate System Model," *Journal of Climate* 14:485–519 [2001].)

ocean or to put available food into the hands of those who need it, it would be perilous to undertake the design and maintenance of a complete life-support system for everyone." Those words could well be truer today than they were then.

In conclusion, let me recount an event that occurred at a climate-change meeting held in New Delhi. Its impact was sharper but not unlike the nonspeech of the ambassador in Toronto a few years earlier. In the midst of a lively discussion about the impacts of climate change, a government official from Bangladesh walked to the front of the room and floated the following thought: "I assume," he said, "that your countries will be willing to accept the two million or so refugees who will have to leave my country as the sea level rises."

6

International Climate-Change Negotiations

The global nature of climate change calls for the widest possible cooperation by all countries and their participation in an effective and appropriate international response.

—Framework Convention on Climate Change, 1992

In 1954 the United States tested a thermonuclear bomb by exploding it in the atmosphere over the western Pacific Ocean. Heavy fallout moved in an unexpected direction and invaded an area open to fishing. When it contaminated a Japanese fishing boat ironically named *Fortunate Dragon,* crew members of that boat and others sickened; some died. The fish on boats in the area were contaminated, and all fish brought to Japanese harbors were viewed with suspicion. That event, combined with the knowledge that any atmospheric test of a nuclear weapon spreads radioactive materials around the world (some were showing up in the teeth of children), focused concern about health effects and triggered negotiations to ban atmospheric nuclear tests.

After nine years of talks and continued citizen interest, the nuclear test ban treaty of October 1963 ended both atmospheric and underwater testing by the United States, the United Kingdom, and the Soviet Union. France and China did not sign the treaty, but the amount of global fallout from weapons tests since that time has remained small.

Nuclear bomb testing was strictly a governmental activity, involving only a few national actors who knew they were tinkering with the most dangerous tool ever developed. Global climate change, by contrast, is created by billions of individual actors—firms that are fueling the very economy of the globe and individual citizens earning their living. The single tragic event of *Fortunate Dragon* contrasts sharply with the millions of small, slow changes wreaked subtly on plants, animals, people, the oceans, and the weather by the gases emitted from fossil-fuel burning, fertilizer use, manufacture of fluorocarbons, cultivation of cattle and rice, and the backyard barbecue. It took nine years after the galvanizing event itself to achieve a ratified nuclear test ban. Not surprisingly, an agreement to make even a small start on slowing the human-induced climate change has already been in negotiation for nearly a decade. It is still in limbo.

In the case of the nuclear test ban, the desired outcome was clear: cease the atmospheric and oceanic explosions used to test nuclear weapons. The desired outcome for addressing climate change is clear in only one sense: it must involve reducing greenhouse gas emissions. How much reduction, how fast, and the fair distribution of effort among countries, individuals, and businesses remains undecided; finding consensus has proved to be an enormous challenge.

Several governments began their consideration of reduced emissions of greenhouse gases in the 1980s; the world began in a formal way to address the issue in 1992. In that year, with the IPCC's first report in hand, delegates to UNCED in Rio decided that the scientific indications of possible harm were definite enough for countries to begin action under international treaties to limit the possibility of a damaging climate change. To that end, delegates adopted a Framework Convention on Climate Change (FCCC) that established the context in which the treaties would be negotiated. The FCCC set as its ultimate objective "stabilization of the greenhouse gas concentrations in the atmosphere at a level that would prevent dangerous anthropogenic interference with the climate system. Such a level should be achieved within a time frame sufficient to allow ecosystems to adapt naturally to climate change, to ensure that food production is not threatened, and to enable economic development to proceed in a sustainable manner."

Though the delegates did not precisely define "dangerous . . . interference," "adapt naturally," or "proceed in a sustainable manner," in general they meant reducing greenhouse gas emissions to a level such that the concentrations of these gases in the air do not continue to climb, and the climate is not continually being pushed to a new set of conditions. Since evidence from the warming during Earth's emergence from the last ice age indicates that a progressive warming disrupts forests and perhaps other ecosystems, we should achieve these reductions soon enough to avoid such disruptions, not only for the benefit of natural ecosystems but also for agricultural activity, given the importance of a reliable food supply.

Delegates signed the FCCC treaty in 1992. The U.S. Senate and equivalent bodies in Canada, Australia, and some developing countries that are particularly vulnerable to climate change (such as Maldives) ratified it promptly. Gradually, more countries, both developed and developing, joined, so that 186 countries had agreed to the treaty by early 1995. But the road from this auspicious beginning to progress on stabilizing the composition of the atmosphere has been a bumpy one indeed.

Stabilizing the atmosphere requires that annual global emissions of each greenhouse gas be brought down to the amount that natural processes can absorb each year. Oceans dissolve carbon dioxide and move it to deep waters or to new limestone deposits, and plant growth uses atmospheric CO_2 as food; so some is captured in growing forests. The rate of absorption increases as the concentration of CO_2 in the atmosphere rises, so that the extra absorption has remained about half the human-induced emission. Thus, to stabilize the atmospheric concentration of CO_2, with global emissions about 30 billion metric tons a year, we need to reduce emissions by at least 15 billion tons a year. Larger reductions may be needed to account for earlier changes in oceans and other systems caused by their previous absorption of this gas; some experts estimate that the required reductions may be as much as 80 percent.

The UNCED delegates recognized that stabilizing the composition of the air would put the world on a long and difficult course, and they laid out procedures for subsequent meetings to address the many open issues. A Conference of Parties (COP), made up of delegates from countries that had signed the FCCC, was assigned responsibility for these further details of the treaty.

The COP Principles

The Rio group adopted several principles to be observed by COP delegates at subsequent meetings. The first required that developed countries take the lead in limiting human-induced climate change. This principle was based on considerations of fairness, in that the developed countries had contributed the majority of the extra greenhouse gases in the air and had greater resources available to deal with the reductions.

The second principle required that "full consideration" be given to developing countries that were especially vulnerable to the adverse effects of climate change, or that would have to bear a disproportionate burden under the steps required to lower emissions.

The third principle said countries should take "precautionary measures" where there were threats of serious or irreversible damage, even if full scientific certainty was lacking.

The Rio delegates also took a concrete, apparently easy step to put the first principle promptly into action: they set a voluntary target for developed countries to drop their greenhouse gas emissions back to 1990 levels by the year 2000. At that time many countries were at or only slightly above their 1990 emission levels, so the goal seemed reasonable.

But achieving it was not easy. Most developed countries discovered internal opposition to the treaty from the coal industry and other businesses—opposition to taking steps to reduce emissions by even a relatively small amount. Economies also surged during the later 1990s, increasing fossil-fuel use. Countries began to complain that returning to 1990 levels by 2000 was not possible; the world would have to set a more "realistic" goal. The United Kingdom did return to its 1990 level of carbon dioxide emissions, aided by a rapid substitution of natural gas from the North Sea for coal, an exchange that reduced carbon dioxide emissions by about half wherever the change was made. A unified Germany profited from its merger and the opportunity to abandon inefficient factories and power plants in the former East Germany. Emissions in Russia also dropped sharply, unfortunately because of economic collapse rather than improved technology or better fuel. This failure of most developed countries to achieve even small decreases taught a valuable lesson: optional goals are not likely to work except in special circumstances.

The COP met in March 1995 in Berlin, then in July 1996 in Geneva. In conformity with the principle that developed countries would go first, the members agreed that developing countries would not be asked to participate in the early reductions. In response to the lesson learned, the delegates agreed that the treaty to be negotiated would specify "legally binding" goals.

The first principle followed, in time and thinking, the very successful treaty to reduce emission of gases that destroy stratospheric ozone. That treaty—the Montreal Protocol—allowed developing countries ten years after developed countries to begin and complete required emission cuts. The COP agreed to a similar provision at Rio and Berlin, but without setting a specific time for the beginning of participation by developing countries. This gap triggered developed-country fears that for an indefinite time the developing countries would have a competitive advantage in international trade, by avoiding the expense of cutting greenhouse gas emissions.

The Distribution of Fossil-Fuel Use

We need to take a look at the distribution of fossil-fuel use to understand why "developed countries first" is a logical, though troublesome, issue in the negotiations. Fossil fuels are not used evenly around the world; prosperous countries use far more than poor countries, with the large developing countries coming up fast. Table 6.1 shows the annual emissions of carbon dioxide from fossil-fuel use by the ten countries with the highest totals, the annual per-capita emissions of these high-emitting countries, and the total cumulative emissions of each of these countries since 1950.

The United States is a clear leader in all three categories, especially in the total emissions over the past half-century, where its total is three times that of the second country. It should be no surprise that other countries expect the United States to take a leading role in any agreement to reduce emissions, whether it wishes to or not. This expectation played a major role in the international negotiations following the adoption of the FCCC; future progress may well depend on the extent to which the United States moves ahead on steps to reduce its emissions.

In 1996 China was second to the United States in annual emissions and India was fifth. China's emissions increased by 4 or 5 percent a year from 1980 to 1997, but in 1998 its emissions dropped by 3.7 percent, perhaps owing to major reductions in the government subsidies for coal. India's emissions increased by more than 7 per-

Rank	Country	Annual emissions	Annual per-capita emissions	Cumulative emissions, 1950–1996
1	United States	5,301	19.7	186,114
2	China	3,364	2.7	57,581
3	Russian Federation	1,580	10.7	62,413
4	Japan	1,168	9.3	31,158
5	India	997	1.0	15,516
6	Germany	861	10.5	42,690
7	United Kingdom	557	9.5	27,168
8	Canada	409	13.7	14,855
9	South Korea	408	9.0	4,988
10	Italy	403	7.0	12,319

TABLE 6.1 Carbon dioxide emissions from fossil fuel use and cement manufacturing (a minor addition) by the ten countries with the largest emission in 1996. Emissions in million metric tons except for per capita emissions in metric tons. (From World Resources Institute, *World Resources, 2000–2001: People and Ecosystems: The Fraying Web of Life* [Washington, D.C.: World Resources Institute, 2000].)

cent a year in the early 1990s, while U.S. emissions rose at 0.4 percent per year. The rapid increases in emissions by the two largest developing countries gave members of the U.S. Senate a reason for opposing any agreement in which China was not given an enforceable target in a definite time frame. They were forgetting, perhaps, their early bipartisan ratification of the FCCC, with its provision that developed countries would lead the way.

China is quite far behind the leading per-capita emitters, allowing Chinese negotiators to remind everyone that each citizen of China is associated with the emission of only one seventh as much CO_2 as each American, an indication that China is far from providing the same level of opportunity, health, and amenity as the United States. China asserts that it would not be fair to ask it to reduce its use of fossil fuel, felt to be necessary if the country is to achieve its rightful place among the prosperous nations of the world. China might also point out that, unlike the United States, it has taken strong and difficult steps both to slow its population growth (thereby making the reduction of these emissions easier in the long run) and to reduce government subsidies for fossil fuels. The conflict between the United States and China relative to greenhouse gases shows how issues of fairness can divide industrialized countries from those that are large but now relatively poor, with aspirations to develop.

As might be expected, the governments of China and India view fairness differently than does the government of Maldives. The big developing countries see it as their right to accelerate their industrialization even though it means additional carbon dioxide emissions. Maldives considers that to be driven from its homeland through no misbehavior of its own would be supremely unfair. The Maldivean government is part of the Association of Small Island States, each member of which is an island nation with a considerable fraction of its usable land area close to sea level. At the negotiating sessions since Rio, this group has strongly asserted that it is time to start reducing emissions, and it asks that negotiations move forward promptly. Unfortunately, the influence of low islands in the negotiations is more nearly proportional to their small GNP than to their occupancy of the moral high ground.

The Kyoto Protocol

With little progress having been made to resolve the issues left to it by the FCCC, the COP meeting scheduled for November 1997 in Kyoto, Japan, became the focus of attention. Preliminary meetings held out the possibility of adopting actual reduction targets, following the rules set down in Rio and the provisos from the Berlin and Geneva meetings. The IPCC Second Assessment Report of climate science had been released by then—a study more explicit in its conclusion about the human role in causing the climate to change than was the initial assessment—and gave added impetus to completing an agreement.

The document negotiated there—the Kyoto Protocol—did specify numerical reductions or emission limitations for developed countries; if ratified by a sufficient number of countries, including the largest emitters, these would have been a small first step toward the Rio goal. Yet the protocol left many details, including enforcement procedures, for later meetings.

The Kyoto accord required that emissions by developed countries during the period 2008 to 2012 average about 5 percent below the 1990 values. (As agreed earlier in Rio and Berlin, developing countries were not expected to join in at this stage.) Delegates from the developed countries negotiated their cuts or limitations with the other delegates, and the result was a wide spread in values. Australia accepted a limitation of 8 percent above 1990, which will require some reduction, since its emissions in the year 2001 are already higher than this level; Iceland is now about 10 percent above 1990 and agreed to that limit; Norway was limited to 1 percent above 1990; New Zealand opted for a return to 1990. Those agreeing to reductions below 1990 included Canada, Hungary, Japan (6 percent), and the United States (7 percent). The group of European countries that negotiates in U.N. forums as the European Union volunteered jointly to reduce emissions 8 percent below their 1990 values—with some countries, notably Germany, making much larger reductions to balance smaller reductions and a few increases by European countries with special problems.

Only a very minor slowing of climate warming would be achieved by the reductions agreed to in Kyoto, a fact recognized by the negotiators. The reasons contributing to a decision to move ahead with a minor step toward the Rio goal, rather than a longer-range schedule with large reductions, likely arose from the realization that any impact on the use of something as essential as the major global fuel would arouse fear of the large secondary economic loss projected by economists, and fierce opposition from the fossil-fuel industry and related businesses. Also, the failure of almost all developed countries to reduce emissions to 1990 levels by the year 2000, as agreed in Rio, reinforced anxiety in the developing world that the large, prosperous countries would not be willing to reduce at all.

Thus, one could consider the Kyoto Protocol a "demonstration project," in which rich countries were required to demonstrate their good faith. They were called upon to produce small actual reductions in their own fossil-fuel use to show their willingness to lead the world toward atmospheric stabilization. This step is a political necessity if poorer countries, resentful of developed countries' wealth and responsibility for climate change, are to be brought into the effort to achieve the Rio goal. Obviously, then, the Kyoto accord has a far larger purpose than the modest negotiated reductions suggest.

The Kyoto Protocol, like the FCCC, left many details for further negotiation. Expectations were focused on the COP meeting scheduled for the fall of 2000 in the Netherlands. But that meeting broke up with no appreciable progress, leaving the situation uncertain until the next meeting in midsummer 2001. In the meantime, a new government was elected in the United States, a government much less convinced than earlier ones that environmental damage is a severe problem for the United States and the world. The new President announced that he was officially withdrawing from the Kyoto Protocol. Since other governments were waiting to see what the most powerful country—and the largest emitter of greenhouse gases—would do, this proclamation threatened to seriously set back negotiations.

In 2001 delegates to the COP met again, this time in Marrakech, Morocco, bringing with them the knowledge that the United States would persist in its determination to boycott the Kyoto Protocol despite the vigorous criticism it had received after the withdrawal announcement—criticism from foreign countries as well as from many of its own citizens.

The delegates from the European Union, Japan, Australia, Canada, and several other developed countries recognized that, with the help of some developing countries, they could amass enough votes to initiate the protocol without the participation of the United States. The delegates did not have time to refine all the lingering details that had been both technically complex and controversial, such as what credits should be allowed for sequestering carbon dioxide or how the sequestering would be verified. They solved such problems by specifying an appropriate credit for each country rather than a process for determining it. At this writing it appears that enough affirmative votes and ratifications are available to bring the treaty to fruition.

American delegates attended the conference, but did not contribute appreciably to the discussion. Although the administration has promised to put forward its own independent emission reduction plan, no such document has yet appeared. The lack of such a plan has been largely obscured by the September 2001 terrorist attack on New York and Washington.

Earlier, while the Kyoto negotiations were under way,

the IPCC completed its Third Assessment Report (TAR) in late 2000 and submitted it to member governments for comments and possible revision before public distribution. As described in Chapter 5, this report included the most unambiguous statement to date about human responsibility for climate warming. It also contained a surprise: it projected a range of possible global average temperature increases by 2100 that reached disturbingly higher than any earlier assessment. These elements of TAR led some observers to expect that the report would stimulate rapid progress on an international treaty. But, as events have demonstrated, credible scientific warnings of future trouble by a large group of climate scientists are not enough to instigate progress in this complex area.

Steps taken in the United States in the 1980s to reduce the sulfur emissions that lead to acid rain illustrate how irrelevant the details of science can be to the policy process. Researchers had assembled considerable evidence on the damage of acid-bearing precipitation and had proposed large reductions in emissions of sulfur dioxide and nitrogen oxides. Electric utilities challenged the findings, complaining that the scientific uncertainty in acid-rain science did not justify the high cost of new machinery to cleanse the sulfur from their smokestack emissions. The U.S. government, apparently agreeing with the utilities, did not take action to slow the emissions; instead, it instituted a ten-year research project to "reduce uncertainties" in the science. Nine years later, shortly before the research project was complete, Congress adopted legislation establishing a "cap-and-trade" system designed to halve sulfur emissions.

In retrospect, this strange behavior tells us that the state of the science was not of primary importance. The deciding issue was how to distribute the costs of cleanup among the states in a politically viable way. Once such a process had been devised, there was no longer any need to wait for better science; it had been adequate all along. After the cap-and-trade legislation was passed, reductions in sulfur emissions proceeded rather faster than the legislation required and at a cost far lower than industry had estimated (although the oxides of nitrogen have yet to be tamed).

The slowing of the destruction of stratospheric ozone by CFCs and related chemicals is a similar story. The chemical industry claimed early in the debate that developing a replacement for CFCs would be difficult and expensive. Some opponents even claimed that without CFCs (which at the time were the basis of all modern refrigeration) food spoilage and deaths from food poisoning would result. Actually, once they were required, replacement chemicals were developed promptly; reductions in use of the offending substances proceeded at low cost, with no reports of ensuing deaths.

It is ironic to hear today's industries, seats of most technical innovation in the modern world, claim that they lack the versatility and inventiveness to adapt to changing conditions—only to find that, when required to do so, they respond much more rapidly and at a far lower cost than they or anyone else had predicted.

Another dimension of the interaction of science and politics involves the ambiguous commitment of voters to environmental concerns. How certain are elected representatives that their voters will support efforts to reduce fossil-fuel use? We know that most voters in the United States consider themselves environmentalists: they turned back a determined effort by a newly elected Congress in 1994 to weaken most forms of environmental protection. However, this same public is puzzled by the notion that climate change in the future needs to be dealt with today, and it confuses climate change with the Antarctic ozone hole. It also balks at the slightest mention of new taxes, particularly on gasoline. Thus the environmental public has not yet communicated to Congress an impatience for the prompt action needed to prepare for the climate change to which we are already committed, and to prevent an even larger change by reducing emissions.

The public has had a great deal of help in achieving this reluctance; vigorous arguments about climate change persist. The arguments within the atmospheric science community are described in Chapter 5. Yet the loudest arguments—and the ones most visible to the public—have come from coal-mine owners, business organizations, nonscientists, and a few atmospheric scientists who have accepted roles as spokesmen for the coal and oil industries. The industry whining witnessed in the acid-rain and stratospheric ozone depletion debates has been prominent, even though several leading firms (including such large oil companies as BP and Shell) have recently changed sides and announced that they feel it necessary to prepare for a future that will involve less reliance on fossil fuels. Criticism is still being leveled at scientists. Some accuse mainstream climate scientists of exaggerating the dangers of climate change in order to obtain research funds, or of being closet revolutionaries attempting to change the form of the U.S. government by bringing the country to the brink of bankruptcy. (I myself was called a public trough scientist by an angry questioner at a talk I gave to a business group in Santa Fe, New Mexico, and I was relieved the term was nothing worse.)

It is evident that the controversy described here is not a scientific debate, but one that uses pieces of science as ammunition in an economic and political war. It is not scientific disagreement or uncertainty that keeps us from a solid international agreement to reduce emission of greenhouse gases; it is political opposition, armed with the belief that stabilizing the climate will cost business, government, and entire economies too much to be worth it.

The Role of Economics

At the heart of the unfolding climate-change debate, in addition to questions about the realism of the scientific models and lingering issues of fairness, is the need for a reliable estimate of the cost of reducing greenhouse gas emissions. Energy experts are of the opinion that low-cost efficiency improvements that would lead to less total fuel use do exist, but economists argue that a major change in one sector of an economy, in this case the energy industry, can ripple through the economy in unexpected ways.

Economic model builders attempting to simulate this ripple effect face many of the same difficulties that climate modelers do, especially the necessity for approximating factors not well known or well measured and for omitting some factors that the computer or the model cannot handle. Economic models, however, are far less complicated than climate models and differ in another important way. The weather gives atmospheric modelers many data sets with which to verify processes simulated in their models, and in addition to the record of the past 140 years, several data sets assembled from proxy data allow comparison of climate models with measured information. The economic modeler is hard pressed to demonstrate realism in predicting something as specific as the economic cost of a fossil-fuel tax. History does not supply many events similar enough to the one being studied, and data from the few that *are* similar have probably been utilized in developing the model, so their use for testing would be circular.

Economic models are employed in a manner parallel to climate models. The modeler first runs the model for a period of simulated time—say, the fifty years from 1990 to 2040—with greenhouse gas emissions continuing along some assumed path. The model is then run again with the emission of greenhouse gases (represented by carbon dioxide) reduced by, for example, a tax on carbon emissions. The comparison of the two calculations is usually reported as the difference in GNP produced by the tax and the lower emissions.

We need to keep in mind that GNP is not a satisfactory representation of human welfare; these calculations need, but sometimes do not get, an accompanying discussion of topics such as the distributional effects of the change, effects on natural-resource depletion, and advantages other than slowing climate change that will accrue from less fossil-fuel use. For example, utilizing less fossil fuel can reduce lung damage in urban areas, a change that tends to decrease GNP because there is less need for medical assistance and certain drugs but that is surely a positive change. Only if the economic model results are interpreted in a sufficiently broad context can they be truly useful in educating policymakers and citizens about the crucial issues surrounding climate change.

Just as climate scientists, in reporting the results of their simplified "double carbon dioxide" model experiments, unintentionally mislead people into thinking that carbon dioxide will double and then stop increasing, economic model results sometimes confuse or mislead the public, and perhaps members of Congress. One economist might report a calculation that shows that reducing emissions will decrease national GNP by 3 percent; another might convert the answer to other numbers and report that the emission reduction will cost $200 billion and eliminate eight hundred thousand jobs. These reports fail to emphasize to the noneconomist that the models show, overall, a rapid growth in GNP and jobs over the fifty years. The calculations actually indicate a slightly longer time to get to a much higher level of economic activity and many more jobs, not spending $200 billion of current income or firing eight hundred thousand current workers, as many readers might assume.

Climate modelers have one great advantage over their economic colleagues. Well-established laws of physics, radiation, chemistry, and physical chemistry largely govern the behavior of the atmosphere and ocean. Economics is not based on any similar set of physical rules, so the governing equations in the economic model are derived from a set of assumptions about human behavior converted into observations such as "With higher prices, consumption will fall." The details of these assumptions, in the case of estimating the cost of reducing fossil-fuel use, make a large difference in the results displayed by the model.

Robert Repetto of the World Resources Institute has analyzed the impact of each of several assumptions commonly used by economic modelers. For example, to calculate the effect of a carbon tax to reduce emissions, the economic modeler must assume what the governments involved will do with the revenue from the tax. If these revenues are placed in the general fund, the calculation will show an additional loss of GNP when the emission is reduced. If instead the money reduces some current taxes (on payroll, capital gains, and the like) that tend to hold back the economy, the greenhouse gas reduction will lessen the loss of GNP or indeed change the answer to a gain. Climate modelers too must make assumptions, such as what process governs the formation of ice in clouds, but none of the assumptions tested has done more than move the calculated warming within a limited range; none changes it to a cooling. Repetto's examination of the effect of the common assumptions of economic modelers shows not only that the results are sensitive to these assumptions, but also that if one chooses all the most favorable assumptions, the gain in GNP is roughly the same as the size of the loss if all the most pessimistic assumptions are chosen.

Another factor that reduces the effective cost of curbing fossil-fuel use is the number of corollary benefits that accrue. These benefits include not only a reduction in the number of extra urban deaths resulting from lung damage and other effects of breathing sulfur dioxide, ozone, and small particles, but also fewer asthma attacks, less obscuration of blue skies and scenic vistas, help in further reducing acid rain, less land disturbance from mining, fewer oil spills in the transportation of petroleum, and a decrease in the power of a few oil-producing states to control the price of oil and related global policies.

A different view of the cost of reducing fossil-fuel use

comes from experts in energy technology. These engineers list many ways in which energy efficiency can be improved at low or negative net cost. For example, a household can replace an older furnace with a new one that delivers the required heat while using considerably less natural gas, so that over a period of several years the higher cost of the efficient furnace is repaid by savings in the fuel bill. Similar calculations have been made for all of the major home appliances. Furnaces yield the largest savings, with washing machines and refrigerators not far behind.

Industries have similar and rather spectacular savings possibilities. As described in Joe Romm's *Cool Companies,* a Dow Chemical plant in Louisiana had made major improvements in its processes and equipment over a number of years and thereby felt that it was using the most modern technology. A staff member convinced the management to conduct a contest among employees to find energy-saving opportunities. The best of the suggestions were selected, and the company invested $1.7 million in the required changes. Somewhat to management's surprise, the energy savings produced a return on investment of 173 percent. To see if all possible savings had been located, the company continued the contest and found new savings each year; in 1989 an investment of $7.5 million produced a return of 470 percent. Many of these savings came from such simple alterations as larger pipes allowing for smaller pumps and hence smaller motors that used less electricity. An unexpected contributor to the large return was additional natural light from outside entering the various work spaces, which decreased the need for electric lighting. The natural lighting saved energy, but it also increased the productivity of employees.

Smaller organizations have achieved similar success. A high school in New York State was able to save half its annual $200,000 energy bill by generating its own electricity and using the waste for winter heating of the building.

The author of *Cool Companies* asserts that if any significant fraction of U.S. companies became "cool" in this sense, "the country as a whole would be able to meet the Kyoto targets while lowering the nation's energy bill by tens of billions of dollars and accelerating economic growth through productivity gains." Romm's analysis is a strong indication that the United States and other developed countries have opportunities for what are now called "no regrets" actions; that is, actions a country will be pleased it took, even if climate change turns out to be less damaging than expected.

Critics who label Romm as too optimistic contend that most companies are not likely to follow the examples of the cool companies, that much current equipment has years of useful life left, and that the efficiency steps these companies might take will result in payback periods of three years or more, too long for most industrial managers. These dissenters also note that saving lives and improving health, elements that would justify action from a societal view, are not considered by industries. Such factors do not enter into their calculation of cost effectiveness, any more than they are considered by a driver investing in a large car or a homeowner failing to make an advantageous investment in an efficient washing machine or furnace. Still, *Cool Companies* shows that cost-effective energy savings can be made at a smaller-than-national scale and suggests the kinds of actions that public policy should encourage.

Thus, the economic case for high national costs is simply not as strong as opponents to action on climate change assert. Clearly, certain industries that have not moved to diversify will experience a loss of sales, and some provision for smoothing the transition may be necessary. Yet some vulnerable companies are taking steps without government incentives. One major oil company, for example, has moved into the solar cell business, a move consistent with the changing physical and policy climate.

Surprises

Another aspect of climate change, recognized only recently, further justifies actions to stem emissions. The study of complex systems (such as an ecosystem or a large nation's electric power grid) has revealed that frequently multiple responses to a single set of external conditions are possible and that the state of such a system is capable of changing from one response to another. The global climate system is, of course, exceedingly complicated, so one would expect that the climate might also have such a capability. Analyses of polar ice cores reinforce such expectations by showing that large and rapid changes in climate occurred during the most recent glaciation, as if a switch were turned on and off several times. Some of these events were apparently caused by changes in major ocean circulations, changes that modified sea-surface temperatures and hence temperatures on adjacent continents.

Everyday experience gives a few examples of surprises in complex systems. If I push harder and harder on a tree limb, it will slowly bend and then suddenly break. As the weather cools in the fall, lakes in some locations gradually respond by a cooling of their surface water. Then, as the air temperature continues to decline, the lake suddenly "turns over"—the heavier cool surface water moves to the bottom, bringing up water that has not cooled as much. The fish, plants, and other life in the lake are rearranged, but having evolved with this annual occurrence they make the necessary adjustments.

The most famous climate surprise, which happened as Earth was warming slowly out of the depth of the most recent ice age, is called the Younger Dryas episode. Europe cooled rather suddenly about thirteen thousand years ago, to such an extent that most of the trees there died. The cooling lasted about eight hundred years, after which warming again took over and continued until Earth reached the current warm, interglacial conditions. This event was identified not by climatologists but by scientists studying fossils in Northern Europe who noted the lack of tree fossils in certain layers. Years later, when cores from the Greenland ice cap and pollen from a Minnesota marsh were interpreted as showing a cold interruption of the gradual warming from the ice age, the dearth of tree fossils was explained.

The fact that the Younger Dryas occurred at a time when the climate system was being driven slowly toward a warmer state suggests that a steady push on the climate, if continued long enough, could produce stresses that would then be relieved by a sudden transition. This suggestion adds some extra interest to stopping the continuing push we are applying to the climate by adding greenhouse gases to the air each year. However, the science of climate surprises is still far from being able to explain the causes or timing of such major events.

It is difficult to tell from the ice core or fossil evidence just how rapidly the Younger Dryas began, but any similarly large change in regional or global climate occurring in a time as short as a decade or year could find present-day society unprepared and extremely vulnerable. It is not yet possible to estimate the likelihood of such surprises in the future, but scholars studying policy responses to greenhouse gas increases have suggested that the greatest benefit from reducing emissions will arise from reducing the probability of unlikely scenarios with extreme adverse consequences. A sudden climate change of large magnitude would certainly qualify for that category.

An unstated assumption throughout this chapter and the preceding one has been that preventing future climate change is wiser than letting it happen. But could a

changed climate actually be a *better* thing? Some analysts—usually from cold northern latitudes, in the tradition of Arrhenius—have emphasized that such a change
could well have benefits as well as detriments. Sturdy environmentalists are made uneasy by such comments, not
because they wish to focus only on damages, but because
they feel that taking advantage of such a human-induced
climate change is merely another step toward human
domination of the natural world, a step being taken without real understanding of its long-range consequences.

Suppose, in a far-fetched example, that as the climate
warms, the agricultural establishment in the midlatitudes
takes advantage of the longer growing season and altered
rainfall regime to plant and nurture a different set of
crops, adapted to the new climate. Communities supporting these agricultural regions will adapt to the changed
circumstances, new communities will grow up around
the most favorable locations for the new crops, and new
businesses will appear to serve the needs of those par-
ticipating in the major crop shifts. We know such changes
can happen—supporting communities have grown up in
the United States around areas of public land made available for cattle grazing. The existence of these communities is a significant obstacle now to reducing the damages to riparian areas caused by excessive grazing. In the
same way, in our hypothetical scenario we will need to
continue to burn enough coal to maintain the changed
climate, even if by then we have found cheaper, cleaner
energy sources that are preferable. Vine Deloria has de-

scribed this problem poetically: "If we subdue nature, we become slaves of the technology by which this task is accomplished." Such a development is indeed a Faustian bargain. We get what we think we want, but with costs we are unlikely to foresee.

The complexities of policy responses to the possibility of a human-induced climate change, as illustrated by the history of international negotiations to reduce greenhouse gas emissions, are certainly greater than those surrounding atmospheric testing of nuclear weapons. Despite several major international reviews of climate science, each more confident than the preceding one that climate change is under way and that human activities are the principal cause, added to a strong statement in the Framework Convention on Climate Change ratified by the United States and most other countries, and nearly a decade of follow-up negotiations, action on agreement is stalled. The details left for further negotiation in the Kyoto Protocol have not been completely supplied, and future success depends on the fragile alliance assembled in Marrakech. Issues of fairness beset the negotiations, with conflicts between the wealthy north and the poor south, between small island states and large developing countries, and between the United States and the rest of the world.

In response to the question "What is holding things up?" one would have to say that the *politics* of climate change is more important than the *science*. Political interests opposing action usually stand behind economic models that, on critical examination, make a far weaker case against action on climate change than is usually understood. In fact, a number of companies have already made investments to reduce carbon emissions and achieved startlingly high returns over short periods. The possibility of surprises wreaking sudden havoc, as occurred during the Younger Dryas, argues against complacency.

Meanwhile, international negotiations carry on, if slowly and fitfully. They continue to be sparked by the commitment of environmentalists, several European countries, solar and wind power industries, nuclear power enthusiasts, large industries looking for closure on what the future rules will be, a growing portion of the American public, and the people of the Republic of Maldives.

7

Creating a Stable Atmosphere

Any parent with a child of five or six years is familiar with the "Why?" period. Everything is subject to question: Why is the sky blue? Why does light scatter in that color? Why are air molecules just that size? Why . . . ?

Elucidating what the world needs to do to stabilize the composition of the atmosphere and avoid the worst effects of climate heating follows a similar train, but the questions are "How?" Those questions and their answers go like this: How do we avoid the worst effects of climate heating? By reducing emissions of greenhouse gases to levels that the atmosphere can absorb without harm. How does the world start reducing greenhouse gas emissions? By using energy much more efficiently than it does today. How do we accomplish that transformation? By getting economic signals to tell the environmental truth. And how do we do that? That question takes longer to answer.

Avoiding the worst effects of climate heating requires ceasing the annual increase in the atmospheric greenhouse gases and the accompanying increase in the force toward larger climate changes. Stabilizing the composition of the atmosphere requires bringing annual global emissions of each greenhouse gas down to the amount that natural processes can absorb each year. That means, for CO_2, reductions to at least half the present rate of emission; some experts see a reduction of 60 to 80 percent required. Other greenhouse gases will need to be limited by various amounts; a small percentage decrease in methane emissions will serve, whereas nitrous oxide will need to go below half its current emissions. Some newly produced, CFC-like compounds (SF6, CF4, C2F6) have estimated lifetimes in the atmosphere of thousands or tens of thousands of years; they will continue to accumulate until their production ceases almost entirely.

Reducing Greenhouse Gas Emissions

Now for the next "How?"—how to reduce greenhouse gas emissions. Our discussion here focuses on carbon dioxide for simplicity, because it dominates emissions, climate effects, and public discussion of climate heating. It also highlights the United States as leading the world in carbon emissions and in energy inefficiency by a developed country.

The emission of carbon dioxide is usually ascribed to three sectors of our economy—transportation, industry, and business and residential. These are the basic elements of the world's "energy economy." In the United States, roughly one third of total emissions come from each sector; land-use change in the United States does not contribute to current emissions. In each of the sectors one can imagine decreasing fossil-fuel use either by reducing fuel-using activities—driving less, heating buildings to lower temperatures, cooling them to higher temperatures, running machinery less often—or, far more desirable, by carrying on the same activities in each sector more efficiently, using less fuel in the process. The most cost-effective reductions in energy use and therefore in emissions are largely concentrated in those homes, businesses, and factories that can replace inefficient equipment (furnaces, air conditioners, windows, electric motors, steam boilers, lights, compressed air equipment, and many others) with equipment that does the same work while using less energy. Potential also lies with technological changes such as computer monitoring and control of energy systems, and switching to fuels with less carbon content— from coal to natural gas, for example, and eventually from fossil fuel of any kind to solar-derived sources, including hydrogen.

The energy economy is the most obvious place to look for fossil-fuel use that produces carbon emissions. But hidden within every product and service in the United States is the energy to produce, transport, and use it. Every building, automobile, machine, head of lettuce, telephone, ream of paper—indeed, every material good and every service—every movie, every university education, all lawn care—also uses energy. Literally everything we do, use, handle, and throw away involves energy and has implications for our climate.

Thus energy efficiency, the obvious tool for prompt reduction in fossil-fuel use, also requires efficiency in the use of materials. Indeed, a world committed to a stable atmospheric composition would create an efficient energy program. It would also create a new materials economy, in which all products were designed to have long useful lives; be easily repaired, reused, or recycled; or break down into components that could be composted in the soils. Industrial processes would have very little waste, of energy or materials, and that waste would be raw material for another industry. Individual factories, industrial complexes, neighborhoods, and entire cities would ultimately be designed to reduce waste, length of commuting, and transportation time, and otherwise use both energy and materials efficiently. Indeed, societies and economies would act like ecosystems.

The Power of Prices

Why do we not already use energy and materials as efficiently as possible? Surely, the less we spend on energy
and materials, the better. Why are industry and individual consumers wasteful in their direct use of energy,
in their vehicles, in heating and cooling buildings, in
fueling machines, or indirectly, through the products
and services that they buy? Two factors contribute to
this situation. First, even though Romm and other analysts show that at current energy prices companies are
missing a fine opportunity for savings, most companies
do not aim at maximum energy-use efficiency. An extensive economic literature explains the reasons, going back to the work of Nobel laureate Herbert Simon,
who showed that buyers frequently prefer a convenient
decision rather than the least expensive one. Most companies find that energy involves a smaller cost than other
categories of expense, so they are not willing to invest the needed management attention to achieve the
highest efficiency in their energy use. Nor do economic
signals reflect environmental harm, including harm to
the climate, so industry and individuals receive inaccu-
rate signals about the costs imposed on society by their
purchases and activities. The price of gasoline does not
capture the harm done by emissions from gasoline engines to urban air quality or to the climate. Thus, vehicle manufacturers, retailers, individual consumers, and

governments have no financial incentives to use gasoline efficiently.

In this diagnosis lies the cure: to create an economy that uses energy and materials efficiently, we must alter the signals sent by the economy so that the environment is taken into account; in other words, we must raise energy costs enough so that industrial managers and householders pay attention to them.

In addition to lack of inclusion of the costs of environmental harm in the price of items, the federal government subsidizes activities that harm the environment directly. The United States condones below-cost sales or leases of federally owned timber, water, power, mining land, and grazing rights. The federal government also underwrites flood insurance, covering areas at high risk of damage from floods and coastal storms. All these activities shift part of the true cost of doing business in resource-related fields—fields strongly connected to the environment—from the businesses and individuals that benefit to the general taxpayer, who generally does not.

In contrast, if the price of something were to tell the ecological truth, coal would no longer be the obvious cheapest source of electricity; natural gas and solar cells would become more competitive. (Wind power already has, even without higher coal prices.) Farmers, miners, and all industry would use water, land, fossil fuels, and minerals more efficiently. People would hesitate to build houses in storm-prone areas. With truth-telling prices everyone would have the incentive to do the right thing both economically and environmentally. The best bargain for individual consumers would become also the best bargain for the environment. In times of ecological truth, manufacturers would have an incentive to make environmentally benign products, as the cost of harmful inputs would be greater than benign ones. Inventors would have an incentive to develop devices that use fuel efficiently, use alternate fuels, or otherwise spare energy and materials. It would be cost effective for firms to do research on alternatives to fossil fuels.

Experience from the "oil shocks" of the 1970s and early 1980s is often cited as evidence of how price increases encourage reductions in per-capita use of a resource, greater overall efficiency, and technological innovation. In 1973 and 1979, in response to political events in the Middle East, the oil-exporting countries, organized as OPEC, cut production and raised the price of petroleum. This in turn cut gasoline and oil supplies in the United States, yielding sharp increases in the price of gasoline. It was feared that the economy as a whole would suffer, as energy use and economic growth had moved in tandem for most of the previous decades of the century. But per-capita use of all energy *fell* during the 1970s and 1980s; GNP grew, perhaps at a slower rate than it would have otherwise; and the average fuel economy of vehicles rose 60 percent. The automobile industry turned out cars that were more fuel efficient, and homes and businesses

across the country responded to tax incentives by install-
ing passive and photovoltaic solar panels, insulating
their buildings, and taking other measures to save energy.

How does one "get the prices right" in a manner more
controlled and fair than waiting for another OPEC oil em-
bargo? One can imagine a variety of methods. The federal
government could decree a price for every object and service in the economy—not the most efficient or politically
acceptable alternative. Another thought, then: the government could declare that all sectors of the economy had
to meet certain standards of energy efficiency—however
they choose to do so. Industries and households that
failed to meet the standard would be fined. Although this
technique has had some success in standards for vehicle
and appliance efficiency, it seems an awkward way to go
about transforming an entire economy.

In contrast to these command and control approaches—the way much environmental cleanup has
been accomplished in the past—are a range of policies
that use the market to do the work that an agency does
with regulations and enforcement. Market-based policy
instruments work by raising the prices of offending goods
and services, thereby making them less attractive and allowing individual businesses and householders to decide whether to buy them or something more environmentally benign. Consumers tend to respond by using
less of something that rises in price.

A number of market-based policy instruments that affect the environment already exist in the United States

and Europe. Some were adopted to raise revenue rather than clean up the environment; others were designed from the outset to achieve an environmental end. The U.S. tax code gives tax credits for ethanol production; imposes excise taxes on cars with low fuel efficiency and ozone-depleting chemicals; taxes crude oil and imported oil, money with which it funds the Oil Spill Liability Trust Fund and Superfund; and allows income and estate tax deductions for land or conservation easement donations.

Probably the most visible market-based environmental policy in the United States is the cap-and-trade scheme, mentioned in Chapter 6, for controlling acid rain. Utilities and other businesses (mostly plants that generate electric power) that burn coal and emit sulfur dioxide are issued permits for a certain amount of sulfur emission, all under a ceiling that declines over the years and is designed to reduce acid rain. Businesses that invest in energy efficiency or alternatives to high-sulfur coal can sell their surplus permits to businesses for which it is more cost efficient to continue to emit sulfur than to invest in efficiency or alternatives. Tradable permits allow emission reductions to proceed at the lowest total cost; industries make financial decisions and tap their own skills according to their own situations. The market creates the conditions in which industry must work—as it always has—and individual companies decide how best to work within those conditions.

At the state and local level, deposit-return charges on bottles and cans prevent litter and encourage recycling of glass and aluminum. Fees charged for trash disposal in landfills or for garbage collection, especially if the fee is proportional to the amount of waste, motivate households and businesses to recycle or otherwise reduce the amount of trash they produce.

Building on these experiences, market-based policy instruments that would likely reduce carbon emissions range from the grand to the specific. Tradable permit schemes could be devised, not for the individual consumer (there are too many of them) but "upstream" at coal mines, oil refineries, or oil-importing businesses, with the permits allowing a certain amount of carbon to pass through these positions along the stream to the final consumer. The ceiling for each permit could be slowly lowered with time. Also, a logical step in getting the prices right is to eliminate subsidies that harm the environment. Indeed, eliminating subsidies and introducing environmental taxes are two aspects of the same policy.

The policy with the greatest potential for transforming an economy that ignores the environment into one that takes it into account, and the simplest approach in some ways, is a revenue-neutral tax shift. A tax shift does not add taxes, but instead shifts them away from factors we wish to encourage, such as employment and investment, to practices we need to discourage, such as emitting carbon compounds into the air and using raw materials wastefully.

People hold varied opinions about taxes. Some want lower taxes in order to keep government smaller and retain more of their earnings in their own pocket. Others want an active government sufficiently funded to take care of poor people, children, and the elderly—or perhaps to fight two wars at once. Almost all agree that to have a government requires some taxation. If the required taxation is arranged to increase the price of practices the country needs to reduce and decrease the cost of practices we value, such as accumulating savings for the future, we will have taken a major step toward getting the prices right—ecologically right.

A set of environmental taxes would have to meet the standard that all taxes should meet. They must be "economically rational," meaning that they must raise revenue at the least overall cost to the economy. Because economic studies show that existing taxes, such as payroll and investment taxes, which environmental taxes would replace, are often a drain on the economy, analysts say that environmental taxes are economically rational. They must also be fair, administratively feasible, and assure a stable revenue stream. Each of these requirements is a real concern. While a tax shift may be designed to be revenue neutral at the national level, without special provisions it would not be revenue neutral to coal companies or to the poor who must buy gasoline for their usually older, less efficient vehicles to drive to work. Administration and revenue stability are issues that have more mundane solutions, but that must be worked out.

In the mid-1990s the U.S. President's Council on Sustainable Development, composed of representatives of business, government, and nonprofit environmental and social organizations, analyzed the promise and challenges of a revenue-neutral tax shift and threw their support behind it. The members recommended the formation of a national commission charged with reviewing "the effect of federal tax and subsidy policies on the goals of sustainable development." They called on such a commission to "make recommendations to the President and Congress on tax reform initiatives that are consistent with the goals of economic prosperity, a healthy environment, and social equity."

A short answer to "How do we achieve energy and materials efficiency?" is "Get the prices right." And the short answer to "How do we get the prices right?" is "A revenue-neutral tax shift" and subsidy reform. These are powerful, efficient policy choices for the difficult, complex problem of climate change—seemingly just one among many environmental problems, but in fact a problem that underlies many of the others. We find that if we start with policies to stabilize the composition of the atmosphere, we move without much delay to the whole of the world's environmental problems—acid rain, urban air pollution, oil spills, species extinction, and overuse of renewable resources. Fossil fuels lie at the heart of the world's industrial economy. Efficiency in fossil-fuel use implicates much of the rest of energy use. Energy implicates materials, as all materials have hidden within them the energy it took to harvest or mine and transport them. Soon one is talking about virtually the whole economy and a much broader range of environmental problems than climate alone. If we were to solve the challenge of climate change, we would find ourselves solving many other environmental problems as well.

Measuring Economic Progress

As critical as tax policy is to getting the prices right, an additional step is equally important in the long run. This step involves our measurement of economic progress. Natural resources—trees, water, air—and the services that ecosystems provide—cleansing, nutrient cycling, pollination—are essentially free in traditional economic terms, never showing up on anyone's balance sheet unless environmental laws force them onto the ledger. As Kenneth Boulding pointed out, the currently used index of economic success—GNP—ignores most of the features of ecosystems and natural resources that matter to the health of the natural world, including the climate. A related measure, Net National Product, is calculated by subtracting from GNP the depreciation of buildings, equipment, and other human-produced assets. The United Nations Statistical Office sets the rules for the calculation of both these accounts. But in the guidelines, this office calls for natural resources to be dealt with only peripherally, not included in the calculation of the two indices. As a result, when an old-growth forest is cut down, GNP goes up because lumber is sold, but no offsetting charge is made for the loss of this natural capital or the negative effect on wildlife and streams. These accounts, which attach no value to reserves of fuels, forests, or fish, tell the leaders that their countries are gaining wealth faster than they actually are. Countries are withdrawing resources from their savings accounts and labeling them as income. The leaders are in the dark about true changes in the wealth of their countries and the implied changes in quality of life enjoyed by their citizens.

The problems with these accounts have long been known, and methods to correct them have been tested in specific circumstances. Data have been collected on resources such as timber stocks, petroleum, and soils; revised accounts have been calculated. One test country, Indonesia, which had been pleased to know that its GNP was growing at more than 7 percent per year, found during this test, using only information about damage to forest, soils, and petroleum reserves, that a more accurate number was somewhat below 4 percent.

A number of developed countries compile accounts on natural-resource stocks, and some use these data in economic models and budgets. So far, none have moved the new information into their national income accounts or related measures of economic success. Developing countries, which have few resources to commit to gathering the necessary data, may suffer the most as they move into the future, believing that they are showing economic gains while the damages to future income through soil erosion and natural-resource depletion are hidden in the inadequate measures of progress.

The two barriers to reforming these accounts are the lack of routine collection of the necessary data and the inertia that inhibits changing a process used widely for many decades. In 1999 a positive step occurred in the United States when, at the request of several members of Congress, the National Academy of Sciences assembled a committee of well-known, mainstream economists to study reformulation of national income accounts. The committee was chaired by William Nordhaus of Yale University, a pioneer in studies of economic issues surrounding climate change, and incidentally someone who attempted to formulate a revision of the GNP many years ago but gave it up as too difficult. The committee prepared a report, entitled "Nature's Numbers," which endorsed the inclusion of natural-resource depletion in the national accounts. The committee went further in also recommending the inclusion of a charge for pollution damages in what are called satellite accounts. It remains to be seen if this report has any impact on national accounting rules.

The Final "How?"

We have discussed several layers of answers to the question, "How do we avoid the worst effects of climate heating?" We have said that the first layer is to reduce greenhouse gas emissions. We accomplish that by becoming vastly more efficient in our use of energy and materials. We find that working on climate change implicates the entire economy and most of the environment. We find that transforming the economy is likely best accomplished by "getting the prices right," by forcing economic signals to tell the truth. All of which bring us to a final "How?" How do we overcome the inevitable and powerful political opposition to changes in the tax code, in subsidies, and in calculation of national income accounts?

We find ourselves again in the realm of the political. It will take political organization beyond anything the environmental movement has accomplished in its three or four decades of experience to make a tax shift a political reality. Thus in the final question about climate change, we find ourselves far from science or even economics. We find ourselves devising political strategies and considering issues as seemingly remote from climate change as campaign finance reform. These are not our specialties, but a complete discussion of what to do about climate change has to include them. We make two recommendations.

First, the removal of subsidies is an essential piece of "getting the prices right," often indistinguishable in substance and effect from a reform of the tax code. Yet subsidies have been studied for much longer than environmental taxes. As the President's Council on Sustainable Development said in 1996, "Their likely economic, environmental, and equity effects are relatively well known." So is the reason they have not come about: in the words of the council, "Intractable political barriers that have proven very difficult to overcome." But the removal of subsidies appeals both to environmentalists—usually considered left of center, especially in the political climate of the United States today—and to analysts from the far right—libertarians who believe in an unfettered market and a limited role for the federal government. These are strange bedfellows, but is it not possible that the two interests might join to present a stronger force for subsidy reform than either has been able to muster in the past? It would require a careful strategy, from the environmental point of view, to minimize potential conflicts and losses. But it is at least worth considering, if not undertaking. Subsidy reform is the thin edge of the wedge of "getting the prices right." Let us start soon to drive it in.

Though it may seem odd to write about campaign finance reform in a book about climate change, it is not as far-fetched as it appears. Industry interests enjoy disproportionate representation at the federal level—undemocratically disproportionate representation, it can be argued. Their ability to make enormous contributions to candidates, often to both candidates for a particular office, guaranteeing the ear of the winner regardless of party, outstrips their appropriate role in a democratic society. Industry interests are capable of stopping reforms of many kinds in their tracks. They are the "intractable political barriers" referred to by the President's Council on Sustainable Development.

We suggest that a full assault on climate change—a successful effort to stabilize the composition of the atmosphere—requires campaign finance reform in the United States. Corporate interests are largely responsible for the presence in the first instance of environmentally harmful subsidies to resource-related industry, and those interests rally at the slightest hint that the subsidies are inappropriate. These interests, working through members of Congress, have even prevented funding of earlier efforts in the Department of Commerce to take resources and the environment into account in calculating GNP. Campaign finance reform that restricts the influence of corporations on policy is probably a necessary step to getting the prices right, first by removing subsidies and then by shifting taxes to discourage activities that harm the environment and encourage activities that help it.

It is not such a new idea that working on climate change has politics at its heart. I received a one-sentence piece of political advice some years ago from a U.S. senator who was much engaged with issues that involved climate change. I offered to prepare a "white paper" for him giving up-to-date answers to the scientific questions he would likely have to consider in congressional and other discussions. His answer was brief. "Don't give me a white paper," he said, "give me a coalition."

Prevention and Adaptation

Getting the prices right and reforming national economic indices to take account of the environment are powerful strategies for transforming economic activities to decrease future greenhouse gas emissions. These strategies are designed to prevent steadily rising greenhouse gas

concentrations and therefore continuously more aggressive climate heating. Preventive strategies have a number
of advantages. They usually work better than cleaning up
after the fact—if such cleanup is possible—and they cost
less. In the case of climate change, they are necessary.
Without significant emission reductions, the force for
warming of the global climate will continue to increase,
moving the climate system further and further into conditions not experienced by Earth in a million years or more.

Preventive strategies alone are not sufficient, however. We can expect to prevent only part of a climate
warming. We are already committed to the portion that
will be induced by the extra greenhouse gases currently
in the atmosphere and by the additional amounts of these
gases that will be emitted during the period it will take to
reduce emissions to levels Earth can routinely absorb.
Indeed, if by some political and engineering magic, the
world stopped all emissions of carbon dioxide and other
heat-trapping gases tomorrow, we would still face climate warming. Higher concentrations of carbon dioxide,
nitrous oxide, and halocarbons, once released into the
air, persist for the better part of a century or more, continuing to trap heat. And after these gases have warmed
the air, it takes several more centuries for the mighty
oceans to draw their share of the warmth. Thus, even if
emissions were to cease, the extra greenhouse gases ac-
cumulated over the past two hundred years would continue to increase global temperature for decades and to
raise sea level for centuries.

When thinking of how society should respond to climate change, we need also to discuss how we might adapt to unavoidable climate change. The issue of adaptation often makes environmentalists uneasy, as if merely raising the question suggests that we will abandon all prevention and surrender to a vastly different climate. It is important to hold the two ideas simultaneously: we must prevent, and because of the way the climate system works and the lengthy time scales involved, we must also adapt. The need to adapt should not take away from the press to prevent—indeed, the more we prevent, the less we will eventually have to adapt. But we are not faced with the ideal option of prevention only.

As we adapt, let us do it right. Human beings, since they first walked upright, have dealt with extreme weather events and changing climates. Droughts and floods have produced famine since time immemorial; the most recent ice age generated changes in the lives of human beings almost beyond our imagination. Doubtless ice age people did adapt, for we are their descendants. They moved to different locations, probably developed warmer clothing and better shelter, and found other ways to carry on. We live today in a largely industrialized world, and the conditions under which we adapt, the tools we use, and the consequences of using those tools are vastly different than they were long ago. Even in the days of adaptation to ice age conditions, humans were capable of causing irreversible environmental impacts.

In North America, large mammals became extinct with the advent of people searching for ways to improve their lives.

One would imagine, at first, that we today are better equipped to adapt to something like climate change than were our ice age ancestors. We are, however, not always very competent at large-scale engineering projects, the tool of choice in our industrial era. Such projects create as well as solve problems. Given our tools and the scale of our activities, our sheer reach—to every ecosystem, mountaintop, and ocean floor—changes the terms of our relationship to Earth and the rules of adaptation.

Industrial society's history is replete with the adverse, unsafe effects of large-scale engineering projects and new technology. Indeed, from ozone-depleting chemicals through vehicle-produced urban smog, increased deaths from toxic chemicals and atmospheric pollution, the rising resistance of bacteria to antibiotics, and the simplification of ecosystems with agricultural activities, the heart of many environmental problems is the unintended consequences of well-meant improvements. Successful adaptation strategies require that we keep this in mind. When someone suggests large-scale engineering projects to adapt to climate change—seawalls around coastal cities, for example, or millions of silver-colored balloons constantly circling high in the atmosphere to reflect enough heat from the sun to cancel the extra greenhouse warming—let us remember our history with engineering and technological side effects and apply our incredible skill at analyzing and simulating the effects of complex proposals to foresee unfortunate side effects in advance.

There is an additional subtlety. Gilbert White, as a young geographer in the 1940s, found in his ground-breaking doctoral study that flood-control structures along the Ohio River increased, rather than reduced, flood damage. It seems that such structures tempt people to build in low areas near the river, inasmuch as the frequency of flood events is reduced. The result is more extensive damage than ever during the extreme floods that break through or overflow the structures. This para-doxical result should be kept in mind as we consider strategies to adapt to climate change.

8

Population and Climate Change Together

Don't be afraid to take big steps. You can't cross a chasm in two small jumps.

—Daniel Lloyd George

As we have spoken to family, friends, and colleagues about this book, one question has dominated (other than "How is it to write a book with your spouse?"). That question is, "How *do* population and climate change interact?"

One of the mechanical ways in which population and climate change interact is, obviously, human consumption of fossil fuels. Without reducing dramatically the amount of fossil fuel that each person uses, continued population growth accelerates climate change, as each new person adds more heat-trapping substances to the atmosphere. By the same token, every time per-capita emissions rise, the negative impact of each person on the climate is multiplied.

The causation arrows point in the opposite direction, too: climate change can amplify troubles faced by rapidly growing populations. Changes in the climate can make food production and economic development more difficult, by producing damaging floods and changing other environmental conditions important to human activities, and by forcing people from their homes and livelihoods through sea-level rise. Indeed, the combination of dense coastal populations and the potential for sea-level rise threatens hundreds of millions, even billions, of people around the world.

These mechanical interactions of population growth and climate change indicate that stabilizing human populations is part of the climate-change solution, as stabilizing the climate is part of the solution to human problems of growth and improved prosperity. Indeed, the same is true of all environmental and human development issues: the new balance we need to strike between human endeavors and Earth's systems requires action on both fronts. It is vital to remember, however, that as critical as stabilizing populations is, it does not have immediate environmental effects. Furthermore, success only guarantees fewer people than there would have been, not fewer people absolutely, except perhaps on very long time scales. Thus efforts to reduce per-capita use of environmentally harmful materials are the only short-term solution.

Apart from these interactions, the relationship between population and climate change that means the most to us is this: we believe that these issues, considered together, inspire two revolutions that are necessary if human beings are to flourish safely on Earth. One, related to population, is a social revolution characterized by greater equity and opportunity, including better health, for the poor of all countries, but with a special emphasis on women and girls. It is our belief that this revolution will create the conditions in which small families make sense: people will be able to have the number of children they want, those children will be healthy and educated, and populations will stabilize, giving human beings a reasonable chance to bring their numbers and their wants into harmony with Earth's ability to supply them.

The second revolution, equal in importance, is a material, economic, and industrial revolution that alters the connection between the way we meet our material needs, on the one hand, and Earth's resources and ecosystems, on the other. This revolution is a technical one, about extreme efficiency in the use of all energy and materials. We must learn to use as little energy as possible—and the safest kind—to heat buildings, move vehicles, and drive machines. Every material product used by human beings should be designed to last essentially forever, to be recycled, or to be composted. Every "waste" then would become a resource. Prices and economic measures must take natural systems into account.

With the social and the technical revolutions that we recommend, we believe that we can alter the destructive course on which we are currently set. Much is required to "save the world," and our two revolutions may give short shrift to aspects of the world's difficulties that others emphasize. But we believe these two revolutions are both essential and capable of turning us around. We do not offer them as the only steps to be taken, but as two large-scale, multifaceted, powerful steps on the road to sustainability.

The Equity Revolution

The revolution required to stabilize the world's population has its roots in the population movement's historical concern with resource depletion, poverty in large families and high-fertility countries, and access to family planning. Yet it goes far beyond this history, with its flavor of panic and blaming, to encompass a more constructive, hopeful agenda—the one framed in Cairo. That agenda calls for putting women at the center of development and improving their health and lives, all the while ensuring access to reproductive health—including family planning. Doing so would move women out of the second-class lives that many of them live today, simultaneously creating the conditions in which populations can stabilize. The question of coercion does not arise, nor does "educating" people in a country directly and specifically to want fewer children. "Take care of the people," the saying goes, "and population will take care of itself." Equally important is this: taking care of the people demands reproductive health, including family planning, and attention to women's lives.

Like the best development visions, the Cairo agenda, while requiring financial support from international agencies and the governments of wealthy industrial countries, has a strong grass-roots component. Indeed, CEDPA's experience in Nigeria allows the hope that despite the donor governments' failure to fund developing-country programs as fully as promised in Cairo, we can make progress because of the energy and devotion of the very women in the Third World who most need help. Bisi Ogunleye was organizing the market women of Ondo State, helping them to improve their lives, well before USAID funded programs in Nigeria.

Her progress would have been slower without the training and organizational skills that CEDPA provided, without U.S.-based funding, and without the access to contraception and other health care made possible by USAID programs. Both are required. It is shameful for wealthy countries to promise funding, then renege on the promise. But we should not imagine that the aid of wealthy countries *creates* the energy for improving women's lives in poor countries. The energy is there already. Funding enables it.

As we create the equity revolution, let us remember

women's lives as a whole. The same women who want birth control and better lives for their children want political participation and more democratic governments. Our equity revolution requires that women participate in building their governments, even (if not especially) infant democracies. Nigeria's 100 Women Groups and CEDPA's work on democracy and governance in Nigeria are models. Where else in the world would government be improved by increased participation of women? Just about everywhere.

The constructive—even indomitable—spirit of CEDPA's partners in Nigeria mirrors changes in attitude and approach that we recommend for American population activists as they work on their own issues related to growth and fertility, in addition to supporting U.S. assistance to groups such as CEDPA. In order to broaden the U.S. population movement to reflect the scope of the Cairo agenda, we recommend not singling out population as the only problem, or even the most important problem, but remembering that it is one of many equally critical problems. We recommend remembering the complexity of the interaction between population and the environment, avoiding determinism and oversimplification and including consumption and social issues. We recommend being constructive rather than punitive—changing the conditions that give rise to high fertility rather than haranguing families to have fewer children. We recommend appreciating the limits of laws, especially legislation that declares a policy of population stabilization. We recommend that the U.S. population movement work wisely on immigration, appreciating the explosive and divisive nature of this hotly political issues. And we urge an appreciation that there are many ways to understand the population issue.

Gender equity is focused most sharply on the fertility component of population issues, the only driving force of global population growth and far more important in most national population growth than immigration. Equity beyond the empowerment of women—higher incomes for all poor people, and more wealth for poor countries as a whole—would affect international immigration by reducing both the critical "push" factor of poverty and the powerful "pull" factor of jobs in industrialized countries. While people leave their countries for reasons other than employment (political and environmental refugees must also be considered), reducing the inequities that drive job-related immigration would strike a blow for a sustained reduction in immigration and thus in population growth in receiving countries. At the same time, higher incomes and empowerment among the poor would create the conditions that reduce population growth in sending countries as well.

The Cairo agenda for population stabilization is often criticized as too much and too costly. In addition, the political alliance that underlies the agenda—feminist reproductive health activists and traditional family planners—is sometimes seen as fragile and contradictory. Feminists have occasionally complained since Cairo that the world is still ignoring race, class, and economic structures as it attempts to improve people's lives. Family planners have complained that broadening the agenda dilutes scarce funding dollars; in fact, funding for family planning suffers in the end, some say.

In our view, the Cairo agenda is the right agenda. To those women who already desire family planning—the 150 million women who do not wish to become pregnant yet are not using family planning, or who want improved services—Cairo says, "Provide high-quality services now." It is a simple matter of health care that people already want. Given funding, family-planning programs—effective ones, with STD and RTI screening and links to other reproductive health care services—stand ready to provide that care.

In settings where families want many children, Cairo says, "Make sure those children are healthy, by delaying and spacing births." This is the beginning of improving the status of women and girls, of creating the conditions in which smaller families will eventually make sense. Healthier children who survive infancy in greater numbers provide a mother more mastery over her life. Such improvement can lead to other forms of mastery, such as better health for the mother, allowing her to care for her family effectively and to earn money. The Cairo agenda urges us always to ask, "What do the women in this place want?" Healthy children? Start there. It is the beginning of the revolution.

It is critical to say that, under the Cairo approach, women's rights—to be treated with respect, as first-class citizens—are more fundamental than family planning, fertility, or population goals. The Cairo coalition is not for those who believe that coercion in family planning or elsewhere is sometimes justified; they should work in other ways. The same is true for those who believe that screening for reproductive tract infections and sexually transmitted diseases is an "extra" that comes after family planning is available everywhere. Screening is integral to it.

Health is the common ground on which the feminist activists and family planners met in Cairo. The health of women is the standard for resolving conflicts. Of course we cannot have it all. Even with infinite funding, women would not be "empowered" instantly. Cultures change slowly, and money is always too scarce. The question we should ask is, "What promotes women's health most cost effectively in a particular place, given the funds available?" Does family planning by itself in a particular setting promote women's health more than no family planning, if funding constraints force a choice between family planning alone and nothing at all? Family planning alone is then the choice. Still, Cairo says one must be absolutely sure that the money available is not better spent on maternal and child health or other aspects of reproductive health. It depends entirely on local conditions, on what women want and on the state of their health. It is crucial to rely on bottom-up, participatory decisionmaking, always asking, "What do people here want most?"

It is our belief that what people want is a revolution, an equity revolution, and that in wanting this, they want a stable population and a new relationship with Earth.

The broadest vision of the equity revolution, involving true economic equity across classes within nations and among nations, is also integral to preventing and adapting to climate change. The resentment of poor nations for wealthy ones is a constant barrier to international agreements that would move the world toward stabilizing the composition of the atmosphere. Inequities within nations emerge in discussions of getting the prices right, when a program is blocked by concerns that higher energy prices will disadvantage poor people. In this way, the equity revolution, while conceived principally to foster population stabilization, would also (though less directly) work toward ameliorating climate change.

The Efficiency Revolution

We call for an efficiency revolution because of what we know and believe. Our moral compass points to action. We know the world is warming. We know that the by-products of our fossil-fuel-based energy economy drive the warming. Complex mathematical models of the atmosphere tell us, with increasing reliability, that if we continue to emit greenhouse gases into the air as we do today, global average temperature is likely to rise by several degrees centigrade over the next hundred years, and sea level is likely to rise a foot and a half.

A warmer climate will stress the unmanaged biosphere as forests, grasslands, and other ecosystems, adapted to one particular climate, struggle to adapt to another. We know that saltwater marshes and mangrove ecosystems will be flooded by sea-level rise.

We know that agriculture is faced with the need to adapt to both rising temperatures and changing rainfall regimes and water supplies. Farmers in prosperous countries have more resources and are more likely to adapt successfully than their counterparts in poor countries.

Such impacts are large enough to demand our concern. In 1992 the global community at UNCED negotiated the Framework Convention on Climate Change. In that document the world agreed to stabilize the concentration of greenhouse gases in the atmosphere, to prevent "dangerous" human-induced alteration of the climate, quickly enough to allow ecosystems to adapt, to protect food production, and to allow sustainable development to proceed. The details of how the world can do this are still under negotiation.

The obstacles to an international agreement to reduce greenhouse gas emissions are many. Countries fight over who should go first, despite the principle, embodied in the FCCC, that wealthy countries should take the lead. Some in the north argue that developing countries must make an effort too. Much of the south argues that climate change, a product of northern activity, should be addressed first by the north. Small island states, most of them underdeveloped, argue that both the north and large southern countries such as China and India should act promptly and decisively to curb emissions.

Perhaps the most powerful obstacle to agreement so far is the prevailing belief that reducing emissions will cost too much. But we know that the economic case against action on climate change is not as strong as its supporters claim. A critical interpretation of the economic models on which the claims are based reveals that what is usually understood as a net cost is actually a brief delay in achieving a GNP significantly larger than it is today. Further, many companies are already investing in energy efficiency, reducing emissions in the process, and achieving high returns on their investments in a short period. Reducing the world's reliance on fossil fuel would bring with it a decrease in urban air pollution; improved health of city dwellers, especially children; a diminishing of acid rain; and a loosening of the grip that oil-exporting countries, especially those in the Middle East, have on international affairs.

We also know that curbing climate change reduces the possibility that the world will be surprised by a sharp and sudden shift in the climate. As a complex system, the climate is capable of making such a shift under changing conditions, as it did during the Younger Dryas. It would probably bring enough chaos and stress to cause the adverse consequences of a slow climate change to pale in comparison.

We know all of this, and we know what we need to do to avoid the worst effects of climate heating. The answer has three levels: reduce greenhouse gas emissions to levels that the atmosphere can absorb without harm, use energy much more efficiently than we do today, and pressure economic signals—both prices and national income accounts—to tell the environmental truth. With a wisely designed revenue-neutral tax shift, prices would tell the environmental truth with no net cost to taxpayers on average, though some firms and households would need help through the transition period. Getting the prices right would unleash the staggering innovative power of the world's industry—probably the most powerful force in the world today, and the only one in control of enough resources, financial and material, to be able to solve the challenge posed by climate change. Reforming national income accounts would provide governments and industries an indicator of economic growth that would reliably signal the prosperity and well-being of both people and nature.

Creating the economic changes required by the efficiency revolution needs governmental action, which in turn calls for political change. We believe that full-scale campaign finance reform, already being urged by many in the United States, is the most direct and powerful way to bring about this needed change. Industry today is blocking subsidy and tax changes that would get the prices right, environmentally right, as it enjoys disproportionate power in legislatures and with presidents and governors. Standing in the way of success on climate change and on a broader efficiency revolution, this disproportionate power we believe, must go.

Prevention of further greenhouse gas emissions through energy and materials efficiency is the most effective, least costly, and most elegant of strategies for dealing with climate change. But we do not have the luxury of prevention only. We will be called on to adapt, as well, given the greenhouse gases that have already been emitted and the time it will take to engineer the transition to efficiency. We need to admit that adaptation is necessary, without allowing it to take the place of present action to prevent future harm. We need to adapt well and wisely, doing better than our history suggests we will.

No one imagines that we will organize and engineer this transition overnight. Even if we break the logjam of international negotiations, overcome the resistance to appropriate prices, and break through international traditions of calculating economic progress, we will be working out the details of the transition for decades. Yet what could be more exciting than to forge a new industrial revolution? To be part of a sparkling generation of leaders, to participate with the best minds, the sharpest innovators, and the wisest philosophers, to create a new world? Such an enterprise is second only to the complexity and beauty of the natural world itself. Let us hasten to begin this new industrial revolution, holding our prospects and our heritage in equal respect.

The central challenge facing the world at the beginning of the twenty-first century derives from the following facts. The world's population is very likely to exceed 10 billion before it stops growing. Ninety percent of that growth will be in Asia, Africa, and Latin America, the countries least able to cope with the growth. At the same time, the global consensus—a morally correct consensus—is that the world's poorer people should have lives that are far more materially generous, with greater social and economic equity, than they have today. They should see "development." At the same time, the sources of material wealth that support and drive development—the physical world, the environment, natural resources—are not infinite, and it is obvious that we are pushing the natural world's ecosystems beyond the point at which they can continue to supply us. This is the dilemma that we face: how to meet the needs of ever more people ever more generously, with a limited, even deteriorating, base of physical resources.

The two revolutions we describe in this book would, we feel, allow the world to escape this bind. All the while that populations grow, the world is essentially walking down the up escalator of development. Everything required to improve people's lives is harder if the number of people is growing, especially if that growth is rapid. A stable population means that development gains actually improve people's lives. Superefficiency in the use of energy and materials, and the substitution of environmentally benign alternatives, mean that living standards can rise without harming the environment. The talents of half the world's population, previously oppressed, will be unleashed and perhaps the greatest environmental threat ever—altering the very fabric of Earth's atmosphere—will be avoided. Given the stakes, given the alternatives, given the promise of our two revolutions, we urge our readers to become rebels. Ralph Waldo Emerson called a revolution "a thought in one person's mind." Have the thought. Join the insurrection.

Dancing in the Crowded Greenhouse

Holding two competing ideas in the mind simultaneously is one of the challenges of an active intelligence.

—F. Scott Fitzgerald

We have a great friend who has worked long and hard on environmental and population issues, in both elective politics and the non-profit world. She told us a story some years ago that affected us deeply.

She participated in a retreat of several days for high-level environmental activists and policymakers, where thoughtful people led and joined in probing discussions. At one point, she was asked if she had hope. Now, this friend has probably the most austere view of the future of the world of any of our environmental friends. She has seen too much of the world's deterioration, the human role in it, and resistance to stemming it, to be sanguine. After a pause, she replied: "No, I don't have hope. But I have great joy."

It is on this paradoxical note that we end our book. In addition to her gritty realism, our friend brings to her work abundant humor, an openness to celebration, and a profound act of will: she simply will not give up. We recommend these qualities to anyone committed to joining the work to stabilize the world's population and stem harmful climate change—indeed, for that matter, any work involving high stakes and enormous odds.

We offer the metaphor of dancing in the crowded greenhouse to develop our notions about humor, celebration, and acts of will. So let us take our places. The music is playing. We are gathered together, many of us, ready to dance in this crowded greenhouse that we wish to change. Let us begin.

Let us dance with our friends.

We in the population and environmental movements have traditionally been a grim group. Who would not be grim, given what we are up against? We have in the past thirty years made progress, however, and we should admit and celebrate it.

On the population side, fertility declines since 1950 translate into national populations smaller by millions—and on a global scale, by hundreds of millions—than we would have otherwise seen. Think of the worsening conditions that hundreds of millions more people would have meant. This success sounds conditional and abstract. It is. But it is also real, and it is worth celebrating.

In recent years the United Nations has revised its population projections for 2050 downward. Where once the "medium projection" of the U.N. demographers envisioned more than 11 billion people in 2050, today their number is closer to 9 billion: more than today, and more than ideal. But fewer than expected, and worth celebrating.

Today women in fifty-one countries with 44 percent of the world's population have fewer than 2.0 children in their lifetimes, long thought—especially by demographers—to be the "lowest" that fertility would go. This reduction has come about in part because of a revolution in the use of modern contraceptives; more than half of the world's women use them, whereas thirty years ago, only a small percentage did. All this is worth celebrating.

Population growth rates are zero or negative in nearly twenty countries, affecting just under 10 percent of the world's population. The list is dominated by Russia and countries of the former Soviet Union and Eastern Bloc, and we need to sort out when desperate economic conditions drive negative population growth rates and when choice does. Still, these developments deserve notice, and celebration.

Examples of success from the environmental world are less far-reaching and less encouraging. But we have

examples, nonetheless. Despite its being thus far largely
rhetorical, rather than practical, we believe that the sheer
existence of Agenda 21, the sweeping blueprint for sustainable development negotiated at UNCED in 1992, is
a success worth celebrating. The language is lofty: "Humanity stands at a defining moment in history . . . No
nation can secure its future alone; but together we can:
in a global partnership for sustainable development."
The scope is comprehensive: the document covers poverty, wealth, health, human settlements, many resources,
many wastes, many forms of degradation, many ecosystems. It also specifies groups that sustainable development must involve if it is to succeed—women, children
and youth, indigenous people, NGOs, workers, business
and industry, and the scientific and technological community. Before we can build a new world, we need a blueprint, and Agenda 21 is an ambitious start. Much work
lies ahead, but this blueprint is worth celebrating.

Two developments that affect the atmosphere directly
are also worth celebrating. Global production of CFCs, the
halocarbons responsible for depletion of stratospheric
ozone, has fallen sharply since 1989, when global CFC
production peaked at just over a million tons. Today, in
response to the Montreal Protocol, which banned most
production of CFCs in industrial countries, and subsequent amendments, the figure is below 150,000 tons. The
problem of stratospheric ozone is far from over. CFCs take
some years to reach the stratosphere and, once there, remain for a century or more. Although the decline has been

sharp, it is somewhat slower than expected. A black market in CFCs and the failure of some countries to comply with the protocol's production phase-out schedule further compromise success on stratospheric ozone. Still, CFC production has indeed fallen sharply, and this is cause for celebration.

Second, it is possible that global emissions of sulfur have stabilized. After rising throughout the twentieth century, emissions have in recent years flattened out. And in some industrialized countries, emissions have fallen sharply—by 80 percent in Austria, nearly 80 percent in Germany, and 75 percent in Norway between 1980 and 1996, for example. Technologies for removing sulfur from the smokestacks of coal-burning power plants, economic downturns in the former Soviet Union and eastern Europe, and emission control policies such as the U.S. tradable permits scheme lie behind the lack of growth in sulfur emissions in recent years. Acid rain continues to plague large portions of European forests, and India's and China's choice of energy technologies— whether clean or dirty—will determine the future of sulfur emissions. But the world has made a start. It is worth celebrating.

We are far from being able to say that the world is turning significantly to a sustainable way of living. But a few signs indicate at least tentative moves in that direction. Global wind-generating capacity has since 1980 been following a trend that resembles the alarming curve of population growth in the past century—but in this case, it is good news. Global shipments of solar cells have followed a similar curve in the past thirty years, rising sharply in the 1990s. Sales of compact fluorescent light bulbs are also increasing rapidly, indicating a commitment to more efficient lighting. These are small developments in the global scheme of things, and they are always dwarfed by "business-as-usual" approaches. But they are good news, all the same.

Many people working in environment and population resist giving their approval to such developments. This metaphor is often mentioned: "If you're in a car speeding toward a brick wall at 60 miles an hour and you slow down to 40, you're still going to kill yourself smashing into the wall!" True. And we can understand why people feel that world population and environmental deterioration are the equivalent of a car speeding toward a brick wall.

In fact, they are *not* a car speeding toward a brick wall. We live on a complex planet, with centuries of history and the enormous weight of momentum from the past. Yes, that momentum is pushing us in a direction that is dangerous and harmful. But does it not make sense, especially given how big the job is and how heavy the burden is, to note and even celebrate successes in changing, and even overcoming, this momentum? Because falling fertility and slowing population growth, though not yet enough, indeed go in the right direction, as do Agenda 21, the Montreal Protocol, a halt in sulfur emissions, and sales of environmentally benign technologies. We are not really speeding toward the brick wall any longer. We are speeding—at a slower rate—toward, perhaps, the shrubbery. We will still get hurt, badly, unless we turn even more sharply—so we plow into an open field, say, or better yet, stop altogether on a smooth paved road.

We need to do this for more than the personal need to celebrate victories. If we fail to admit—before those who oppose us point it out—that fertility is indeed falling, that population growth rates are slowing, that contraceptive use is rising, we are open to the charge that we are exaggerating the problem. The same is true for environmental improvements, on those rare occasions when they happen. We need to seize that territory before our critics do.

We also need to seize it first because the press and some analysts misinterpret the slightest hint of progress as complete success, and conclude that the job is over. The past few years have seen several stories in major newspapers asserting that "the population explosion is over," on the basis that growth rates have slowed and fertility is falling. The failure to appreciate the difference between absolute numbers and changing rates of growth is maddening indeed. We have to be there, with the ability to hold two competing ideas in our minds simultaneously, pointing out that indeed we have made progress, and indeed we need to make a lot more.

So let us dance with our friends, celebrating victories, large and small.

Let us also dance with our enemies, with those who disagree with us and fight us.

This approach may not seem humorous or celebratory, but it is smart. As we dance with our enemies, we have the chance to observe them up close. As we feel that we know their weaknesses—their beliefs that human beings can take over nature and manage it successfully, that women are second-class citizens—let us learn their strengths.

Let us look closely and determine what our opponents get right. Is the natural world just a little more resilient than we environmentalists think? The idea is worth considering. It is far from a license for further violence against the natural world, but it is a basis for hope about Earth's eventual recovery.

Are markets indeed powerful tools for distributing resources? If so, can we use them on our side? We already know that the answer is yes, and new environmental policies from tradable permits for sulfur emissions to an environmental tax shift are already starting to work well.

Are people indeed our greatest resource? In fact, yes. Most people themselves want fewer children; when healthy and empowered, they choose to have fewer children. People are indeed population stabilization's most promising resource.

Are business and industry other great resources? In fact, yes. As business and industry have been the most powerful in harming the environment, their power must be tapped to save the environment. Without them, we have very little hope of creating a sustainable world.

Is religion a powerful force? Yes, indeed. It is probably

unwise to be entirely and exclusively secular in our alternatives to religion-based traditions that keep women as second-class citizens or that see the world as the dominion of humans alone. It is also unwise to fail to mention the divine quality of nature, of creation. Human beings are religious creatures, and it is foolhardy to exclude notions of the divine from our vision of the new world.

Dancing with our enemies will not be as much fun as dancing with our friends. Yet we can learn a lot. And perhaps our enemies will learn to like us, on the dance floor of the crowded greenhouse.

We urge everyone involved in population and the environment to dance with themselves, as well. We must be kind to ourselves as we try to save the world. Thousands of issues are involved; we can be overwhelmed, or we can appreciate the abundance of issues on which we can work. Each of us must choose among the many areas something that we love and that we can handle. For example, even though we are deeply committed to protecting children from violence, we cannot work directly on that goal for very long without wearing down. It is just too hard. So we put our energies elsewhere, where we can work longer and more effectively.

Dancing alone in the crowded greenhouse also means doing the emotional work required to stay constructive and effective. Whether our job deals with it, or we volunteer a little time, or we simply believe in it and vote accordingly, any level of activism on population and the environment, as on any of the "big problems" like war, poverty, or social injustice, requires doing a piece of psychological work. Without it, we risk being so angry, so desperate, or so depressed that we compromise our effectiveness.

The piece of work is to do what is needed to reconcile ourselves to a terrible contradiction: that we are utterly committed to changes that are absolutely necessary but may never come about. We may lose! We are not sure what the chances are. Some days, it seems we have far better than a fifty-fifty chance of winning. Other days, collapse is imminent. We have to recognize both possibilities, or the chance of failure will destroy us. We have seen informed, dedicated people so twisted by anger over the path the world is following that they are not only completely ineffective, they are positively destructive. We have seen students hotly interested in the whole package of issues at the beginning of the semester who sink into despair at midterm. Even some of the original thinkers in both population and environment, in our opinion, undermine themselves with sarcasm, which is a variant of anger. Some laugh in response, but others they might have reached are put off.

Let us do the piece of work. Talking to friends and advisers can help, especially people who seem to have accomplished the reconciliation, at least for now. Whatever the technique for dealing with difficulties and sorrows, it must be employed in this work. It is not incidental, dispensable, or extra. It is central. Indeed, it is more: it is an obligation of active intelligence and the price of commitment.

As we have danced in our own crowded greenhouse over the years, we have found a single rule to be enormously helpful. It is this: the only sin is giving up. This rule comes with a dry joke, too. You are only allowed to give up on alternate Thursdays. And, please, try to coordinate with your dancing partner, so that you do not both give up on the same day.

When your Thursday is over, do what you must: reach deep, dig into your most profound beliefs about how the world works and how you fit into it, mourn the sorrows and the losses. Then get back to work, with joy.

Bibliographic Essay

Chapter 1. One Vision of the Year 2050

In recent years various authors have published possible or suggestive scenarios for important events and changes in the twenty-first century or for the period up to the year 2050. Our first chapter adds one to the list. For an informative review of the usefulness of scenarios and of examples constructed by individuals, committees, industries, or government agencies see Allen Hammond, *Which World: Scenarios for the Twenty-First Century*, Island Press, 1998.

Most of the numbers in Chapter 1 are invented. We were guided in our invention of population figures by United Nations, *World Population Prospects: The 1994 Revision, Annex Tables* (published informally in 1994 by the United Nations, Population Division of the Department for Economic and Social Information and Policy Analysis), and various annual editions of the Population Reference Bureau's *World Population Data Sheet* (Washington, D.C.: Population Reference Bureau).

Chapter 2. The New World of Population Policy

Joel Cohen's *How Many People Can the Earth Support?* was published in 1995 by W. W. Norton, New York. The material cited is at pp. 5–6.

Early sources of population rhetoric containing envi-
ronmental and resource-scarcity arguments include Paul
Ehrlich, *The Population Bomb* (New York: Ballantine
Books, 1968) and Lester Brown, *The Twenty-Ninth Day*
(New York: W. W. Norton, 1971).

Thomas Malthus first published *An Essay on the Principle of Population* (Harmondsworth, England: Penguin
Books, 1970) in 1798. See pp. 249–250 for the "moral
restraint" point. For earlier European concern with population growth and economic resources, see Cohen, *How Many
People Can the Earth Support?* pp. 6–7.

The coitus interruptus reference is Genesis 38:8–10.

John Riddle's works on contraceptives and abortifacients in early medical texts are *Contraception and Abortion from the Ancient World to the Renaissance* (Cambridge, Massachusetts: Harvard University Press, 1992) and
*Eve's Herbs: A History of Contraception and Abortion in the
West* (Cambridge, Massachusetts: Harvard University Press,
1997).

For the presence of abortion in people's lives in many
cultures and times, see the U.S. Supreme Court's opinion
in *Roe* v. *Wade,* 410 U.S. 113 (1973), pp. 130–141, written
by Justice Harry Blackmun. For infanticide, see William
Langer, "Infanticide: A Historical Survey," *History of Childhood Quarterly* 1:353–365 (1973–1974); William Harris,
"The Theoretical Possibility of Extensive Infanticide in the
Greco-Roman World," *Classical Quarterly* 32:114–116
(1982); and Barbara Kellum, "Infanticide in England in the
Later Middle Ages," *History of Childhood Quarterly* 1:367–
388 (1973–1974).

Material on Francis Place can be found in Garrett
Hardin, ed., *Population, Evolution, and Birth Control: A
Collage of Controversial Ideas* (San Francisco: W. H. Free-
man, 1969), pp. 188–191 and 192–193. See also Peter
Fryer, *The Birth Controllers* (New York: Stein and Day,
1966), pp. 43–57.

For the history of the modern family planning movement, with an emphasis on the United States, see, for example, James Reed, *The Birth Control Movement and American Society: From Private Vice to Public Virtue* (Princeton: Princeton University Press, 1982); Hardin, *Population, Evolution, and Birth Control,* pp. 198–203; and Paul Ehrlich and Anne Ehrlich, *Population, Resources, Environment: Issues in Human Ecology* (San Francisco: W. H. Freeman, 1970), pp. 234–235. For a biography of Margaret Sanger, see Ellen Chesler, *Woman of Valor: Margaret Sanger and the Birth Control Movement in America* (New York: Simon and Schuster, 1992). For a biography of Marie Stopes, see Ruth Hall, *Passionate Crusader: The Life of Marie Stopes* (New York: Harcourt Brace Jovanovich, 1977).

For social scientists' early views of family planning, see Paul Demeny, "The Populations of the Underdeveloped Countries," *Scientific American,* September 1974, pp. 149–159 at 152, and Paul Demeny, letter to the editor, *Scientific American,* May 1975, pp. 6–7.

On the argument that family planning is not enough to solve the population problem, see Kingsley Davis, "Population Policy: Will Current Programs Succeed?" *Science* 158:730–739 (1967); Kingsley Davis, "Zero Population Growth: The Goal and the Means," in Mancur Olson and Hans Landsberg, eds., *The No-Growth Society* (New York: W. W. Norton, 1973), pp. 15–30; and Ehrlich and Ehrlich, *Population, Resources, Environment,* pp. 251–252.

For other measures, see Bernard Berelson, "Beyond Family Planning," *Studies in Family Planning,* February 1969, pp. 1–16. See also Ehrlich and Ehrlich, *Population, Resources, Environment,* pp. 252–256. For a widely known theoretical analysis favoring "coercive" measures to stem population growth, see Garrett Hardin, "The Tragedy of the Commons," *Science* 162:1243–48 (1968).

For the history of events leading to the creation of the U.S. foreign assistance program in family planning, see

Phyllis Piotrow, *World Population Crisis: The United States Response* (New York: Praeger, 1973), pp. 12–100. For the history of the Agency for International Development's population program, see Peter Donaldson, *Nature Against Us: The United States and the World Population Crisis, 1965–1980* (Chapel Hill: University of North Carolina Press, 1990).

The original legislation that created the domestic U.S. family planning program is *Family Planning Services and Population Research Act of 1970,* Public Law 91-572. The act can be read as passed in *United States Code and Congressional and Administrative News,* 91st Congress—Second Session, 1970, vol. 1, *Laws* (St. Paul, Minnesota: West Publishing Company, 1970), pp. 1748–53.

Part of the legislative history of Title X can be found at *United States Code and Congressional and Administrative News,* 91st Congress—Second Session, 1970, vol. 3, *Legislative History, Proclamations, Executive Orders, Reorganization Plans, Tables, and Index* (St. Paul, Minnesota: West Publishing Company, 1970). Piotrow, *World Population Crisis,* also discusses events leading to the passage of Title X; see pp. 98 and 194–198. See also "United States: Report of the President's Committee on Population and Family Planning," *Studies in Family Planning,* April 1969, pp. 1–4.

For the U.S. share of international population assistance from 1965 to 1980, see Donaldson, *Nature Against Us,* pp. 49–50. For the 1995 figure, see United Nations Population Fund (UNFPA), *Global Population Assistance Report, 1995* (New York: United Nations, 1997), p. 13.

The source for "mass distribution of contraceptives" and "technical fix" is Donaldson, *Nature Against Us,* pp. 53 and 55. For a discussion of unmet demand, see John Bongaarts, "The KAP-Gap and the Unmet Need for Contraception," *Population and Development Review* 17:293–313 (1991).

Figures on current contraceptive prevalence and family

size are from Population Reference Bureau, *2000 World Population Data Sheet* (Washington, D.C.: Population Reference Bureau, 2000). For early figures on contraceptive prevalence and average family size, see Alene Gelbard, Carl Haub, and Mary Kent, *World Population Beyond Six Billion,* Population Bulletin, vol. 54, no. 1 (Washington, D.C.: Population Reference Bureau, March 1999), p. 13. Also of interest is John Bongaarts, W. Parker Mauldin, and James Phillips, "The Demographic Impact of Family Planning Programs," *Studies in Family Planning* 21:299–310, at pp. 300–301 (1990). A useful summary of regional fertility declines between 1970 and 1995 can be found in United Nations, *The World's Women, 1995: Trends and Statistics* (New York: United Nations, 1995), p. 15.

For an examination of whether or not family planning programs actually change the number of children that people want, see Ronald Freedman, "Do Family Planning Programs Affect Fertility Preferences? A Literature Review," *Studies in Family Planning* 28:1–13 (1997).

The Mauldin and Ross study is W. Parker Mauldin and John Ross, "Family Planning Programs: Efforts and Results, 1982–89," *Studies in Family Planning* 22:350–367 (1991). The figures cited are drawn from text and tables on pp. 357–359.

Fertility rates and average GNP per capita for Colombia, Bangladesh, Italy, Hong Kong, Bulgaria, and the Czech Republic are from *2000 World Population Data Sheet.*

For a discussion of why poverty provides a supportive environment for high fertility, and a brief treatment of the fertility–infant mortality link, see World Bank, *World Development Report, 1994* (New York: Oxford University Press, 1994), pp. 51–52. For the complex aspects of poverty and their interactions with fertility, see, for instance, Gelbard et al., *World Population Beyond Six Billion,* p. 27. For a brief summary of the connection between women's education and fertility, see, for example, World Resources Institute, *World Resources, 1994–1995: A Guide to the*

Global Environment (New York: Oxford University Press, 1994), p. 32. For a survey of the issues surrounding women's lives and their fertility, and a summary of findings about the causal connections, see Nafis Sadik, "Investing in Women: The Focus of the '90's," in Laurie Ann Mazur, ed., *Beyond the Numbers: A Reader on Population, Consumption, and the Environment* (Washington, D.C.: Island Press, 1994), pp. 209–226.

Jodi Jacobson, "Women's Reproductive Health: The Silent Emergency," Worldwatch Paper 102 (Washington, D.C.: Worldwatch Institute, 1991), and National Research Council, *Reproductive Health in Developing Countries: Expanding Dimensions, Building Solutions* (Washington, D.C.: National Academy Press, 1997), are the principal sources for the section on women's reproductive health.

Figures on RTIs are from National Research Council, *Reproductive Health in Developing Countries,* pp. 40 and 45–48.

For information on the Safe Motherhood Initiative, see Anne Tinker and Marjorie Koblinsky, *Making Motherhood Safe* (Washington, D.C.: World Bank, 1993).

See Jodi Jacobson, "Women's Reproductive Health," pp. 38–51, for an analysis of limited family planning programs.

For a treatment of coercion in some family planning programs, see Betsy Hartmann, *Reproductive Rights and Wrongs: The Global Politics of Population Control* (Boston: South End Press, 1995).

See Jyoti Singh, *Creating a New Consensus on Population* (London: Earthscan Publications, 1998) for the history, chronology, and issues involved in the International Conference on Population and Development, including the importance of feminist activists and the emergence of the reproductive health approach.

The text of the "Women's Declaration on Population Policies" can be found in *Information Kit: Women's Perspectives on Population Issues,* published by Isis International for circulation prior to the ICPD in Cairo in September 1994. Jodi Jacobson's work includes "Women's Reproductive Health." Judith Bruce's includes "Fundamental Elements of the Quality of Care: A Simple Framework," *Studies in Family Planning* 21:61–91 (1990).

For the history of U.N. population conferences, see Singh, *Creating a New Consensus on Population,* and Lori Ashford, *New Perspectives on Population: Lessons from Cairo,* Population Bulletin, March (Washington, D.C.: Population Reference Bureau, 1995).

The official document negotiated at Cairo is United Nations, *International Conference on Population and Development,* Cairo, Egypt, 5–13 September 1994, A/CONF. 171/13. Eight of its sixteen chapters can also be found in *Population and Development Review* 21:187–213 (1995).

U.S. population funding levels since 1993 are taken from a table prepared by the U.S. Agency for International Development, "U.S. Funding for Population and Reproductive Health Assistance: FY 1993–1998 Obligations (millions of dollars)."

Chapter 3. Putting Cairo to Work

Figures on Nigeria's population are from Population Reference Bureau, *2000 World Population Data Sheet* (Washington, D.C.: Population Reference Bureau, 2000).

An interview with Peggy Curlin in the Washington offices of CEDPA on November 17, 2000, is the source of both her story and parts of Bisi Ogunleye's. Interviews on the same date with Elizabeth Keys MacManus and with Joyce Holfeld, a USAID officer who worked with MacManus in Nigeria, are the source of the MacManus story.

Some of the material on CEDPA-Nigeria is taken from sources published by CEDPA in booklet form: annual reports of the organization since 1994, and *Women on the Move,* published in Lagos in September 1997 by the CEDPA Nigeria field office. Information is also available about

CEDPA-Nigeria in a quarterly newsletter, *The CEDPA Network: News for Alumni and Associates,* available from CEDPA at 1400 16th Street, N.W., Suite 100, Washington, DC 20036, telephone (202) 667-1142. CEDPA's website, at *www.cedpa.org,* is an additional source.

Some details about COWAN's work; its geographic spread in Nigeria; the number of women reached through the democracy and governance initiative; and confirmation of details regarding Nigerian elections, elements of programs, and funding figures were provided by Dr. Entyantu Ifenne, resident adviser to the CEDPA-Nigeria field office, in December 2000.

Otherwise, all the figures and stories in Chapter 3 are taken from unpublished materials found in CEDPA's Washington office: project proposals, from Nigerian organizations to CEDPA in Washington and from CEDPA-Washington to the U.S. Agency for International Development; progress reports on numerous projects; annual reports since 1975 on file in the Washington office; correspondence between the various grassroots Nigerian groups and the CEDPA headquarters; applications for training; and reports of conferences. Some of these materials, with no title and few dates, are difficult to cite.

The most useful file materials were these: the most recent proposal to USAID for reproductive health programs in Nigeria under ENABLE; the April 1996 proposal from CEDPA and Johns Hopkins to USAID for the democracy and governance program in Nigeria, entitled "Towards Civil Society: Building the Capacity and Participation of Women's NGOs in Nigeria"; the year 2000 proposal to USAID from CEDPA for democracy and governance programs; "Nigeria Democracy and Governance Initiative Final Result for Phase II, ENABLE Project," March 1998–February 1999; proposal submitted by the National Council of Women's Societies, Plateau State branch, to CEDPA in 1995; and the proposal submitted by the Grassroots Health Organization of Nigeria to CEDPA in 1997.

Chapter 4. U.S. Population Activism in the New Century

See Chapter 2 above for full citations for Ehrlich's *Population Bomb,* Brown's *Twenty-Ninth Day,* and Hardin's "Tragedy of the Commons."

Figures for U.S. fertility in 1960 are from U.S. Department of Commerce, *Statistical Abstract of the United States, 1997* (Washington, D.C.: Government Printing Office, 1997), p. 77. The current China fertility figure is from Population Reference Bureau, *2000 World Population Data Sheet.*

Lester Thurow's quotation is from his article, "Why the Ultimate Size of the World's Population Doesn't Matter," *Technology Review,* vol. 89, no. 22, August 1986.

For an exhaustive treatment of unintended pregnancy in the United States, see Institute of Medicine, *The Best Intentions: Unintended Pregnancy and the Well-Being of Children and Families* (Washington, D.C.: National Academy Press, 1995).

For the link between child sexual abuse and adolescent pregnancy, see Debra Boyer and David Fine, "Sexual Abuse as a Factor in Adolescent Pregnancy and Child Maltreatment," *Family Planning Perspectives,* vol. 24, no. 1, January/February 1992, pp. 4–11.

The 1999 population policy bill was H. Con. Res. (House Concurrent Resolution) 17.

Chapter 5. A Warming World

For descriptions of typical proxy measurements see H. H. Lamb, *Climate: Present, Past, and Future,* vol. 2 (London: Metheun, 1977), and La Marche, "Tree-Ring Evidence of Past Climatic Variability," *Nature,* vol. 276 (1978).

Kenneth Boulding's essay was published as "Fun and Games with the Gross National Product: The Role of Misleading Indicators in Social Policy," in H. W. Helfrich, Jr., ed., *Environmental Crises: Man's Struggle to Live with Himself* (New Haven: Yale University Press, 1970).

Many economic models of costs use as their output Gross Domestic Product (GDP) instead of Gross National Product (GNP). GDP is defined as GNP minus foreign receipts by national companies. The difference is not material to the discussion here, so for simplicity I use GNP throughout.

Boulding brought clarity as well as humor to any group with which he was involved. During one discussion of environmental affairs, he quietly penned the following poem:

> With development extended to the whole of planet earth
> What started with abundance may conclude in dismal
>   dearth.
> And it really will not matter then who started it or ran it
> If development results in an entirely plundered planet.

Many fine texts are available to explain the science of climate change and the greenhouse effect at various levels of detail and sophistication. A few of these are Warren Washington and Clare Parkinson, *An Introduction to Three-Dimensional Climate Modeling* (Mill Valley, California: University Science Books, 1986); John Firor, *The Changing Atmosphere: A Global Challenge* (New Haven: Yale University Press, 1990); Kevin Trenberth, ed., *Climate System Modeling* (Cambridge: Cambridge University Press, 1992); and Thomas Graedal and Paul Crutzen, *Atmospheric Change: An Earth System Perspective* (New York: W. W. Freeman, 1993).

The status of climate-change science is described in volume 1 of the reports of the Intergovernmental Panel on Climate Change in 1990, 1995, and 2001. Volume 2 of each assessment covers the impacts of climate change. These reports are published by Cambridge University Press with the following names: 1990—*Climate Change;* 1995—*Climate Change, 1995;* and 2001—*Climate Change, 2001.*

The career of Louis Agassiz is described in the *New*

Encyclopedia Britannica (1990). A modern biography is *A Lifetime in Science* by Edward Laurie (1960).

The simultaneous development by Charles Darwin and Alfred Wallace of evolution as the explanation for the origin of species is described in *The Song of the Dodo* by David Quammen (New York: Simon and Schuster, 1996).

The controversy over continental drift is the subject of the book by Naomi Oreskes, *The Rejection of Continental Drift* (New York: Oxford University Press, 1999).

Schedules of meetings and reports of actions of the Intergovernmental Panel on Climate Change (IPCC) are found at *http://www.meto.gov.uk/sec5/CR_div/ipcc*.

The impacts of climate change expected in the United States are described in National Assessment Synthesis Team, *Climate Change Impacts on the United States: The Potential Consequences of Climate Variability and Change* (Washington, D.C.: U.S. Global Change Research Program, 2000). For additional references for climate-change impacts, see volume 2 of the IPCC assessments.

Chapter 6. International Climate-Change Negotiations

The nuclear test ban treaty was the first international agreement covering a global source of atmospheric pollution. The treaty negotiations went on with little progress for seven years after the *Fortunate Dragon* incident and then, as seems to have happened to the Kyoto agreement, were completely stalled by competing worries. In the test ban case, the Soviet Union resumed atmospheric tests after having earlier instituted a voluntary cessation, and the United States resumed underground tests following its voluntary moratorium in 1961—each uneasy lest the other gain a military advantage. The history of this treaty is described in John Firor and Stephen Rhodes, "Political and Legislative Control of Air Pollution," in C. N. Hewitt and W. T. Sturges, eds., *Global Atmospheric Chemical Change* (New York: Elsevier Applied Science, 1993).

The texts of the various environmental treaties and lists of signatories can be found at *http://www.un.org*.

The data in Table 6.1, is from *World Resources, 2000–2001,* a joint publication of the World Resources Institute, the United Nations Environment Programme, the United Nations Development Programme, and the World Bank (New York: Oxford University Press, 2000).

The cap-and-trade system assigns permits allowing a certain quantity of sulfur emissions by power plants and others. Any emitter able to reduce emissions below the permitted amount may sell its excess permits to an emitter that finds it expensive to reduce its emission to the level permitted. This system puts the reductions largely in the hands of those who can achieve the highest efficiency at lowest cost. By the gradual decrease in the value of each permit, the national emission is slowly brought down to a much lower level.

A review of sixteen widely used economic models applied to cost estimates for reducing greenhouse gas emissions, and the role of the assumptions made in these models, is given in Robert Repetto and Duncan Austin, *The Costs of Climate Protection: A Guide for the Perplexed* (Washington, D.C.: World Resources Institute, 1997). A discussion of how the presentation of economic-model results may mislead noneconomists is in Stephen Schneider, "Degrees of Certainty," *Research and Exploration,* vol. 9, no. 2, pp. 173–190 (1993).

Joe Romm's book is *Cool Companies: How the Best Businesses Boost Profits and Productivity by Cutting Greenhouse Gas Emissions* (Washington, D.C.: Island Press, 1999).

Chapter 7. Creating a World with a Stable Atmosphere

Data on relative energy use by sectors is from the Energy Information Agency web site, *http://www.eia.doe.gov*.

Discussions and examples of environmental tax shifts include A. T. Durning and Yoram Bauman, *Tax Shift* (Seattle: Northwest Environment Watch, 1998); R. Repetto, R. C. Dower, R. Jenkins, and J. Geoghegan, *Green Fees: How a Tax Shift Can Work for the Environment and the Economy* (Washington, D.C.: World Resources Institute, 1992); and Population and Consumption Task Force, President's Council on Sustainable Development, *Population and Consumption* (Washington, D.C.: President's Council on Sustainable Development, 1996).

The correction of the Indonesian national income accounts is described in Robert Repetto et al., *Wasting Assets: Natural Resources in National Income Accounts* (Washington, D.C.: World Resources Institute, 1989). A similar study of accounts in Costa Rica appears in Raul Solorzano et al., *Accounts Overdue: Natural Resource Depreciation in Costa Rica* (Washington, D.C.: World Resources Institute, 1991).

Failure of flood-control projects is discussed in Gilbert White, "Human Adjustment to Floods," University of Chicago Department of Geography Research Paper no. 29 (1945), and G. F. White et al., "Changes in Urban Occupancy of Flood Plains in the United States," Research Paper no. 57 (1958).

Chapter 8. Population and Climate Change Together

For an exhaustive examination of the technical interactions of climate change and population growth, see Brian O'Neill, F. Landis MacKellar, and Wolfgang Lutz, *Population and Climate Change* (Cambridge: Cambridge University Press, 2001).

See Judith Jacobsen, "Population, Consumption, and Environmental Degradation: Problems and Solutions," *Colorado Journal of International Environmental Law and Policy,* vol. 6, no. 2, Summer 1995, pp. 255–272, for a discus-

sion of the impossibility of treating environmental problems in the short term with population solutions.

For the argument that the Cairo coalition is fragile, see
Dennis Hodgson and Susan Cotts Watkins, "Feminists and
Neo-Malthusians: Past and Present Alliances," *Population
and Development Review,* vol. 23, no. 3, September 1997,
pp. 469–523.

For a useful technical analysis of "escaping the bind,"
see Ernst Von Weizsacker et al., *Factor Four: Doubling
Wealth, Halving Resource Use* (London: Earthscan Publications, 1999).

Afterword

Many statistical sources provide historical fertility data;
the source of fertility in the developing world in 1950 is
United Nations, *World Population Prospects: The 1994
Revision, Annex Tables,* p. 122. Current fertility and population figures are taken from Population Reference Bureau,
2000 World Population Data Sheet (Washington, D.C.: Population Reference Bureau, 2000). An accessible source of
information about U.N. population projections is Carl
Haub, "U.N. Projections Assume Fertility Decline, Mortality Increase," *Population Today,* vol. 26, no. 12, December 1998, pp. 1–2. *Population Today* is published by the
Population Reference Bureau, *www.prb.org.* For an over-
view of world population projections by various groups,
see John Bongaarts and Rodolfo A. Bulatao, eds., *Beyond
Six Billion: Forecasting the World's Population* (Washington, D.C.: National Academy Press, 2000), pp. 17–19.

Agenda 21 can be found at *http://iisd1.iisd.ca/
rio+5/agenda* or in published form as United Nations, *The
Global Partnership for Environment and Development: A
Guide to Agenda 21* (New York: United Nations, 1993). The
quoted language is from Chapter 1.

Global CFC production trends may be found in Lester
Brown et al., *Vital Signs, 1998: The Environmental Trends*

That Are Shaping Our Future (New York: W. W. Norton, 1998), pp. 70–71.

Information on sulfur emissions is taken from Lester Brown et al., *Vital Signs, 1996: The Environmental Trends That Are Shaping Our Future* (New York: W. W. Norton, 1996), pp. 70–71, and World Resources Institute, *World Resources, 2000–2001* (Oxford: Oxford University Press, 2001), p. 284.

Information on wind-generating capacity, sales of solar cells, and sales of compact fluorescent light bulbs is from *Vital Signs, 1998,* pp. 58–63.

Index